JEFF FALLOW is an illustrator and writer based
'For me the Swinging Sixties meant sh
School. There wasn't much Flower Power in th   village of
Netherburn, Lanarkshire.

My awkward teenage years in Airdrie in the '70s doubtless prepared
me for my prodigal 20s in Glasgow in the '80s, drifting from job to job
(usually graphic design, but also a spell in the Civil Service) and dropping
in and out of college courses.

I finally grew-up in Fife in the '90s, settling into family life,
graduating from Duncan of Jordanstone Art College and struggling to
become an illustrator and a writer, working on historical comic books for
Luath and for London-based publishers Writers & Readers'.

Fallow's political cartoons have been published in the *Scots
Independent*, *CND Today* and local newspapers. His first book,
Revolting Scotland, upon which old Scotland new Scotland is based, was
published in 1992. He has recently illustrated *Stanislavski for Beginners*
by David Allen. He has written and illustrated *Scotland for Beginners*
and *Wales for Beginners*, and has illustrated *London for Beginners* by
Nita Clarke, all to be published in 1999.

old **Scotland**
new **Scotland**

JEFF FALLOW

Luath Press Limited

EDINBURGH

www.luath.co.uk

First Published as *Revolting Scotland* 1992
Revised, Extended and Updated 1998

The paper used in this book is acid-free, neutral sized and recyclable.
It is made from low chlorine pulps produced in a low energy, low
emission manner for sustainable forests.

Printed and bound by
Bell & Bain Ltd., Glasgow

Typeset by
S. Fairgrieve, Edinburgh 0131 658 1763

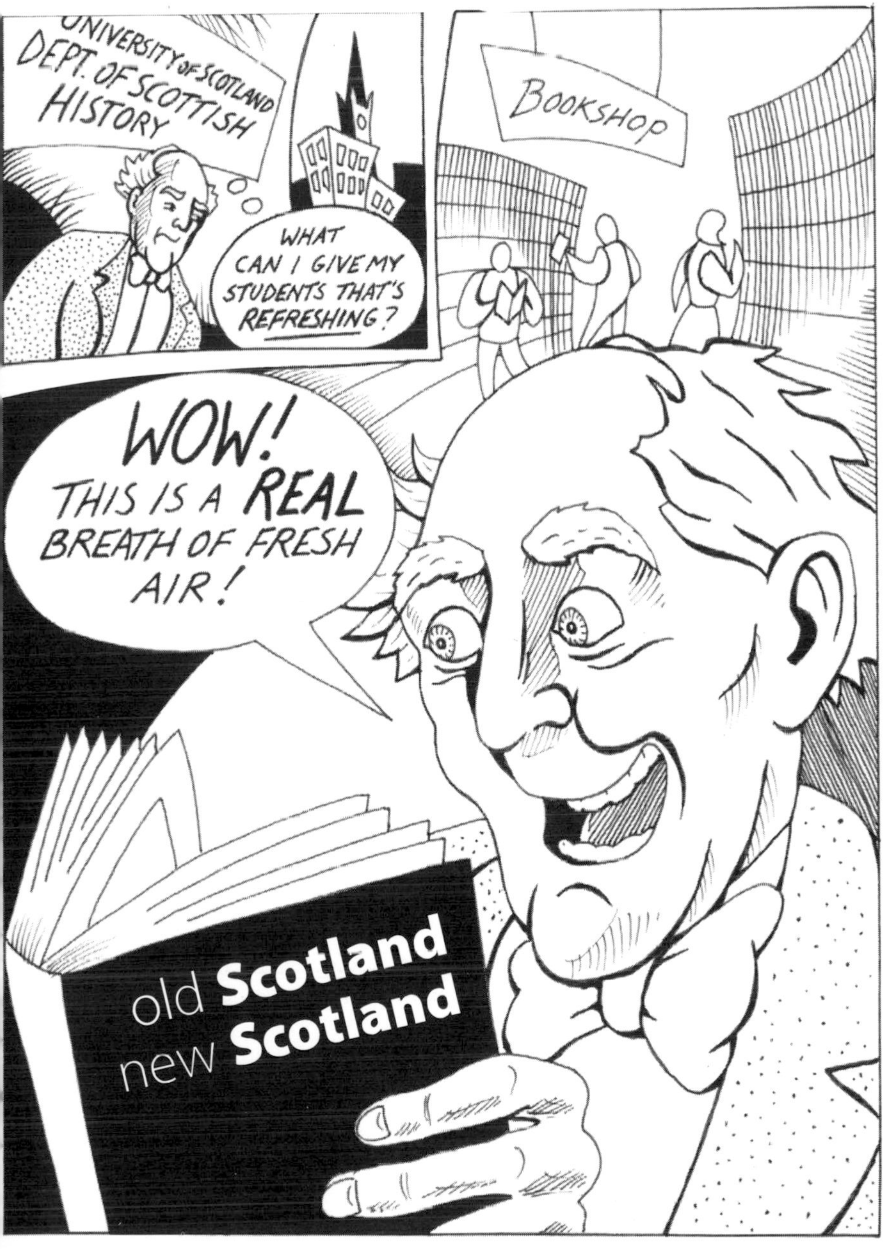
UNIVERSITY OF SCOTLAND
DEPT. OF SCOTTISH HISTORY
WHAT CAN I GIVE MY STUDENTS THAT'S REFRESHING?
BOOKSHOP
WOW! THIS IS A REAL BREATH OF FRESH AIR!
old Scotland
new Scotland

Dedicated to the memory of Hugh I. Orr (1916 - 1990)
socialist, patriot, artist, friend

A few words from the author

THIS BOOK IS A RADICAL history of Scotland, its place within the United Kingdom, and its inseparable struggles for democracy, national identity and home rule, presented in graphic form. It is a revised, updated version of my earlier book *Revolting Scotland*. A lot has happened since its publication in 1992, most importantly the realisation of a degree of home rule.

Unlike other cartoon books on Scottish history, this is no silly lighthearted look at our relationship with the 'Auld Enemy'. Too many people associate Scottish history with tartan trivia or outworn romantic myth. This book aims to blast that stubborn idea. It looks at Scotland's relationship with England, yes, but England is certainly not my enemy, nor indeed is it Scotland's, whose only real enemy in recent years has been its lack of self-confidence. Whether or not this changes will depend on the people of Scotland and how they choose to use their new parliament.

Jeff Fallow
October 1998

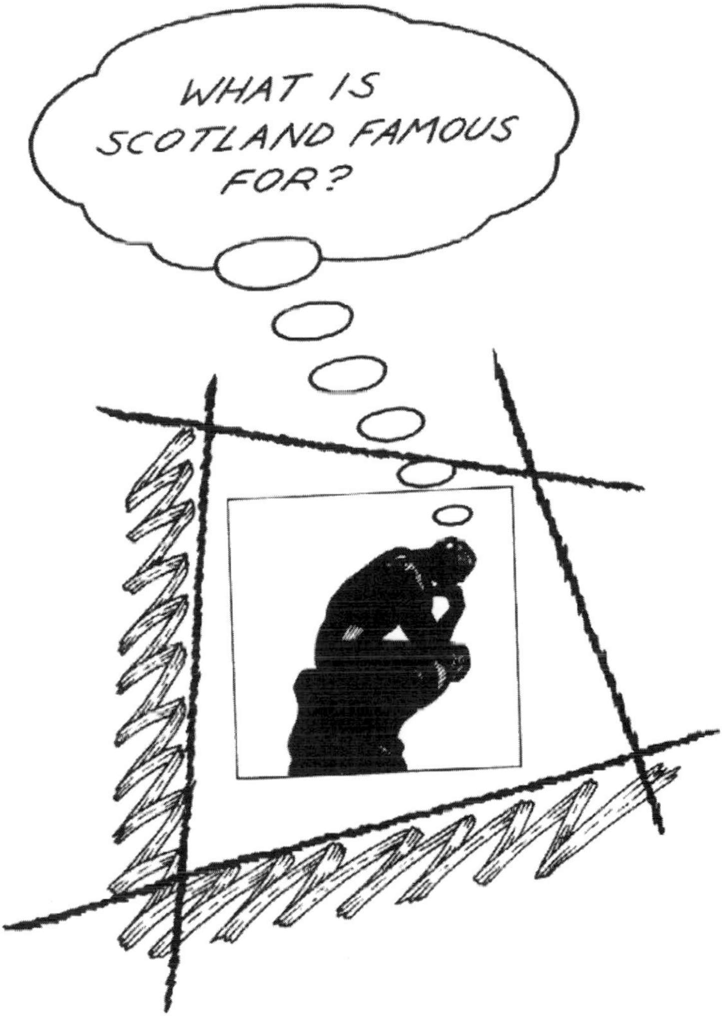
WHAT IS
SCOTLAND FAMOUS
FOR?

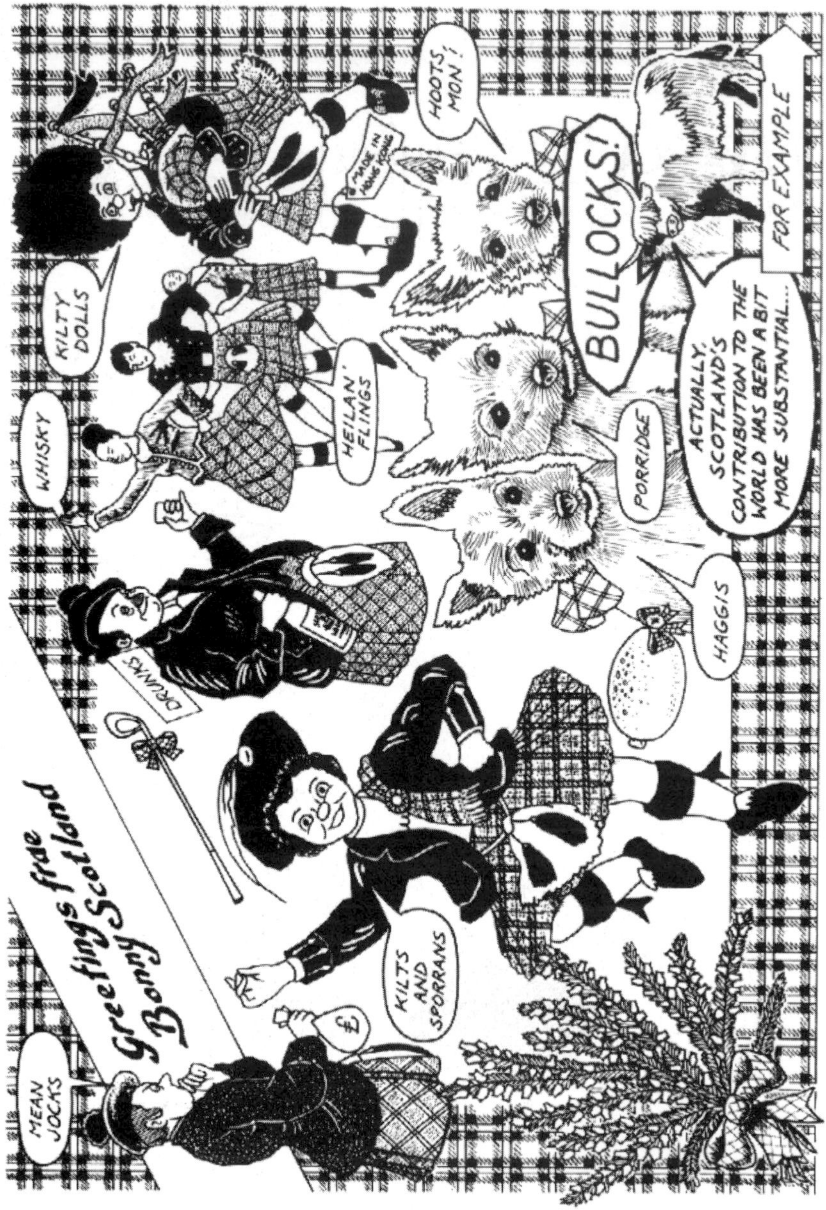
Greetings frae Bonny Scotland
MEAN JOCKS
KILTS AND SPORRANS
DRUNKS
WHISKY
HEILAN' FLINGS
KILTY DOLLS
MADE IN HONG KONG
HOOTS, MON!
HAGGIS
PORRIDGE
BULLOCKS!
ACTUALLY, SCOTLAND'S CONTRIBUTION TO THE WORLD HAS BEEN A BIT MORE SUBSTANTIAL...
FOR EXAMPLE

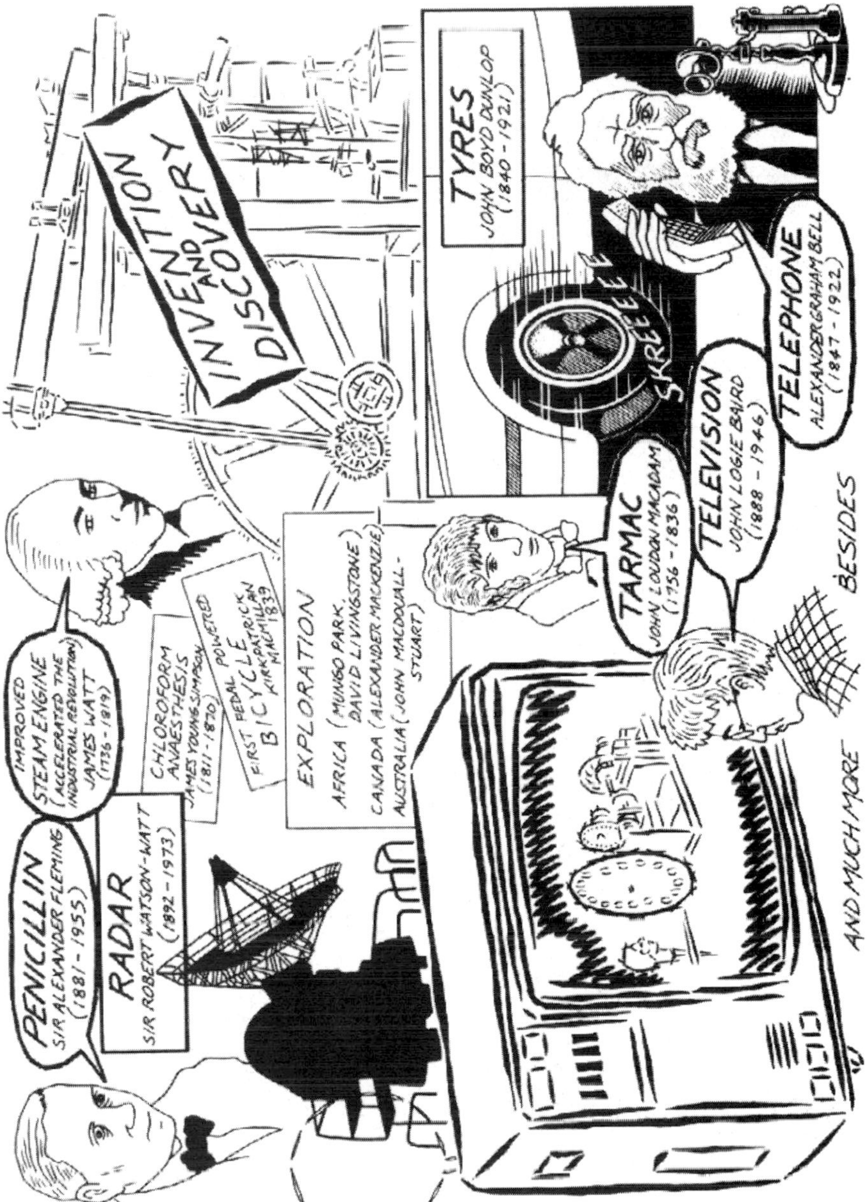
INVENTION AND DISCOVERY
PENICILLIN SIR ALEXANDER FLEMING (1881 - 1955)
IMPROVED STEAM ENGINE (ACCELERATED THE INDUSTRIAL REVOLUTION) JAMES WATT (1736 - 1819)
RADAR SIR ROBERT WATSON-WATT (1892 - 1973)
CHLOROFORM ANAESTHESIS JAMES YOUNG SIMPSON (1811 - 1870)
FIRST PEDAL POWERED BICYCLE KIRKPATRICK MACMILLAN 1839
EXPLORATION
AFRICA (MUNGO PARK, DAVID LIVINGSTONE)
CANADA (ALEXANDER MACKENZIE)
AUSTRALIA (JOHN MACDOUALL-STUART)
TYRES JOHN BOYD DUNLOP (1840 - 1921)
SKREEEEEE
TARMAC JOHN LOUDON MACADAM (1756 - 1836)
TELEVISION JOHN LOGIE BAIRD (1888 - 1946)
TELEPHONE ALEXANDER GRAHAM BELL (1847 - 1922)
BESIDES
AND MUCH MORE

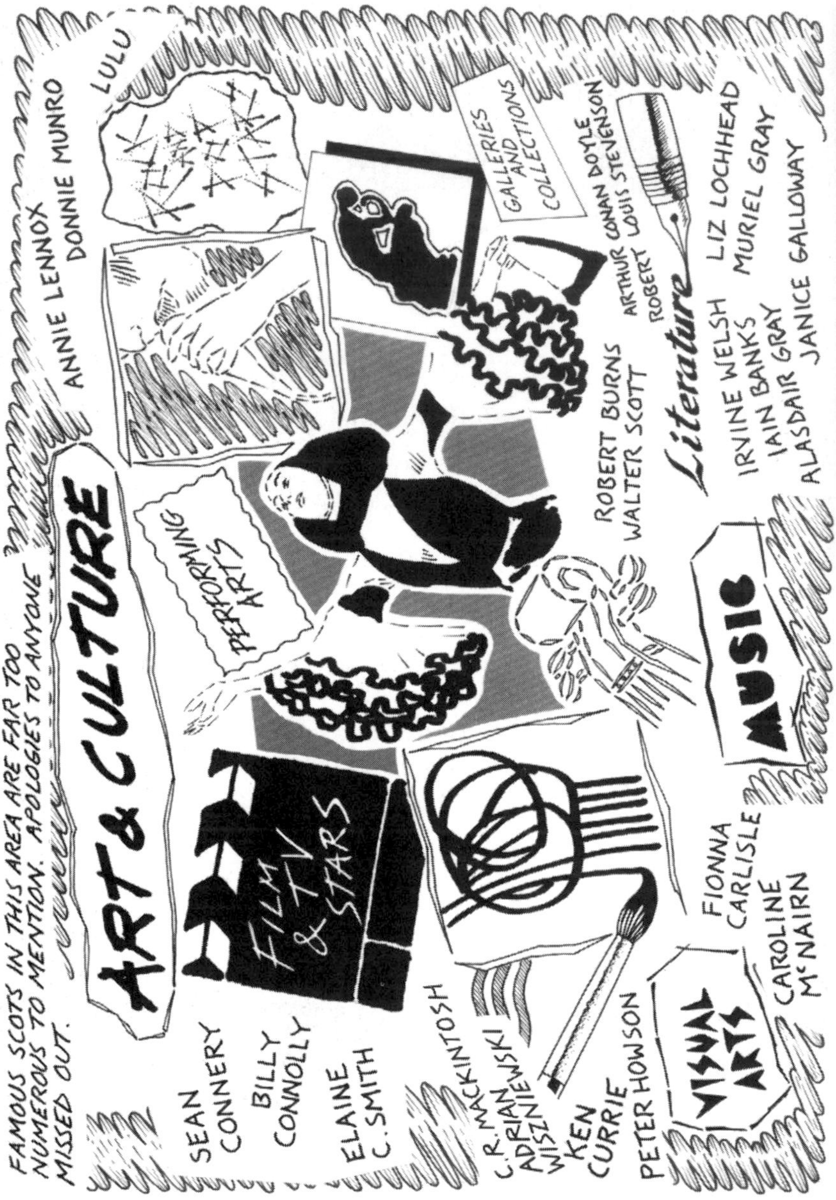
FAMOUS SCOTS IN THIS AREA ARE FAR TOO NUMEROUS TO MENTION. APOLOGIES TO ANYONE MISSED OUT.
ART & CULTURE
FILM & TV STARS
SEAN CONNERY
BILLY CONNOLLY
ELAINE C. SMITH
PERFORMING ARTS
ANNIE LENNOX
DONNIE MUNRO
LULU
GALLERIES AND COLLECTIONS
ARTHUR CONAN DOYLE
ROBERT LOUIS STEVENSON
ROBERT BURNS
WALTER SCOTT
Literature
IRVINE WELSH
IAIN BANKS
ALASDAIR GRAY
JANICE GALLOWAY
LIZ LOCHHEAD
MURIEL GRAY
MUSIC
C.R. MACKINTOSH
ADRIAN WISZNIEWSKI
KEN CURRIE
PETER HOWSON
VISUAL ARTS
FIONNA CARLISLE
CAROLINE McNAIRN

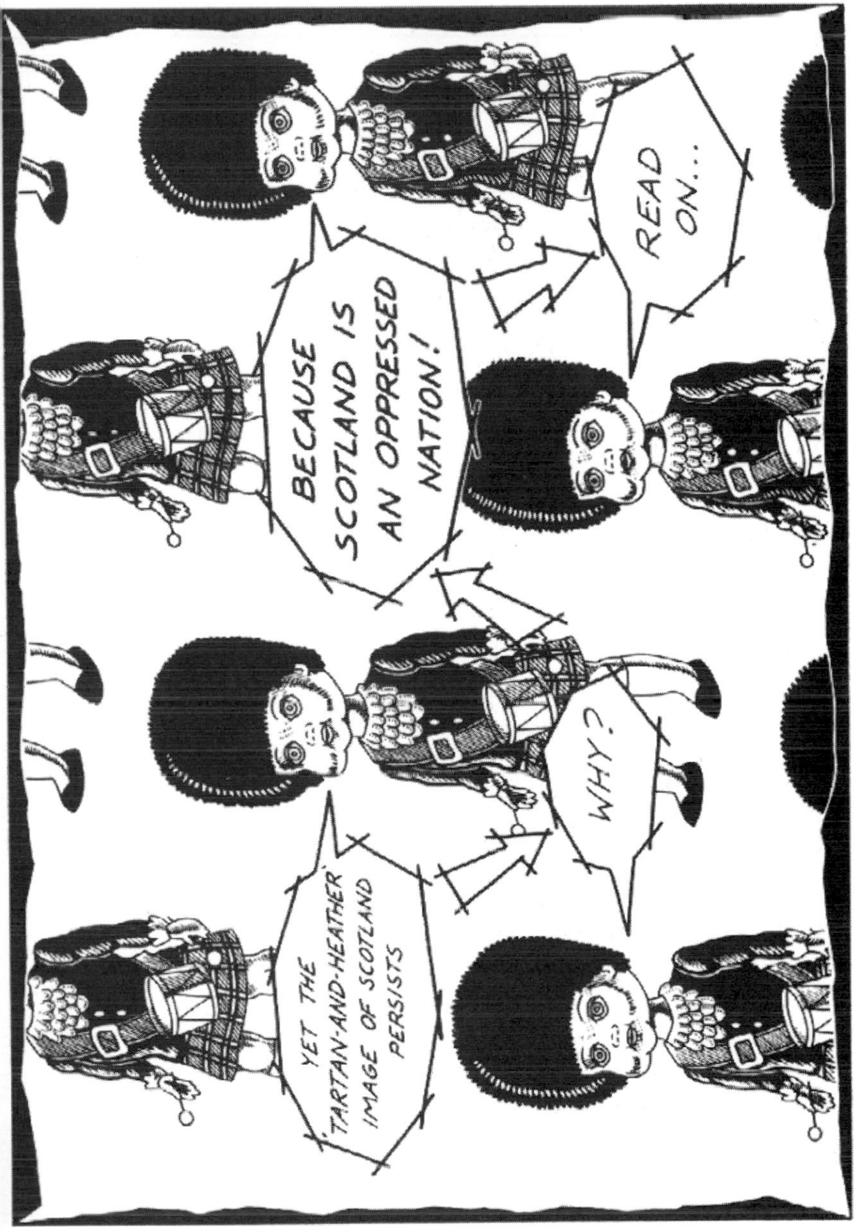
YET THE 'TARTAN-AND-HEATHER' IMAGE OF SCOTLAND PERSISTS
WHY?
BECAUSE SCOTLAND IS AN OPPRESSED NATION!
READ ON...

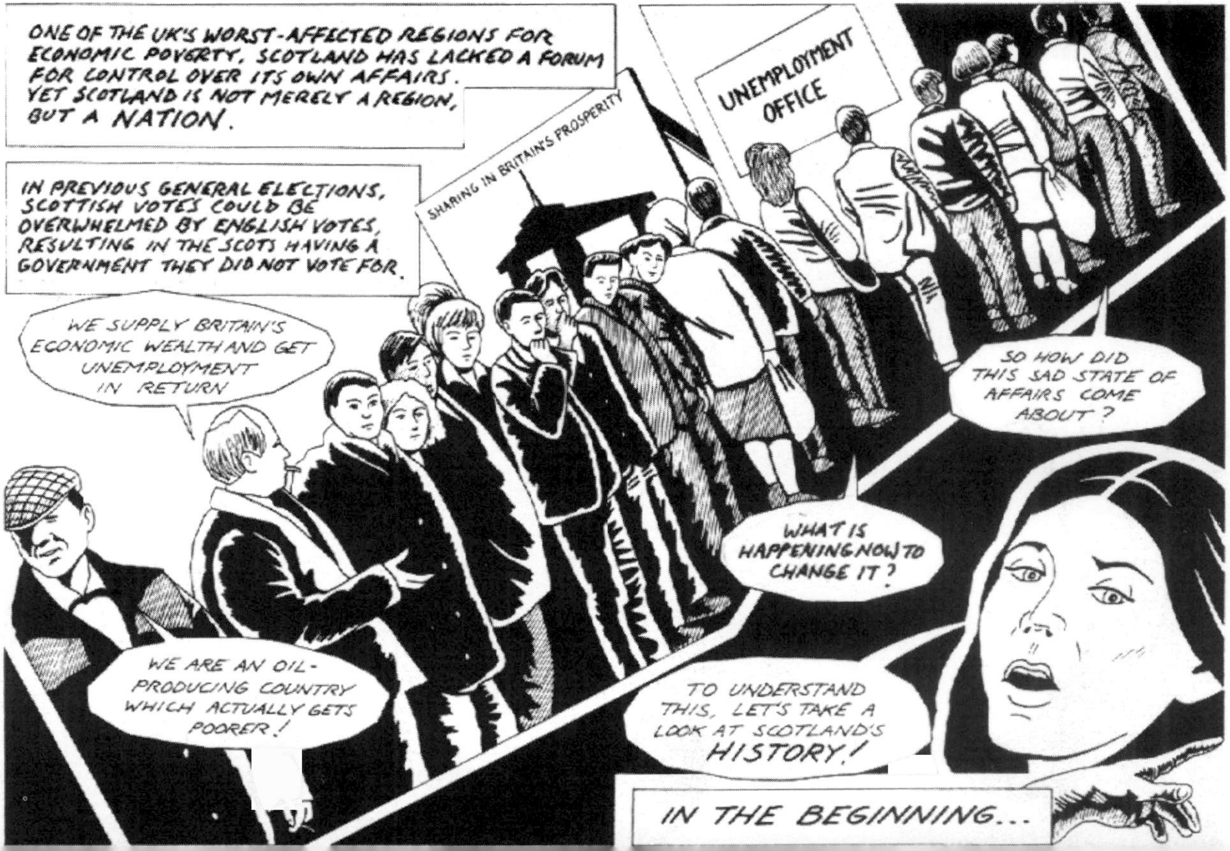
ONE OF THE UK'S WORST-AFFECTED REGIONS FOR ECONOMIC POVERTY, SCOTLAND HAS LACKED A FORUM FOR CONTROL OVER ITS OWN AFFAIRS. YET SCOTLAND IS NOT MERELY A REGION, BUT A NATION.
IN PREVIOUS GENERAL ELECTIONS, SCOTTISH VOTES COULD BE OVERWHELMED BY ENGLISH VOTES, RESULTING IN THE SCOTS HAVING A GOVERNMENT THEY DID NOT VOTE FOR.
SHARING IN BRITAIN'S PROSPERITY
UNEMPLOYMENT OFFICE
WE SUPPLY BRITAIN'S ECONOMIC WEALTH AND GET UNEMPLOYMENT IN RETURN
WE ARE AN OIL-PRODUCING COUNTRY WHICH ACTUALLY GETS POORER!
SO HOW DID THIS SAD STATE OF AFFAIRS COME ABOUT?
WHAT IS HAPPENING NOW TO CHANGE IT?
TO UNDERSTAND THIS, LET'S TAKE A LOOK AT SCOTLAND'S HISTORY!
IN THE BEGINNING...

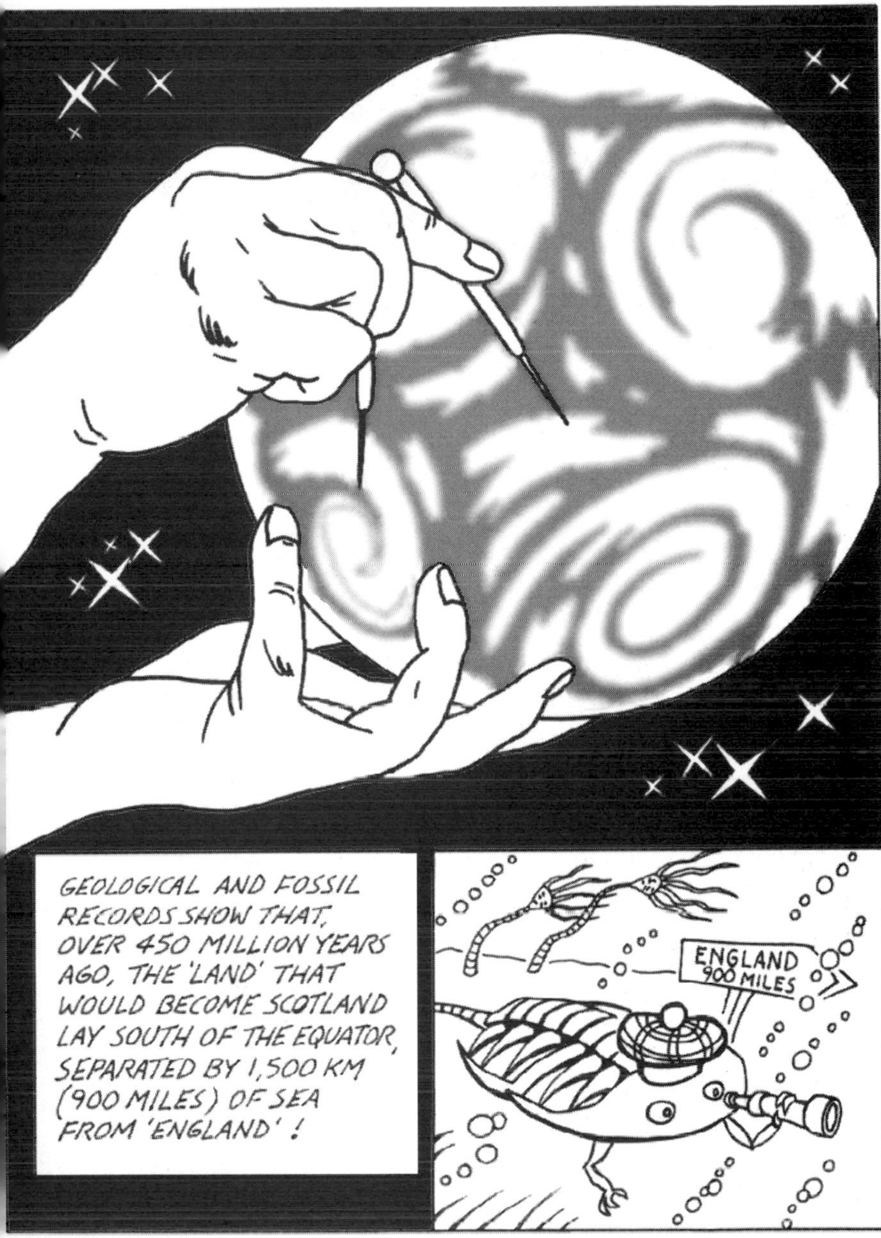
GEOLOGICAL AND FOSSIL RECORDS SHOW THAT, OVER 450 MILLION YEARS AGO, THE 'LAND' THAT WOULD BECOME SCOTLAND LAY SOUTH OF THE EQUATOR, SEPARATED BY 1,500 KM (900 MILES) OF SEA FROM 'ENGLAND' !
ENGLAND 900 MILES

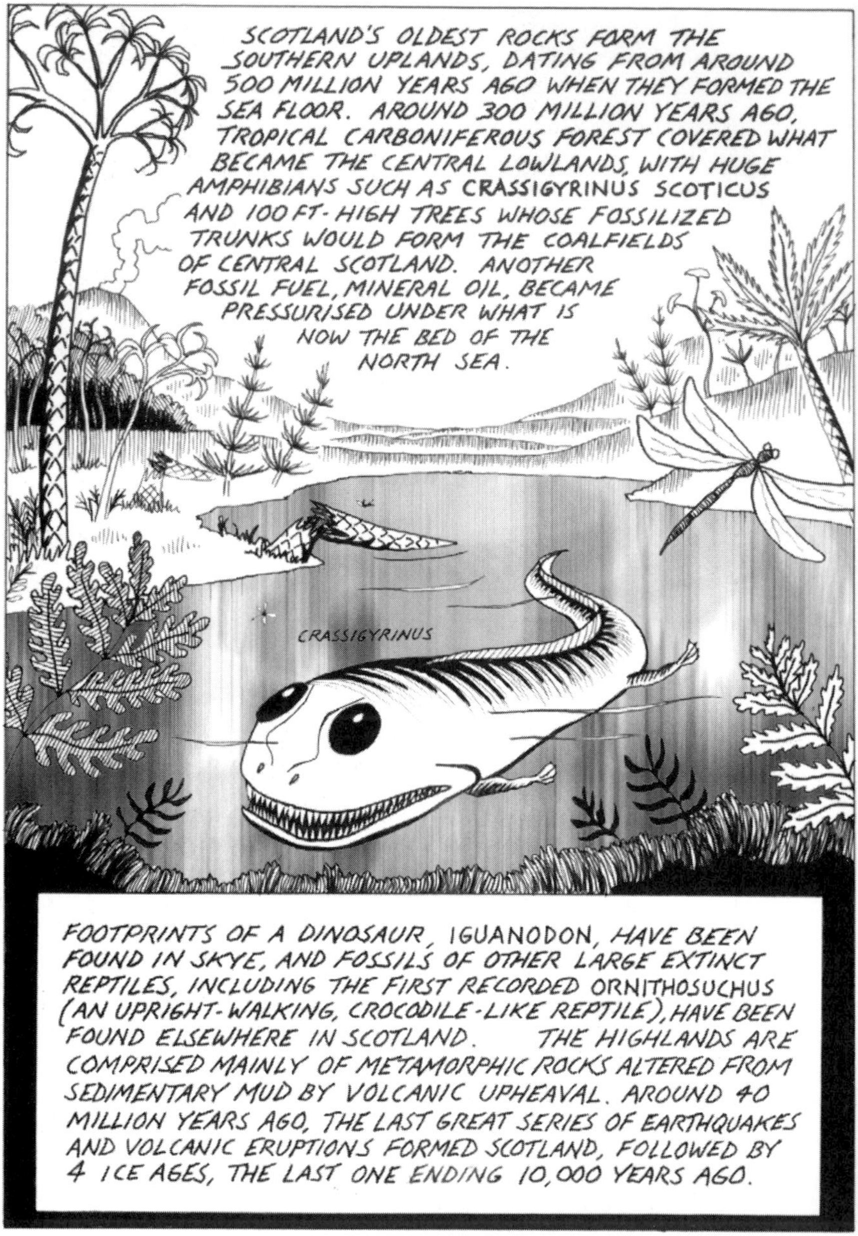
SCOTLAND'S OLDEST ROCKS FORM THE SOUTHERN UPLANDS, DATING FROM AROUND 500 MILLION YEARS AGO WHEN THEY FORMED THE SEA FLOOR. AROUND 300 MILLION YEARS AGO, TROPICAL CARBONIFEROUS FOREST COVERED WHAT BECAME THE CENTRAL LOWLANDS, WITH HUGE AMPHIBIANS SUCH AS CRASSIGYRINUS SCOTICUS AND 100 FT-HIGH TREES WHOSE FOSSILIZED TRUNKS WOULD FORM THE COALFIELDS OF CENTRAL SCOTLAND. ANOTHER FOSSIL FUEL, MINERAL OIL, BECAME PRESSURISED UNDER WHAT IS NOW THE BED OF THE NORTH SEA.
CRASSIGYRINUS
FOOTPRINTS OF A DINOSAUR, IGUANODON, HAVE BEEN FOUND IN SKYE, AND FOSSILS OF OTHER LARGE EXTINCT REPTILES, INCLUDING THE FIRST RECORDED ORNITHOSUCHUS (AN UPRIGHT-WALKING, CROCODILE-LIKE REPTILE), HAVE BEEN FOUND ELSEWHERE IN SCOTLAND. THE HIGHLANDS ARE COMPRISED MAINLY OF METAMORPHIC ROCKS ALTERED FROM SEDIMENTARY MUD BY VOLCANIC UPHEAVAL. AROUND 40 MILLION YEARS AGO, THE LAST GREAT SERIES OF EARTHQUAKES AND VOLCANIC ERUPTIONS FORMED SCOTLAND, FOLLOWED BY 4 ICE AGES, THE LAST ONE ENDING 10,000 YEARS AGO.

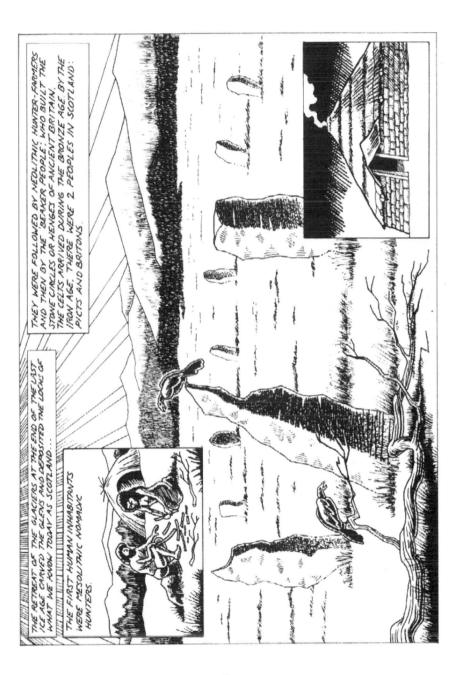

THE RETREAT OF THE GLACIERS AT THE END OF THE LAST ICE AGE CARVED THE GLENS AND DEPOSITED THE LOCHS OF WHAT WE KNOW TODAY AS SCOTLAND....

THE FIRST HUMAN INHABITANTS WERE MESOLITHIC NOMADIC HUNTERS.

THEY WERE FOLLOWED BY NEOLITHIC HUNTER-FARMERS AND THEN BY THE BEAKER PEOPLE, WHO BUILT THE STONE CIRCLES OR HENGES OF ANCIENT BRITAIN. THE CELTS ARRIVED DURING THE BRONZE AGE BY THE IRON AGE, THERE WERE 2 PEOPLES IN SCOTLAND: PICTS AND BRITONS.

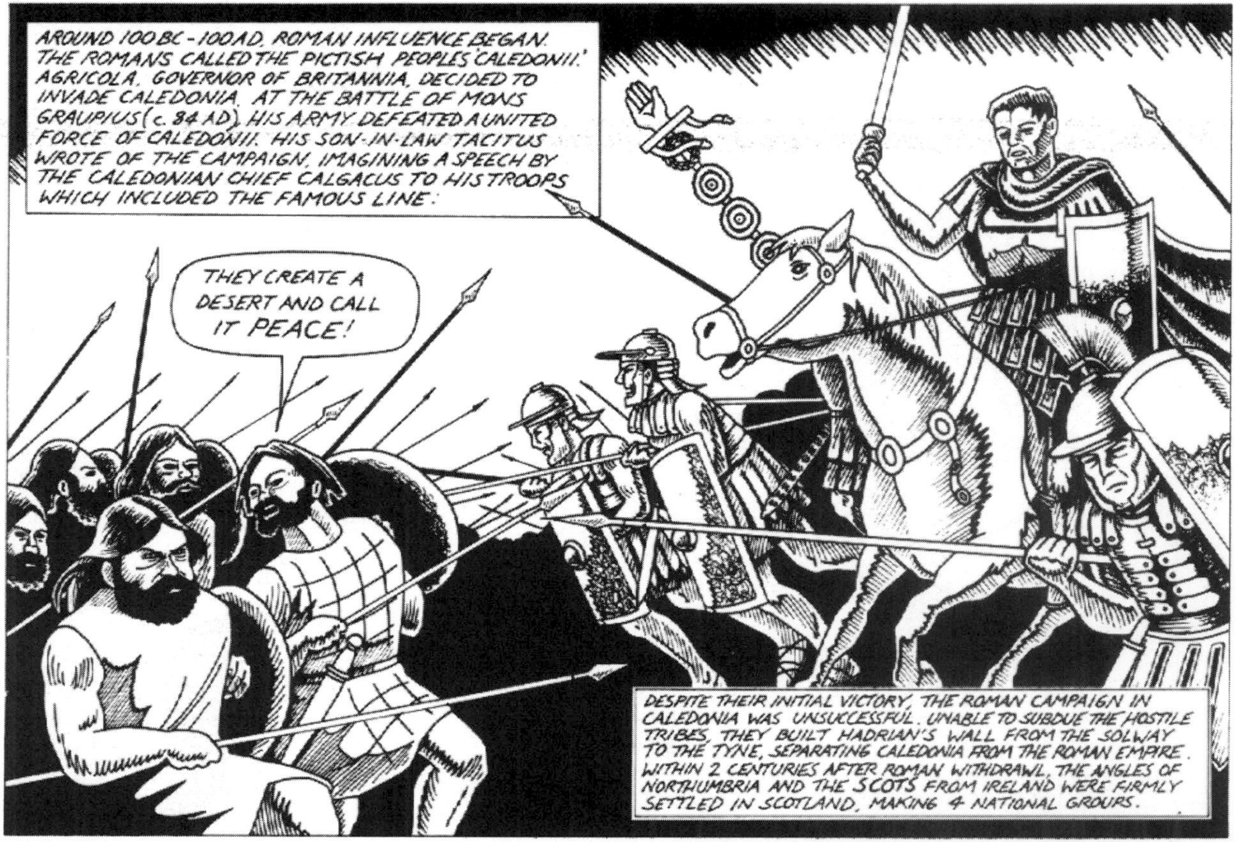
AROUND 100 BC - 100 AD, ROMAN INFLUENCE BEGAN. THE ROMANS CALLED THE PICTISH PEOPLES 'CALEDONII.' AGRICOLA, GOVERNOR OF BRITANNIA, DECIDED TO INVADE CALEDONIA. AT THE BATTLE OF MONS GRAUPIUS (c. 84 AD) HIS ARMY DEFEATED A UNITED FORCE OF CALEDONII. HIS SON-IN-LAW TACITUS WROTE OF THE CAMPAIGN, IMAGINING A SPEECH BY THE CALEDONIAN CHIEF CALGACUS TO HIS TROOPS WHICH INCLUDED THE FAMOUS LINE:
THEY CREATE A DESERT AND CALL IT PEACE!
DESPITE THEIR INITIAL VICTORY, THE ROMAN CAMPAIGN IN CALEDONIA WAS UNSUCCESSFUL. UNABLE TO SUBDUE THE HOSTILE TRIBES, THEY BUILT HADRIAN'S WALL FROM THE SOLWAY TO THE TYNE, SEPARATING CALEDONIA FROM THE ROMAN EMPIRE. WITHIN 2 CENTURIES AFTER ROMAN WITHDRAWL, THE ANGLES OF NORTHUMBRIA AND THE SCOTS FROM IRELAND WERE FIRMLY SETTLED IN SCOTLAND, MAKING 4 NATIONAL GROUPS.

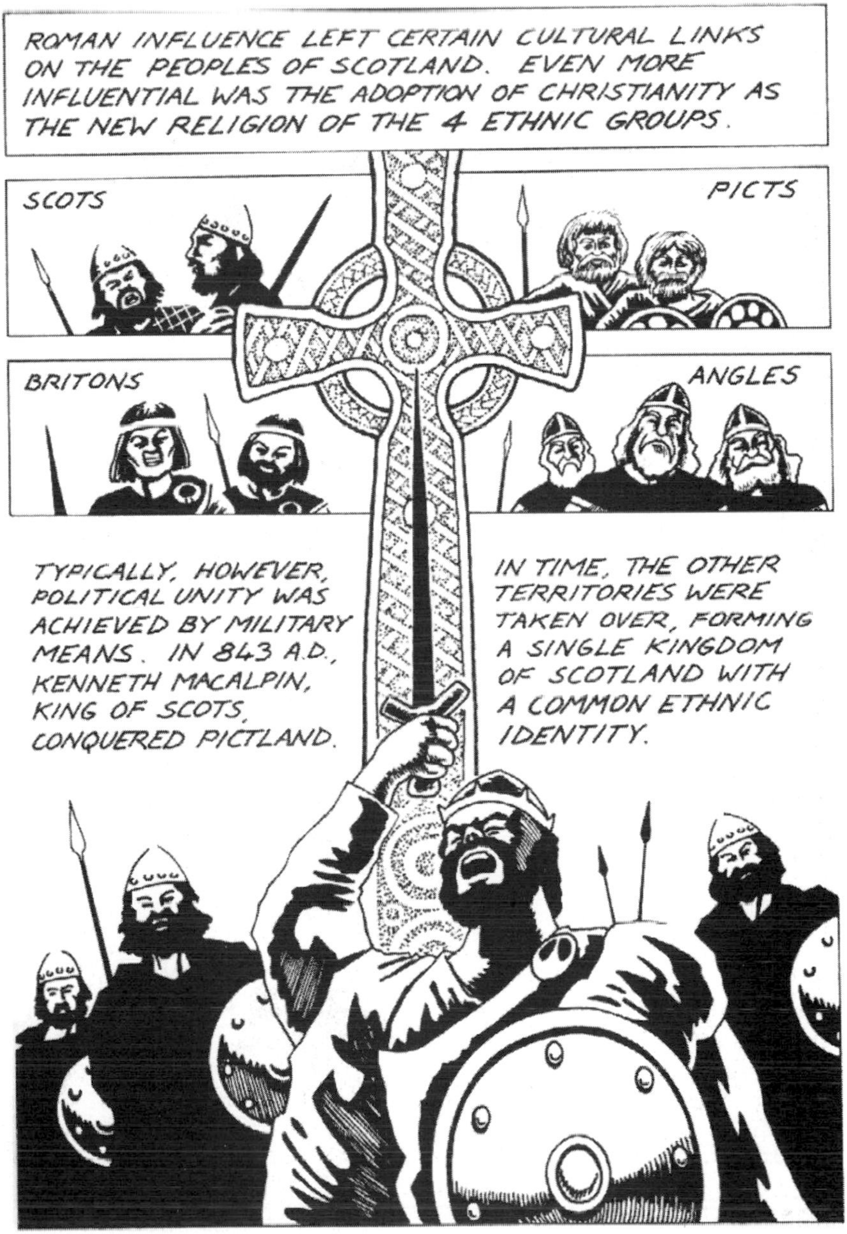
ROMAN INFLUENCE LEFT CERTAIN CULTURAL LINKS ON THE PEOPLES OF SCOTLAND. EVEN MORE INFLUENTIAL WAS THE ADOPTION OF CHRISTIANITY AS THE NEW RELIGION OF THE 4 ETHNIC GROUPS.
SCOTS
PICTS
BRITONS
ANGLES
TYPICALLY, HOWEVER, POLITICAL UNITY WAS ACHIEVED BY MILITARY MEANS. IN 843 A.D., KENNETH MACALPIN, KING OF SCOTS, CONQUERED PICTLAND.
IN TIME, THE OTHER TERRITORIES WERE TAKEN OVER, FORMING A SINGLE KINGDOM OF SCOTLAND WITH A COMMON ETHNIC IDENTITY.

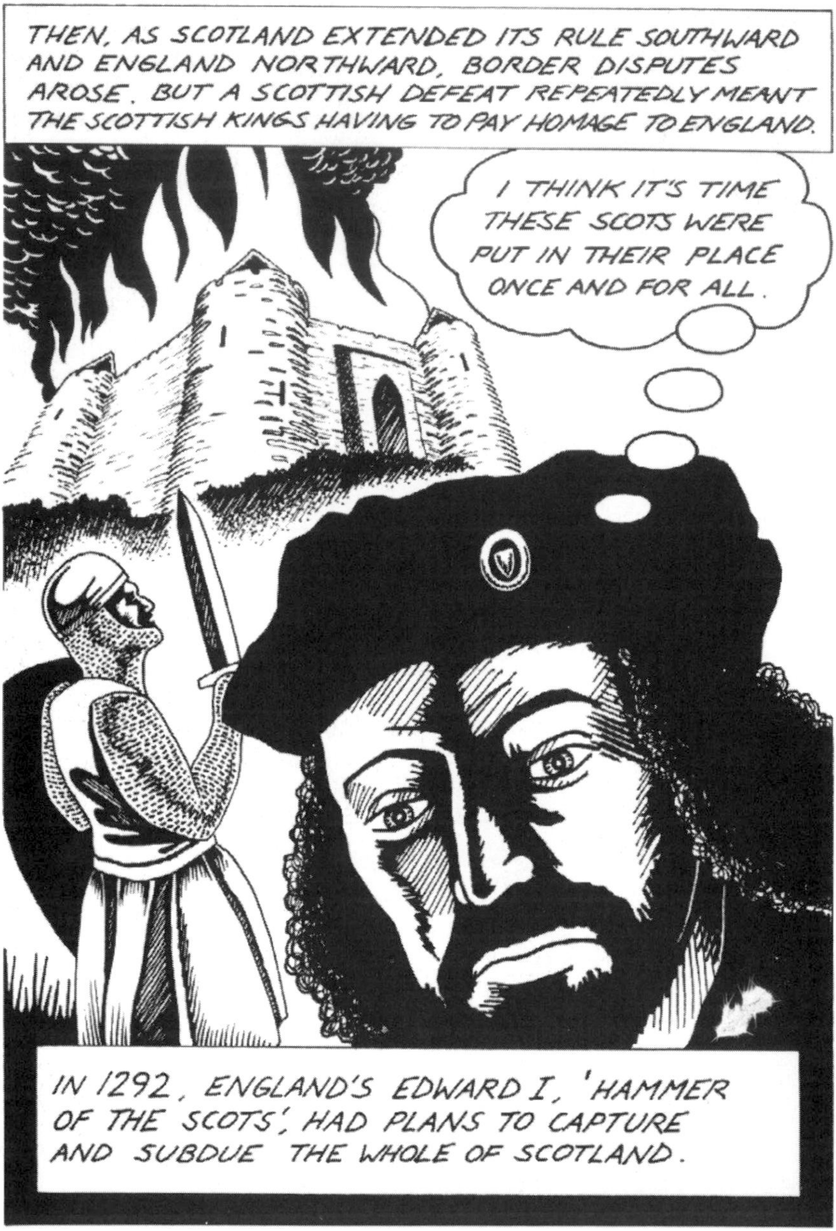
THEN, AS SCOTLAND EXTENDED ITS RULE SOUTHWARD AND ENGLAND NORTHWARD, BORDER DISPUTES AROSE. BUT A SCOTTISH DEFEAT REPEATEDLY MEANT THE SCOTTISH KINGS HAVING TO PAY HOMAGE TO ENGLAND.
I THINK IT'S TIME THESE SCOTS WERE PUT IN THEIR PLACE ONCE AND FOR ALL.
IN 1292, ENGLAND'S EDWARD I, 'HAMMER OF THE SCOTS', HAD PLANS TO CAPTURE AND SUBDUE THE WHOLE OF SCOTLAND.

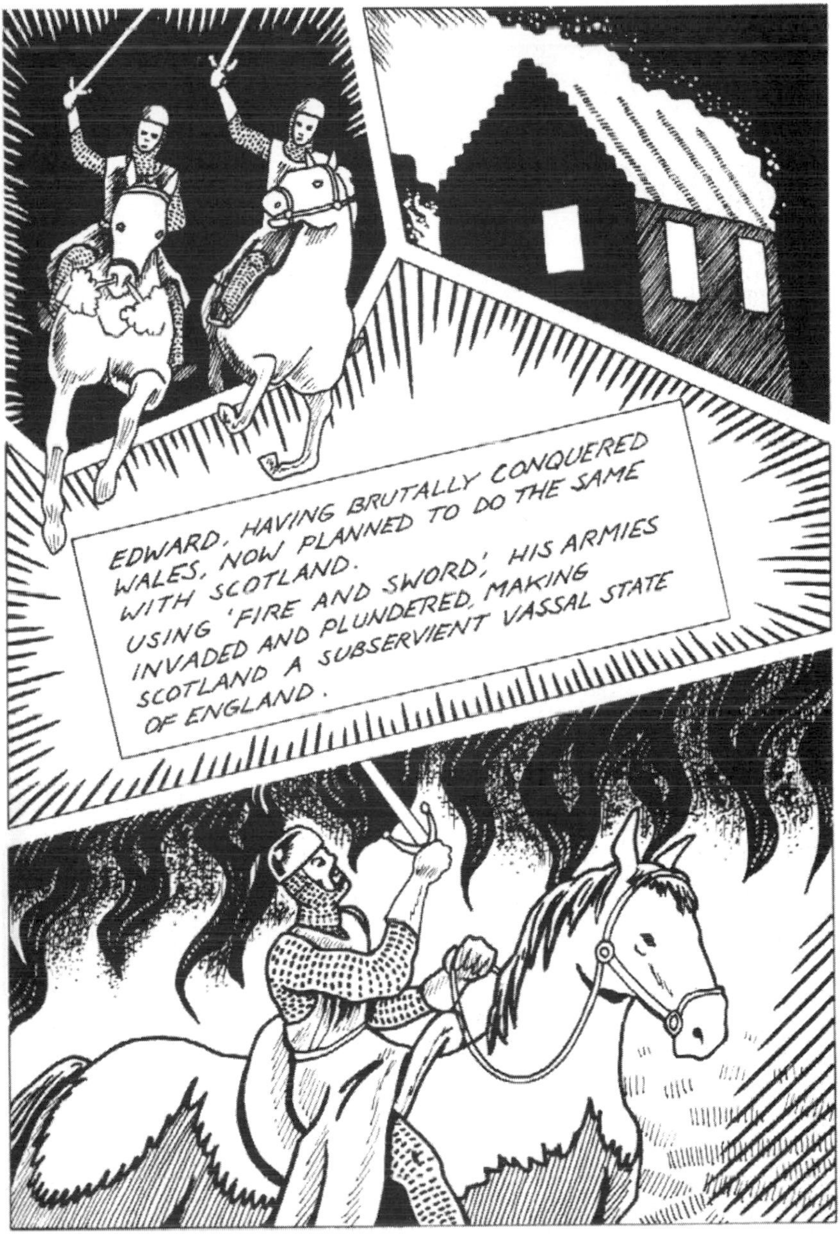
EDWARD, HAVING BRUTALLY CONQUERED WALES, NOW PLANNED TO DO THE SAME WITH SCOTLAND.
USING 'FIRE AND SWORD', HIS ARMIES INVADED AND PLUNDERED, MAKING SCOTLAND A SUBSERVIENT VASSAL STATE OF ENGLAND.

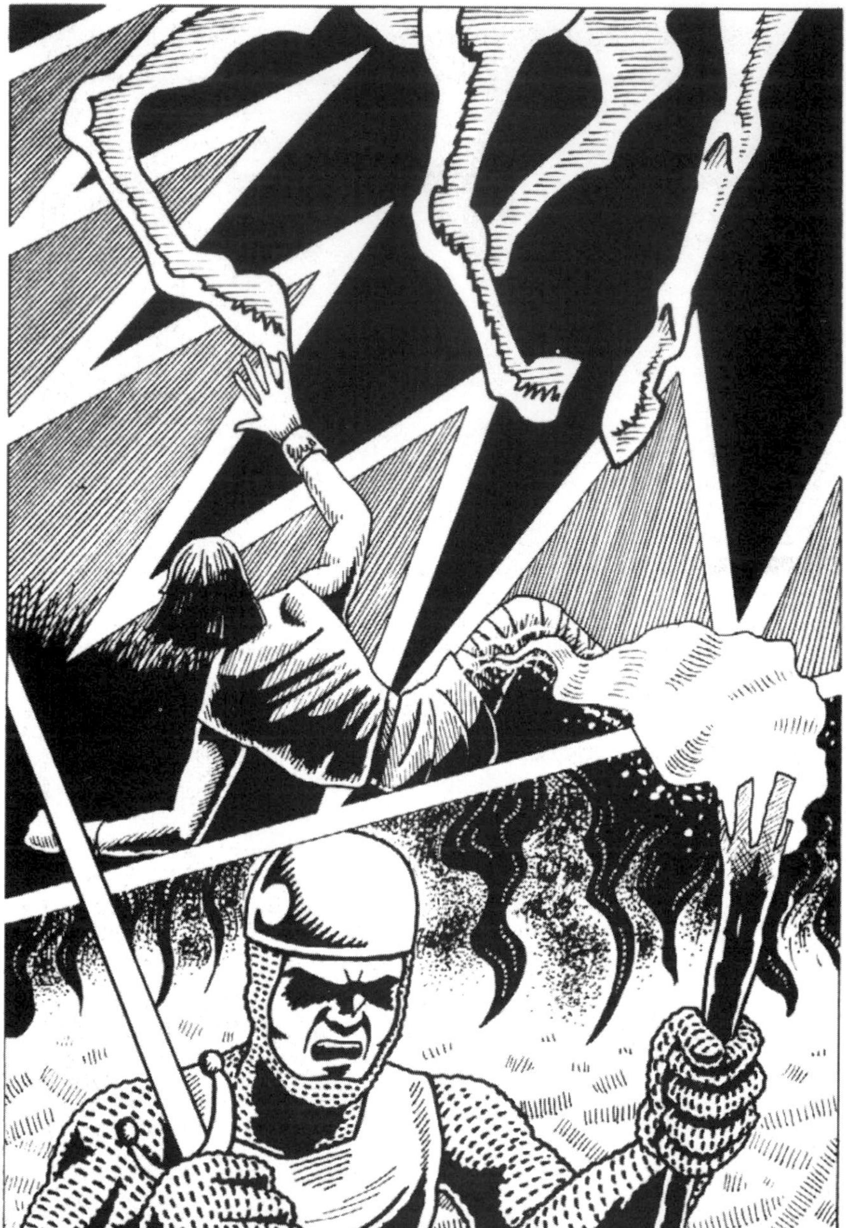

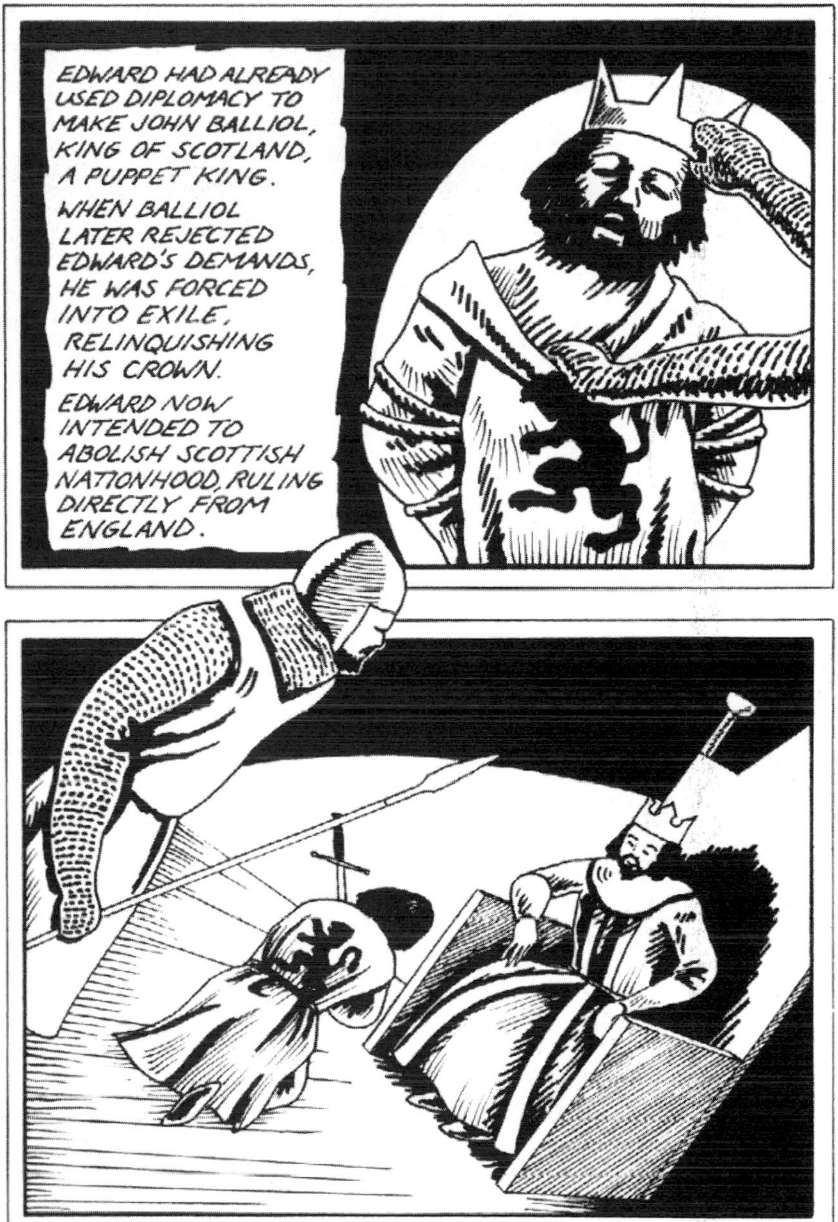
EDWARD HAD ALREADY USED DIPLOMACY TO MAKE JOHN BALLIOL, KING OF SCOTLAND, A PUPPET KING.
WHEN BALLIOL LATER REJECTED EDWARD'S DEMANDS, HE WAS FORCED INTO EXILE, RELINQUISHING HIS CROWN.
EDWARD NOW INTENDED TO ABOLISH SCOTTISH NATIONHOOD, RULING DIRECTLY FROM ENGLAND.

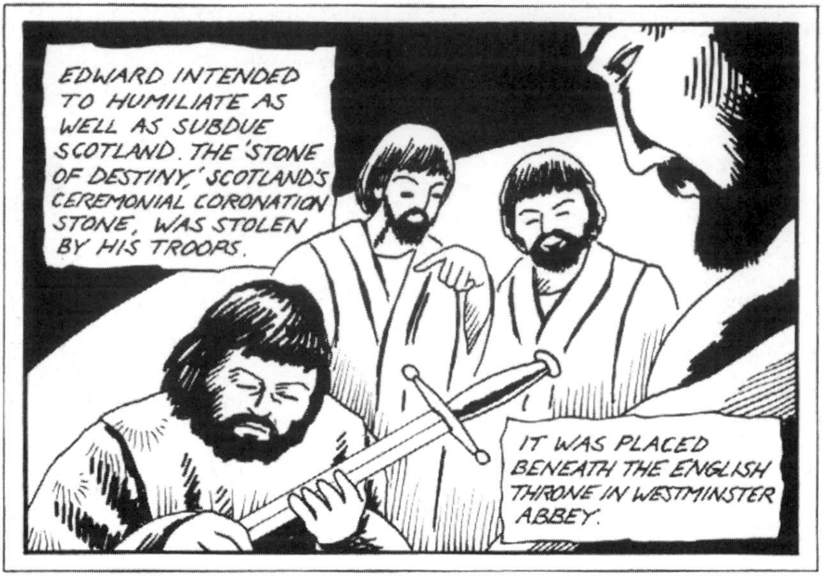
EDWARD INTENDED TO HUMILIATE AS WELL AS SUBDUE SCOTLAND. THE 'STONE OF DESTINY,' SCOTLAND'S CEREMONIAL CORONATION STONE, WAS STOLEN BY HIS TROOPS.
IT WAS PLACED BENEATH THE ENGLISH THRONE IN WESTMINSTER ABBEY.

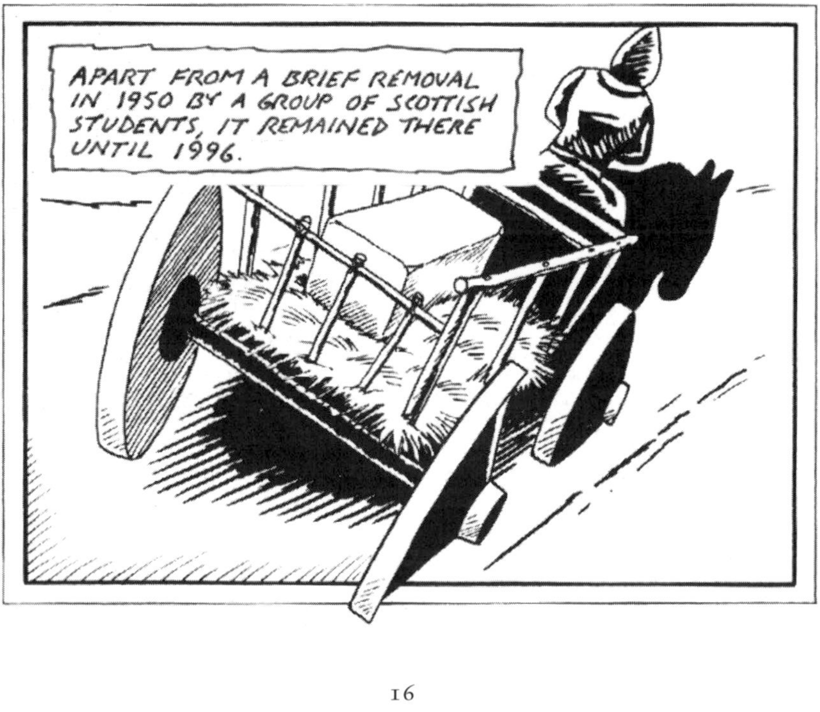
APART FROM A BRIEF REMOVAL IN 1950 BY A GROUP OF SCOTTISH STUDENTS, IT REMAINED THERE UNTIL 1996.

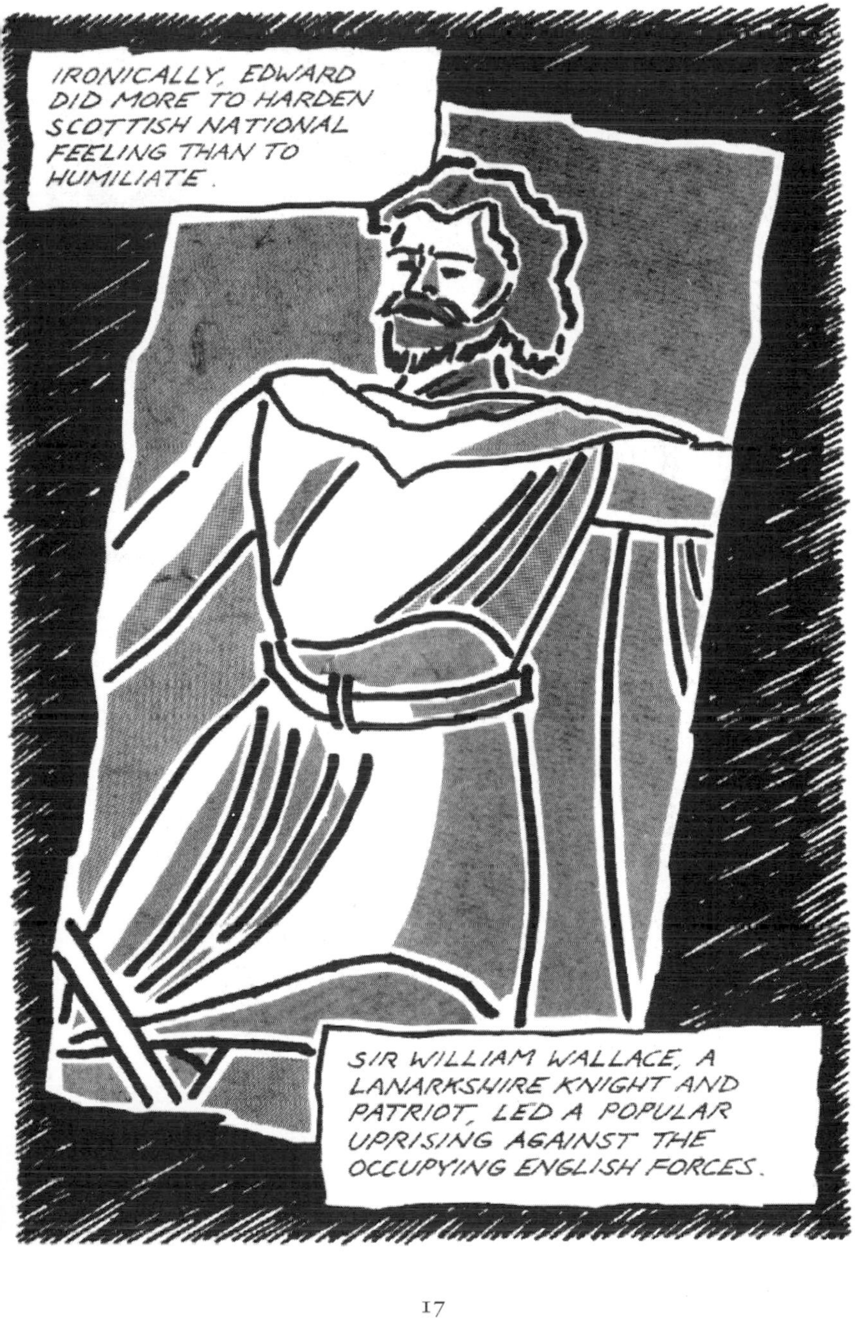
IRONICALLY, EDWARD DID MORE TO HARDEN SCOTTISH NATIONAL FEELING THAN TO HUMILIATE.
SIR WILLIAM WALLACE, A LANARKSHIRE KNIGHT AND PATRIOT, LED A POPULAR UPRISING AGAINST THE OCCUPYING ENGLISH FORCES.

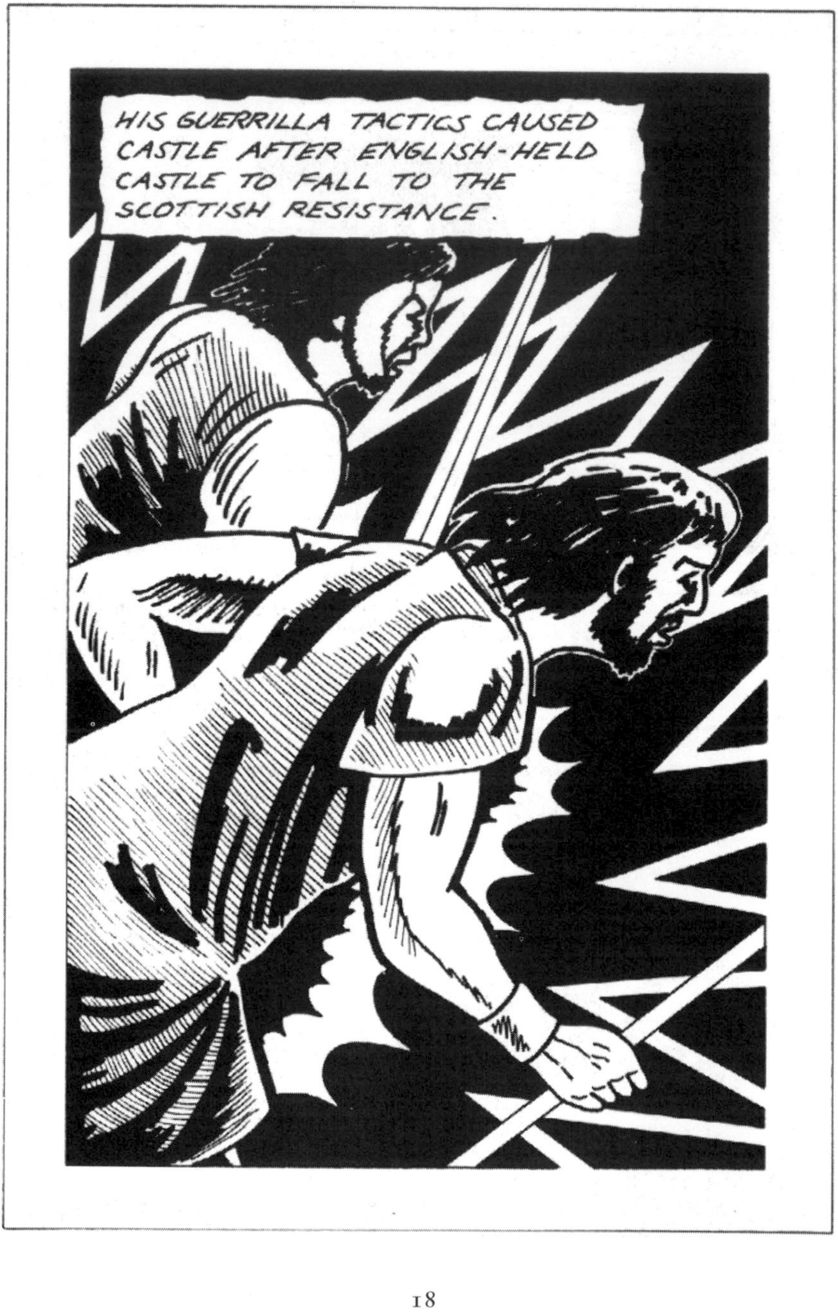
HIS GUERRILLA TACTICS CAUSED CASTLE AFTER ENGLISH-HELD CASTLE TO FALL TO THE SCOTTISH RESISTANCE.

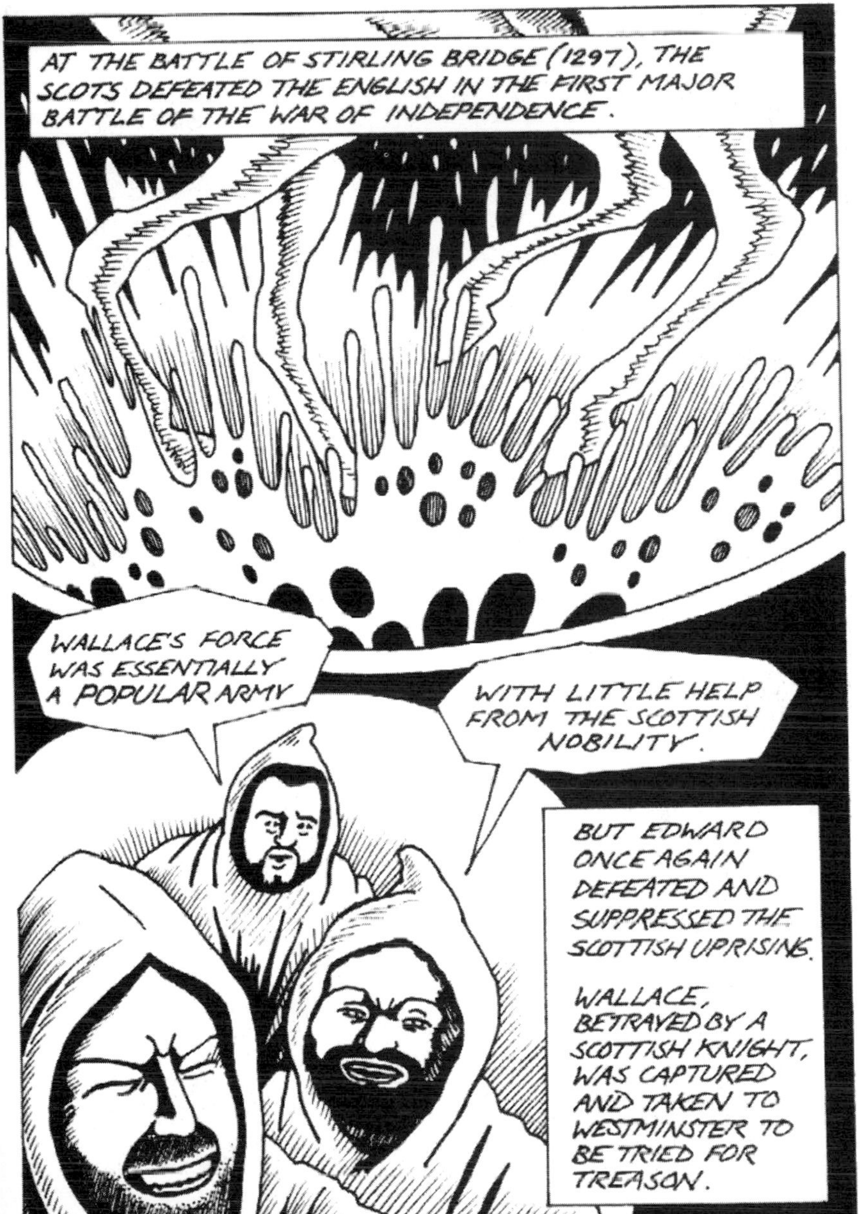
AT THE BATTLE OF STIRLING BRIDGE (1297), THE SCOTS DEFEATED THE ENGLISH IN THE FIRST MAJOR BATTLE OF THE WAR OF INDEPENDENCE.
WALLACE'S FORCE WAS ESSENTIALLY A POPULAR ARMY
WITH LITTLE HELP FROM THE SCOTTISH NOBILITY.
BUT EDWARD ONCE AGAIN DEFEATED AND SUPPRESSED THE SCOTTISH UPRISING.
WALLACE, BETRAYED BY A SCOTTISH KNIGHT, WAS CAPTURED AND TAKEN TO WESTMINSTER TO BE TRIED FOR TREASON.

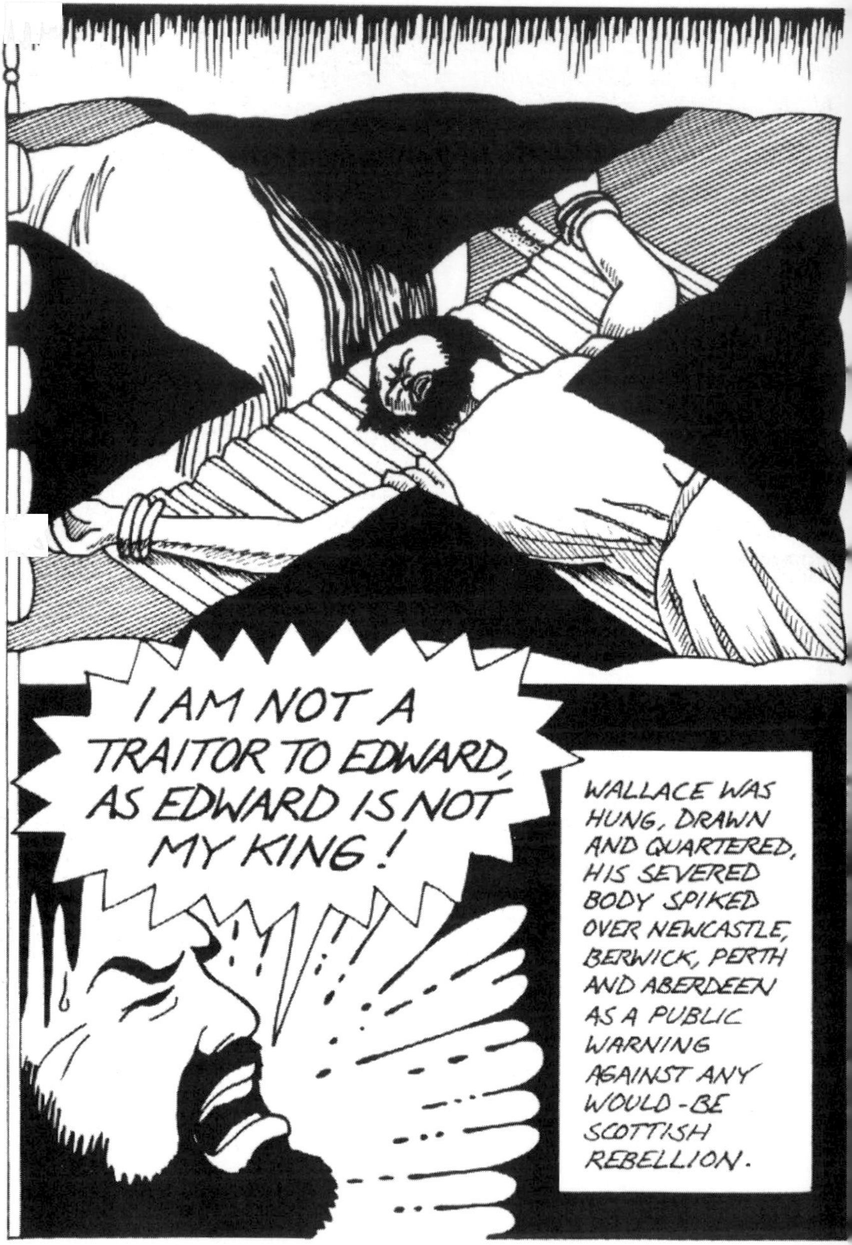
I AM NOT A TRAITOR TO EDWARD, AS EDWARD IS NOT MY KING!
WALLACE WAS HUNG, DRAWN AND QUARTERED, HIS SEVERED BODY SPIKED OVER NEWCASTLE, BERWICK, PERTH AND ABERDEEN AS A PUBLIC WARNING AGAINST ANY WOULD-BE SCOTTISH REBELLION.

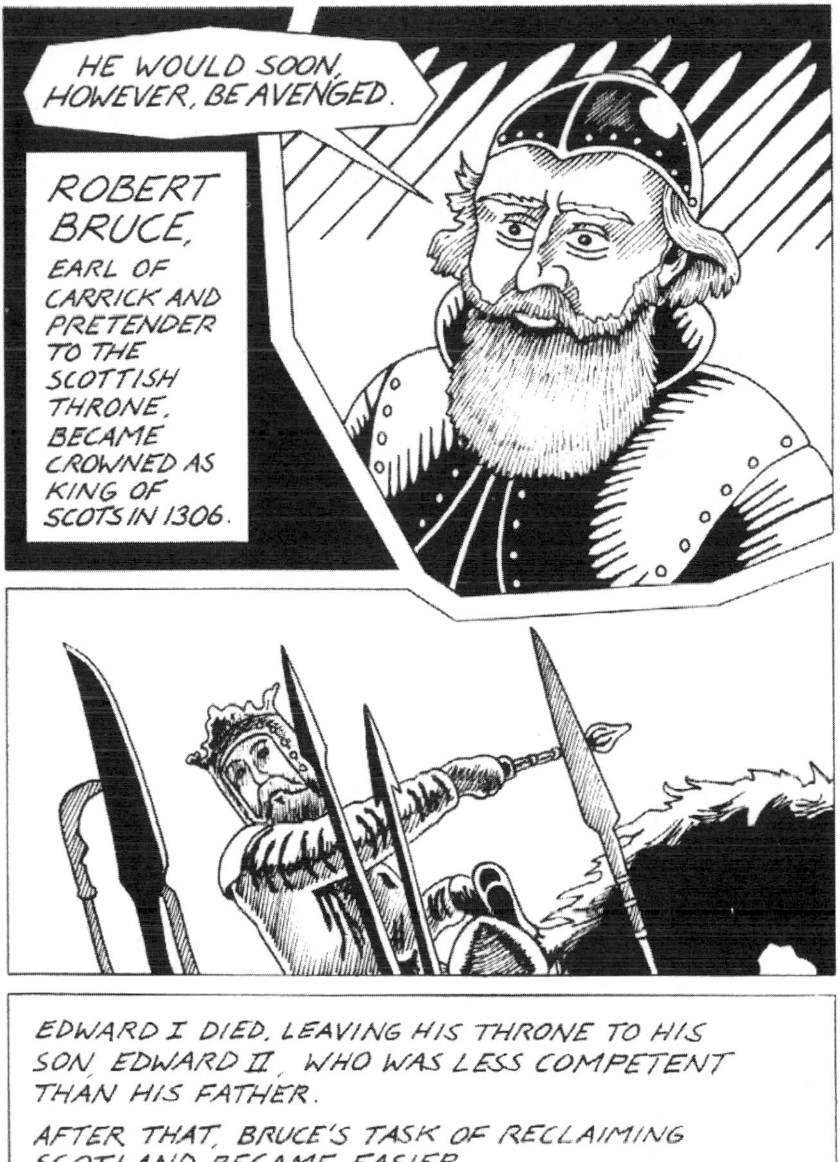
HE WOULD SOON, HOWEVER, BE AVENGED.
ROBERT BRUCE, EARL OF CARRICK AND PRETENDER TO THE SCOTTISH THRONE, BECAME CROWNED AS KING OF SCOTS IN 1306.
EDWARD I DIED, LEAVING HIS THRONE TO HIS SON, EDWARD II, WHO WAS LESS COMPETENT THAN HIS FATHER.
AFTER THAT, BRUCE'S TASK OF RECLAIMING SCOTLAND BECAME EASIER.

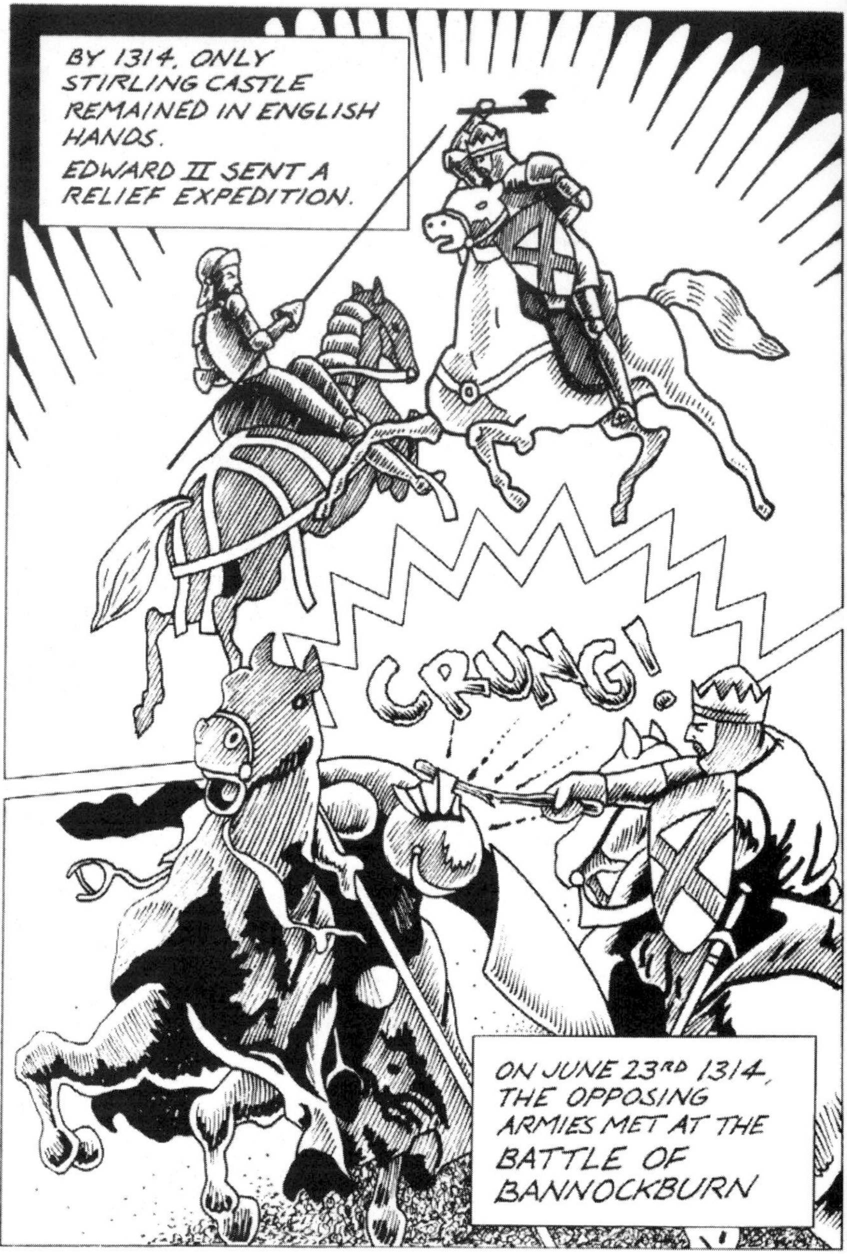
BY 1314, ONLY STIRLING CASTLE REMAINED IN ENGLISH HANDS.
EDWARD II SENT A RELIEF EXPEDITION.
CRUNG!
ON JUNE 23RD 1314, THE OPPOSING ARMIES MET AT THE BATTLE OF BANNOCKBURN

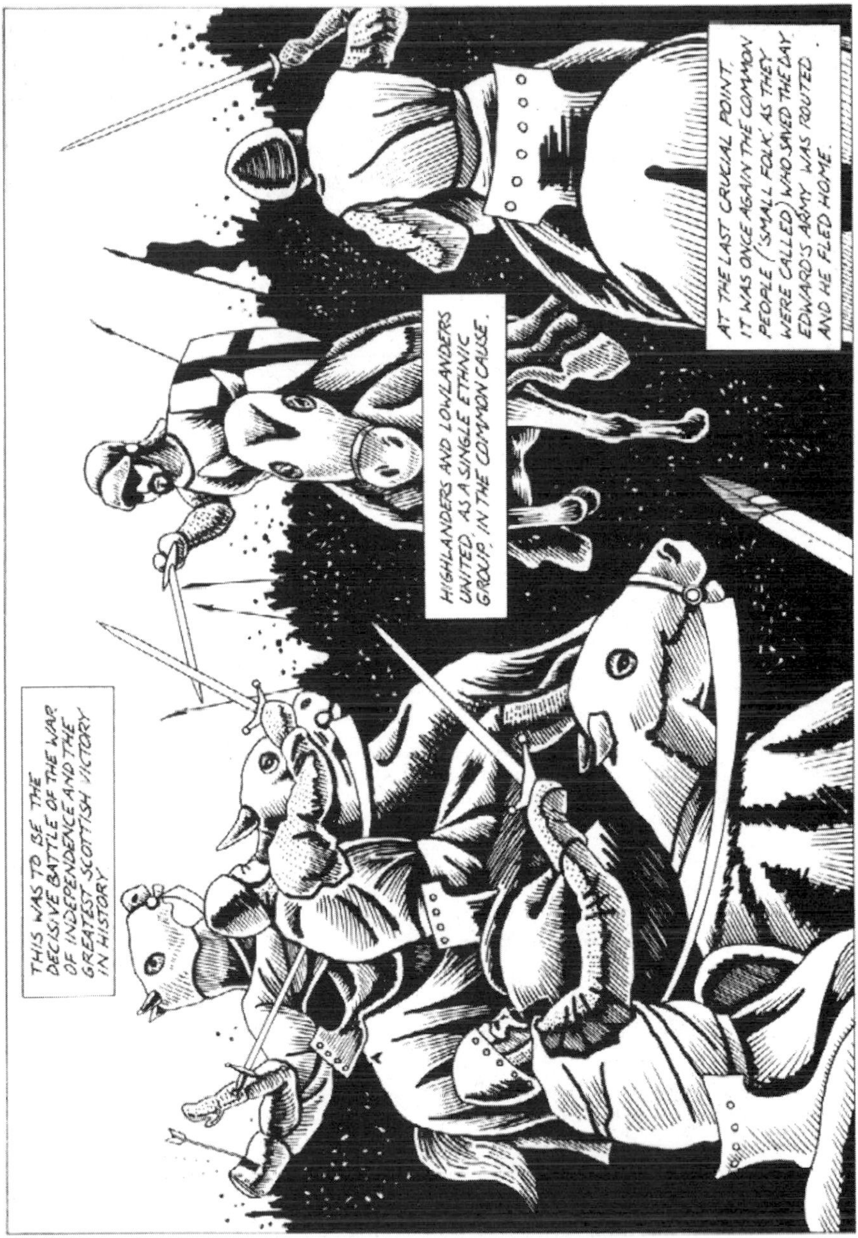
THIS WAS TO BE THE DECISIVE BATTLE OF THE WAR OF INDEPENDENCE AND THE GREATEST SCOTTISH VICTORY IN HISTORY
HIGHLANDERS AND LOWLANDERS UNITED, AS A SINGLE ETHNIC GROUP, IN THE COMMON CAUSE.
AT THE LAST CRUCIAL POINT IT WAS ONCE AGAIN THE COMMON PEOPLE ('SMALL FOLK' AS THEY WERE CALLED) WHO SAVED THE DAY. EDWARD'S ARMY WAS ROUTED AND HE FLED HOME.

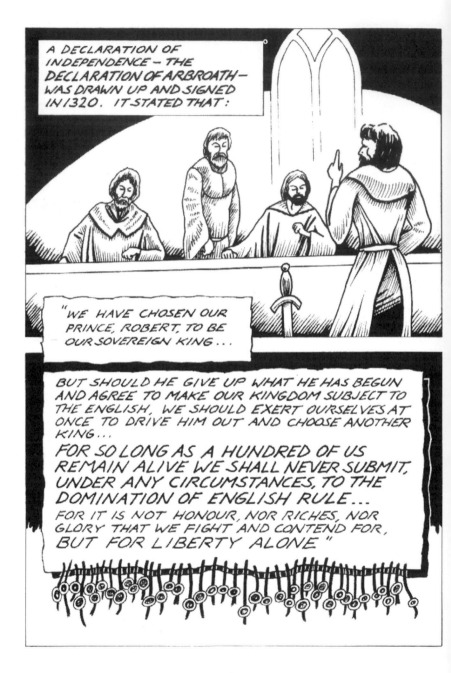

A DECLARATION OF INDEPENDENCE — THE DECLARATION OF ARBROATH — WAS DRAWN UP AND SIGNED IN 1320. IT STATED THAT:

"WE HAVE CHOSEN OUR PRINCE, ROBERT, TO BE OUR SOVEREIGN KING...

BUT SHOULD HE GIVE UP WHAT HE HAS BEGUN AND AGREE TO MAKE OUR KINGDOM SUBJECT TO THE ENGLISH, WE SHOULD EXERT OURSELVES AT ONCE TO DRIVE HIM OUT AND CHOOSE ANOTHER KING...

FOR SO LONG AS A HUNDRED OF US REMAIN ALIVE WE SHALL NEVER SUBMIT, UNDER ANY CIRCUMSTANCES, TO THE DOMINATION OF ENGLISH RULE...

FOR IT IS NOT HONOUR, NOR RICHES, NOR GLORY THAT WE FIGHT AND CONTEND FOR, BUT FOR LIBERTY ALONE"

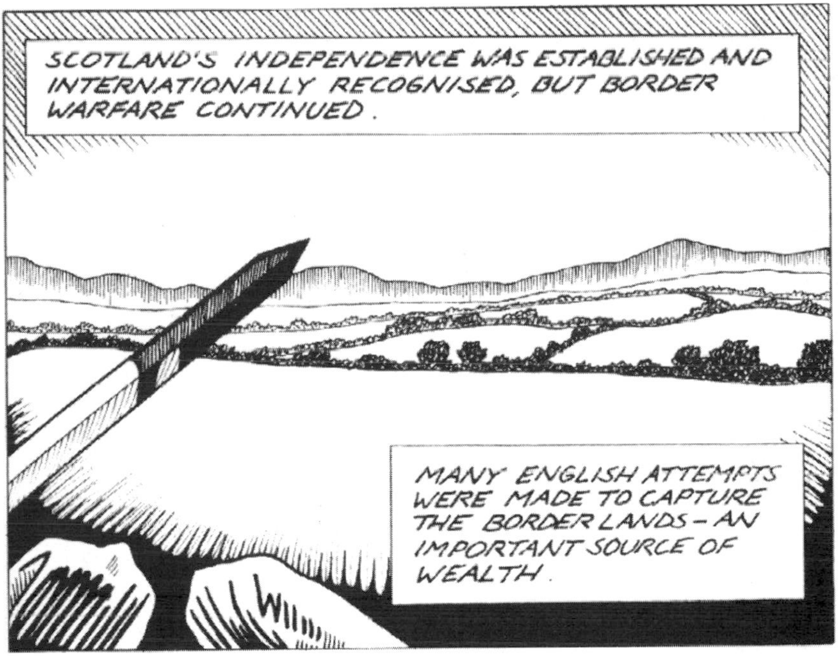
SCOTLAND'S INDEPENDENCE WAS ESTABLISHED AND INTERNATIONALLY RECOGNISED, BUT BORDER WARFARE CONTINUED.
MANY ENGLISH ATTEMPTS WERE MADE TO CAPTURE THE BORDER LANDS – AN IMPORTANT SOURCE OF WEALTH.

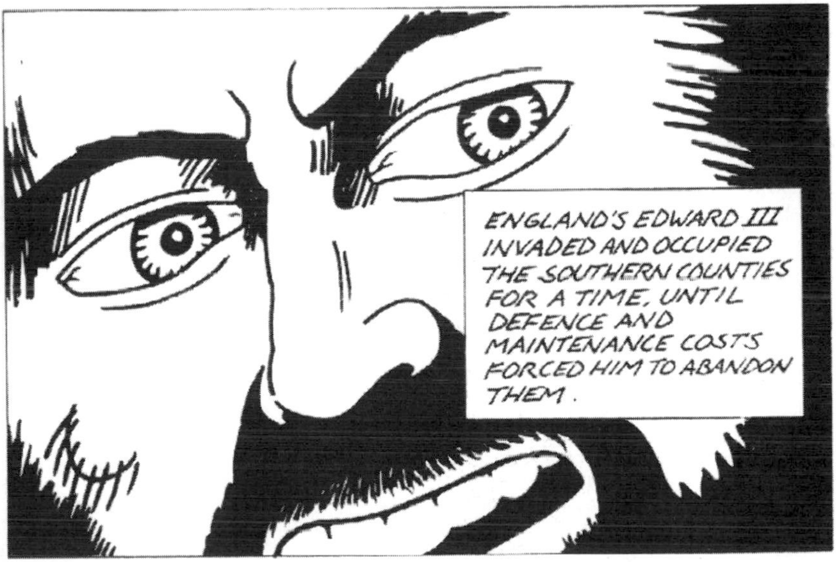
ENGLAND'S EDWARD III INVADED AND OCCUPIED THE SOUTHERN COUNTIES FOR A TIME, UNTIL DEFENCE AND MAINTENANCE COSTS FORCED HIM TO ABANDON THEM.

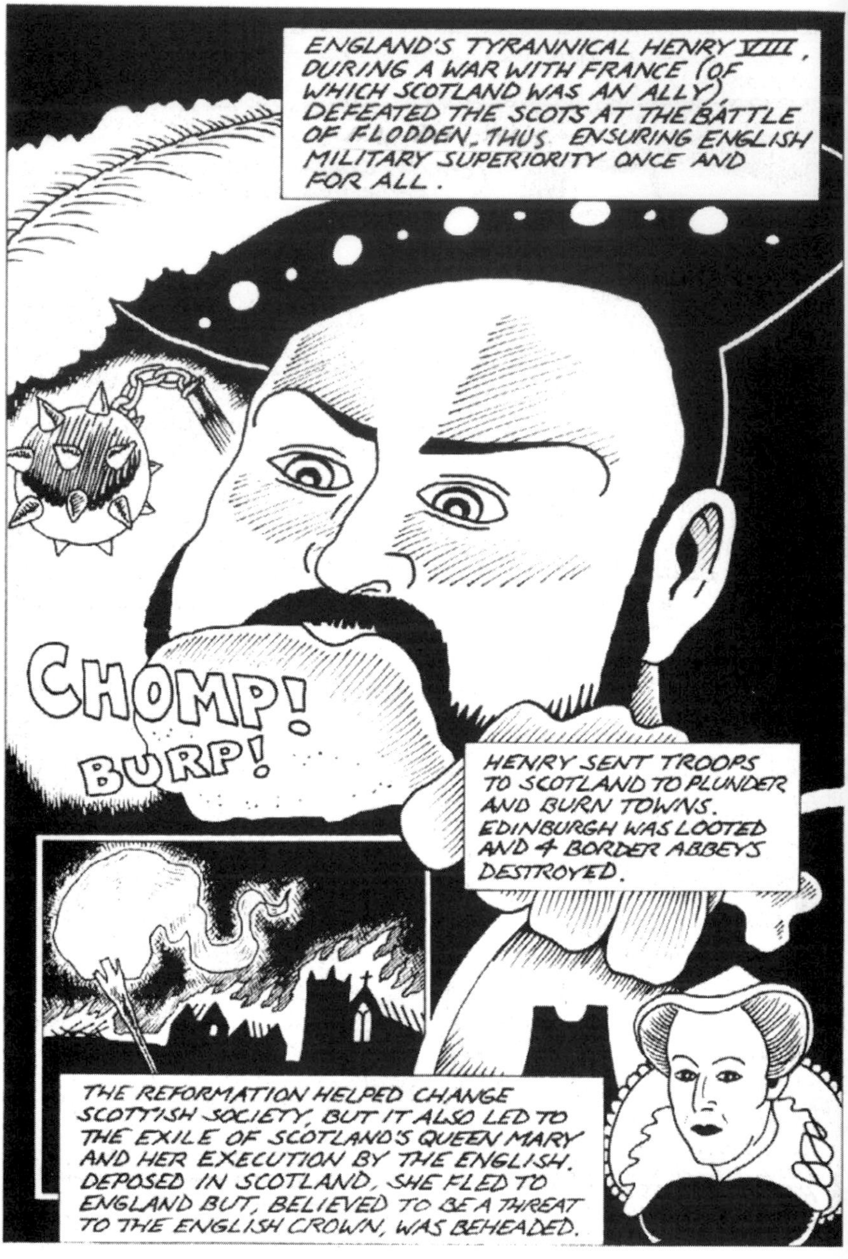
ENGLAND'S TYRANNICAL HENRY VIII, DURING A WAR WITH FRANCE (OF WHICH SCOTLAND WAS AN ALLY), DEFEATED THE SCOTS AT THE BATTLE OF FLODDEN, THUS ENSURING ENGLISH MILITARY SUPERIORITY ONCE AND FOR ALL.
CHOMP!
BURP!
HENRY SENT TROOPS TO SCOTLAND TO PLUNDER AND BURN TOWNS. EDINBURGH WAS LOOTED AND 4 BORDER ABBEYS DESTROYED.
THE REFORMATION HELPED CHANGE SCOTTISH SOCIETY, BUT IT ALSO LED TO THE EXILE OF SCOTLAND'S QUEEN MARY AND HER EXECUTION BY THE ENGLISH. DEPOSED IN SCOTLAND, SHE FLED TO ENGLAND BUT, BELIEVED TO BE A THREAT TO THE ENGLISH CROWN, WAS BEHEADED.

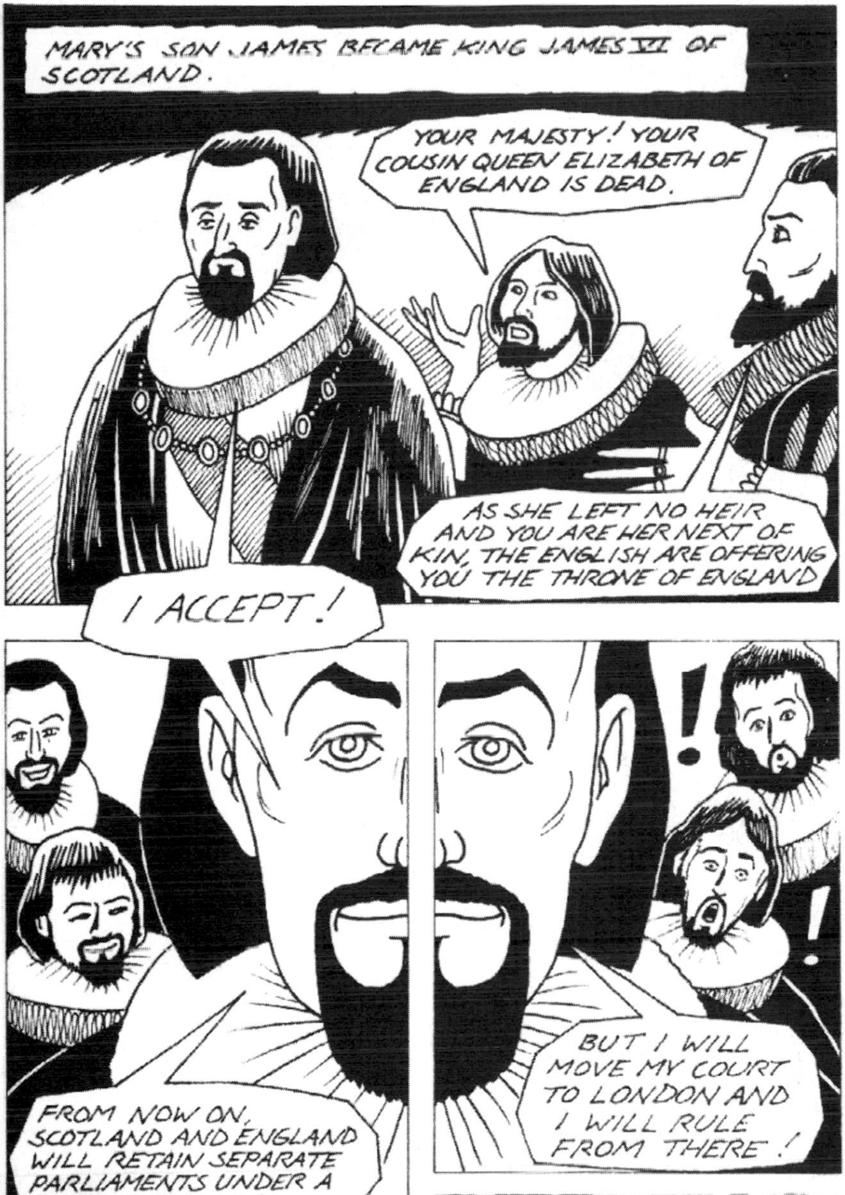
MARY'S SON JAMES BECAME KING JAMES VI OF SCOTLAND.
YOUR MAJESTY! YOUR COUSIN QUEEN ELIZABETH OF ENGLAND IS DEAD.
AS SHE LEFT NO HEIR AND YOU ARE HER NEXT OF KIN, THE ENGLISH ARE OFFERING YOU THE THRONE OF ENGLAND
I ACCEPT!
FROM NOW ON, SCOTLAND AND ENGLAND WILL RETAIN SEPARATE PARLIAMENTS UNDER A SINGLE CROWN...
!
!
BUT I WILL MOVE MY COURT TO LONDON AND I WILL RULE FROM THERE!
UNION OF CROWNS: 1603

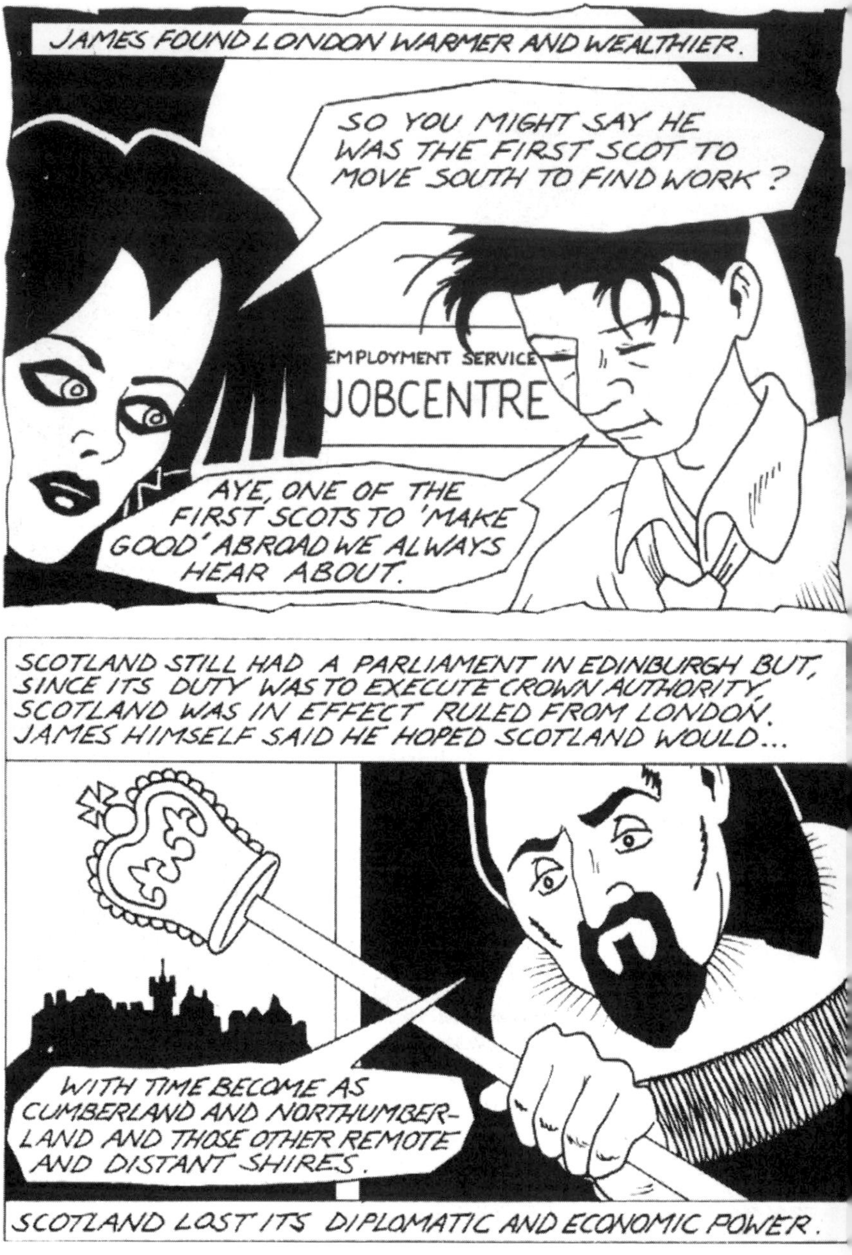
JAMES FOUND LONDON WARMER AND WEALTHIER.
SO YOU MIGHT SAY HE WAS THE FIRST SCOT TO MOVE SOUTH TO FIND WORK?
EMPLOYMENT SERVICE
JOBCENTRE
AYE, ONE OF THE FIRST SCOTS TO 'MAKE GOOD' ABROAD WE ALWAYS HEAR ABOUT.
SCOTLAND STILL HAD A PARLIAMENT IN EDINBURGH BUT, SINCE ITS DUTY WAS TO EXECUTE CROWN AUTHORITY, SCOTLAND WAS IN EFFECT RULED FROM LONDON. JAMES HIMSELF SAID HE HOPED SCOTLAND WOULD...
WITH TIME BECOME AS CUMBERLAND AND NORTHUMBERLAND AND THOSE OTHER REMOTE AND DISTANT SHIRES.
SCOTLAND LOST ITS DIPLOMATIC AND ECONOMIC POWER.

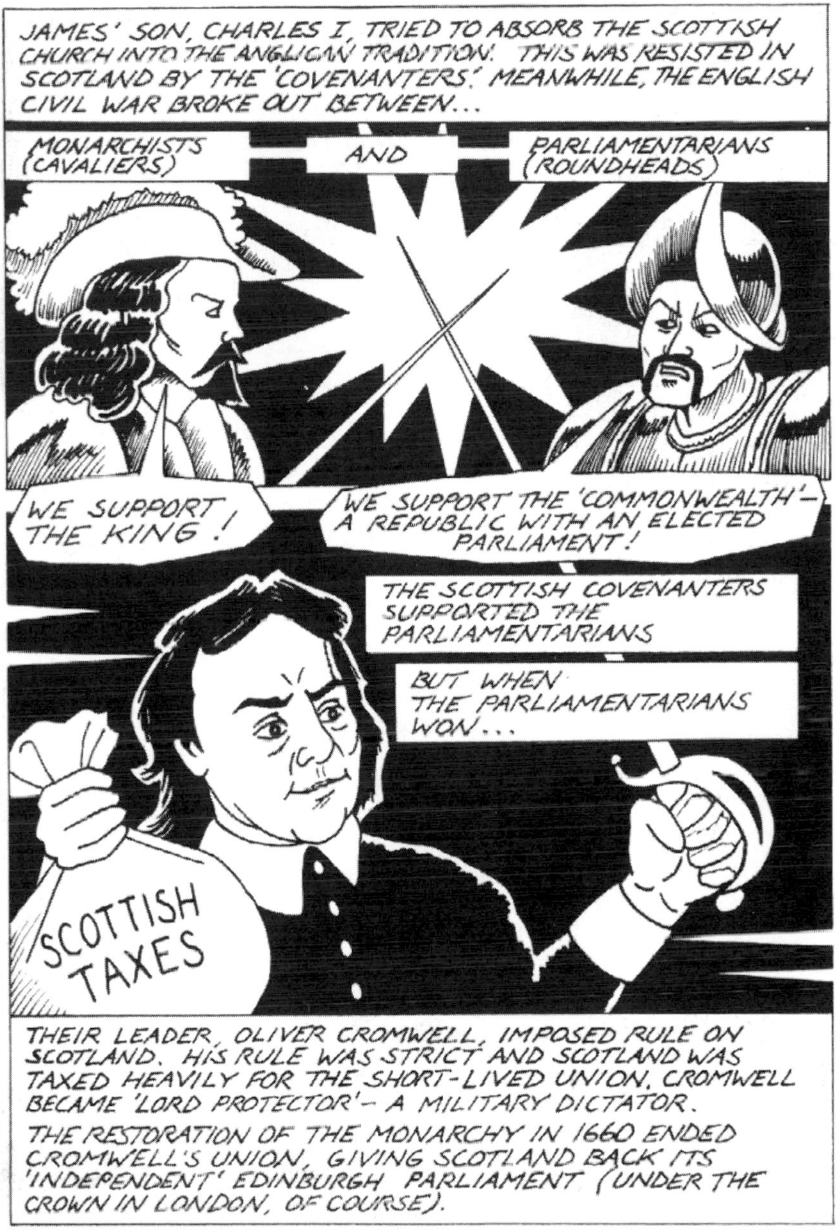
JAMES' SON, CHARLES I, TRIED TO ABSORB THE SCOTTISH CHURCH INTO THE ANGLICAN TRADITION. THIS WAS RESISTED IN SCOTLAND BY THE 'COVENANTERS.' MEANWHILE, THE ENGLISH CIVIL WAR BROKE OUT BETWEEN...
MONARCHISTS (CAVALIERS)
AND
PARLIAMENTARIANS (ROUNDHEADS)
WE SUPPORT THE KING!
WE SUPPORT THE 'COMMONWEALTH'– A REPUBLIC WITH AN ELECTED PARLIAMENT!
THE SCOTTISH COVENANTERS SUPPORTED THE PARLIAMENTARIANS
BUT WHEN THE PARLIAMENTARIANS WON...
SCOTTISH TAXES
THEIR LEADER, OLIVER CROMWELL, IMPOSED RULE ON SCOTLAND. HIS RULE WAS STRICT AND SCOTLAND WAS TAXED HEAVILY FOR THE SHORT-LIVED UNION. CROMWELL BECAME 'LORD PROTECTOR'– A MILITARY DICTATOR.
THE RESTORATION OF THE MONARCHY IN 1660 ENDED CROMWELL'S UNION, GIVING SCOTLAND BACK ITS 'INDEPENDENT' EDINBURGH PARLIAMENT (UNDER THE CROWN IN LONDON, OF COURSE).

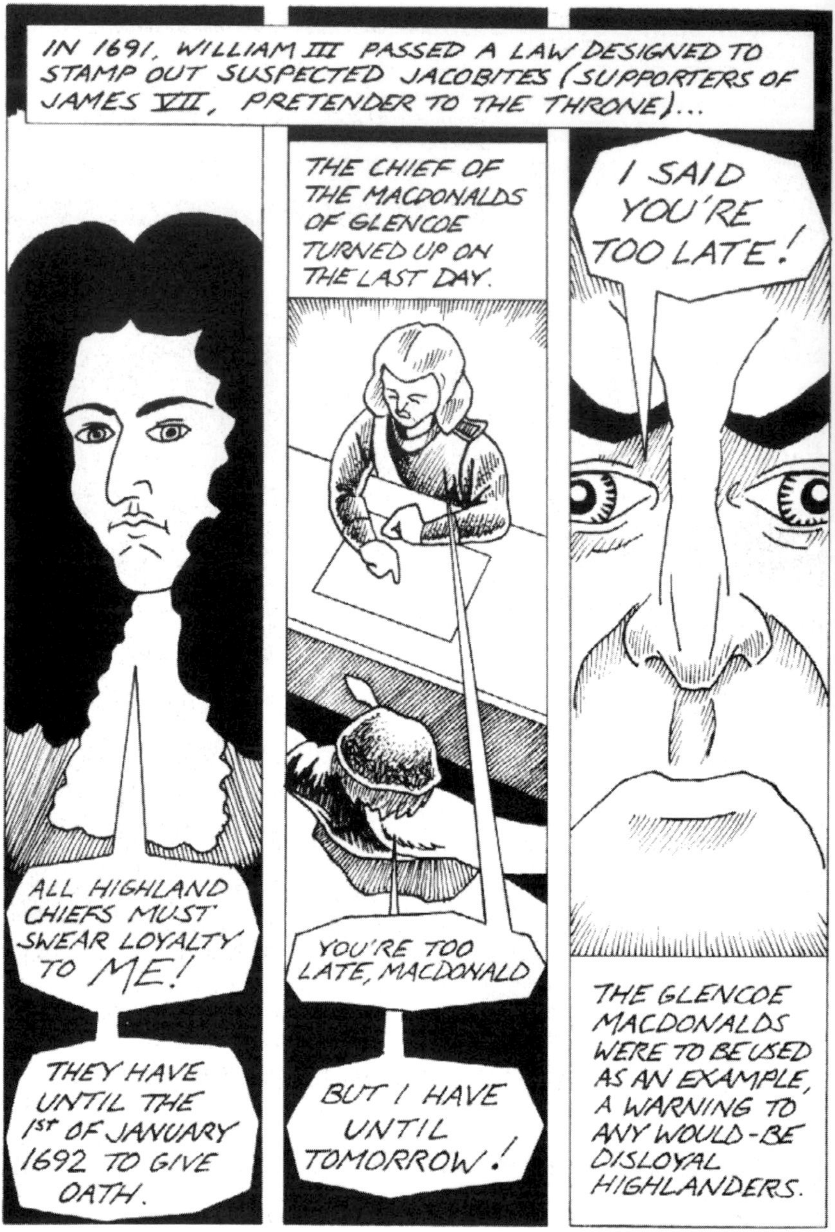
IN 1691, WILLIAM III PASSED A LAW DESIGNED TO STAMP OUT SUSPECTED JACOBITES (SUPPORTERS OF JAMES VII, PRETENDER TO THE THRONE)...
ALL HIGHLAND CHIEFS MUST SWEAR LOYALTY TO ME!
THEY HAVE UNTIL THE 1st OF JANUARY 1692 TO GIVE OATH.
THE CHIEF OF THE MACDONALDS OF GLENCOE TURNED UP ON THE LAST DAY.
YOU'RE TOO LATE, MACDONALD
BUT I HAVE UNTIL TOMORROW!
I SAID YOU'RE TOO LATE!
THE GLENCOE MACDONALDS WERE TO BE USED AS AN EXAMPLE, A WARNING TO ANY WOULD-BE DISLOYAL HIGHLANDERS.

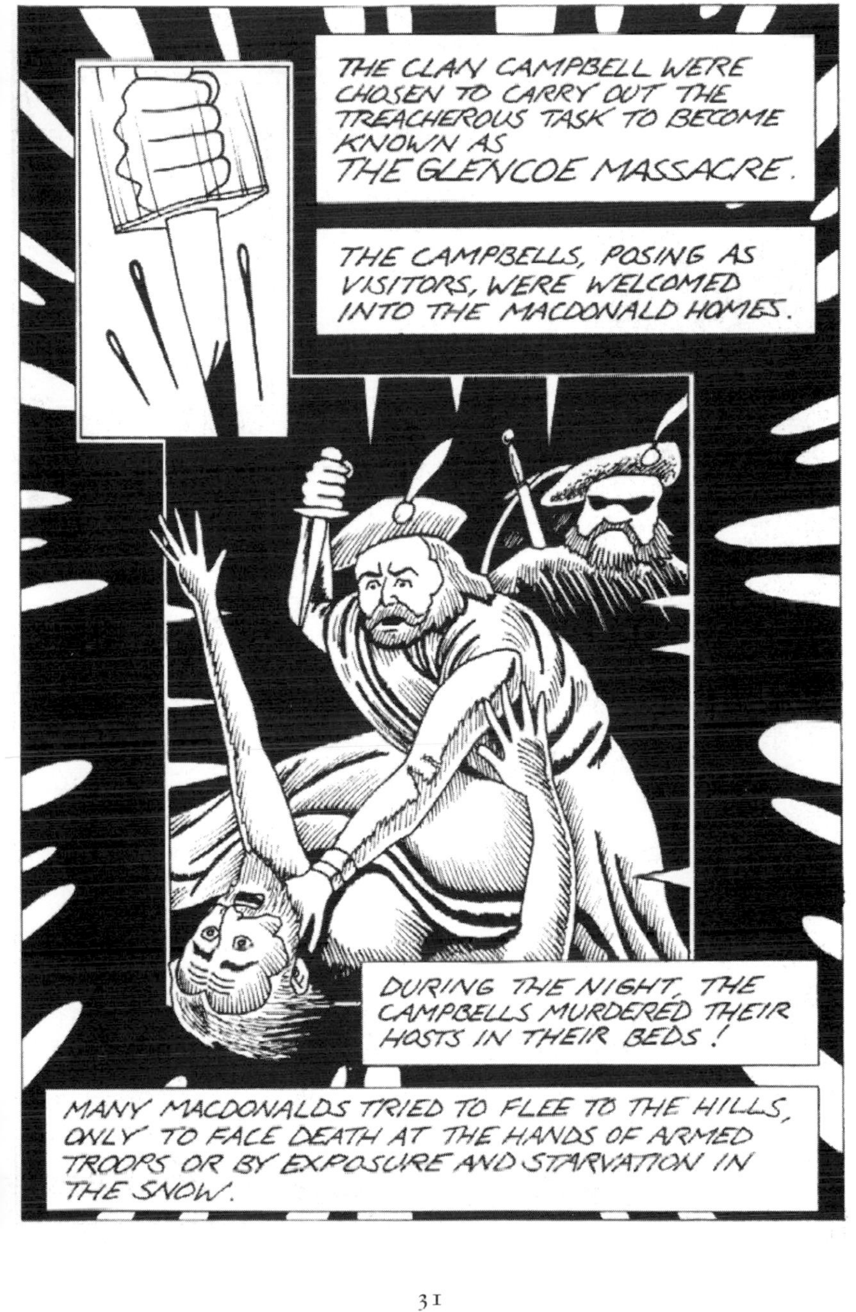
THE CLAN CAMPBELL WERE CHOSEN TO CARRY OUT THE TREACHEROUS TASK TO BECOME KNOWN AS THE GLENCOE MASSACRE.
THE CAMPBELLS, POSING AS VISITORS, WERE WELCOMED INTO THE MACDONALD HOMES.
DURING THE NIGHT, THE CAMPBELLS MURDERED THEIR HOSTS IN THEIR BEDS!
MANY MACDONALDS TRIED TO FLEE TO THE HILLS, ONLY TO FACE DEATH AT THE HANDS OF ARMED TROOPS OR BY EXPOSURE AND STARVATION IN THE SNOW.

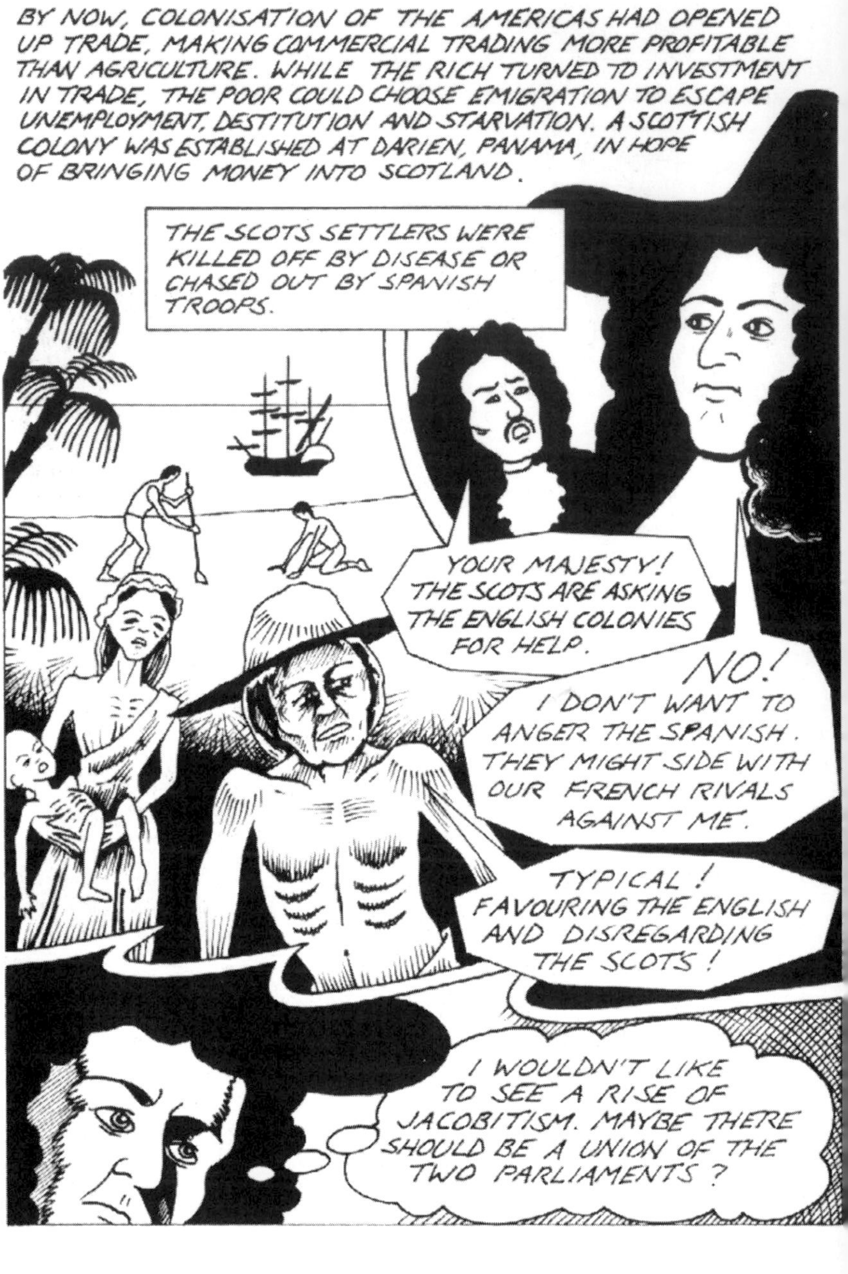
BY NOW, COLONISATION OF THE AMERICAS HAD OPENED UP TRADE, MAKING COMMERCIAL TRADING MORE PROFITABLE THAN AGRICULTURE. WHILE THE RICH TURNED TO INVESTMENT IN TRADE, THE POOR COULD CHOOSE EMIGRATION TO ESCAPE UNEMPLOYMENT, DESTITUTION AND STARVATION. A SCOTTISH COLONY WAS ESTABLISHED AT DARIEN, PANAMA, IN HOPE OF BRINGING MONEY INTO SCOTLAND.
THE SCOTS SETTLERS WERE KILLED OFF BY DISEASE OR CHASED OUT BY SPANISH TROOPS.
YOUR MAJESTY! THE SCOTS ARE ASKING THE ENGLISH COLONIES FOR HELP.
NO! I DON'T WANT TO ANGER THE SPANISH. THEY MIGHT SIDE WITH OUR FRENCH RIVALS AGAINST ME.
TYPICAL! FAVOURING THE ENGLISH AND DISREGARDING THE SCOTS!
I WOULDN'T LIKE TO SEE A RISE OF JACOBITISM. MAYBE THERE SHOULD BE A UNION OF THE TWO PARLIAMENTS?

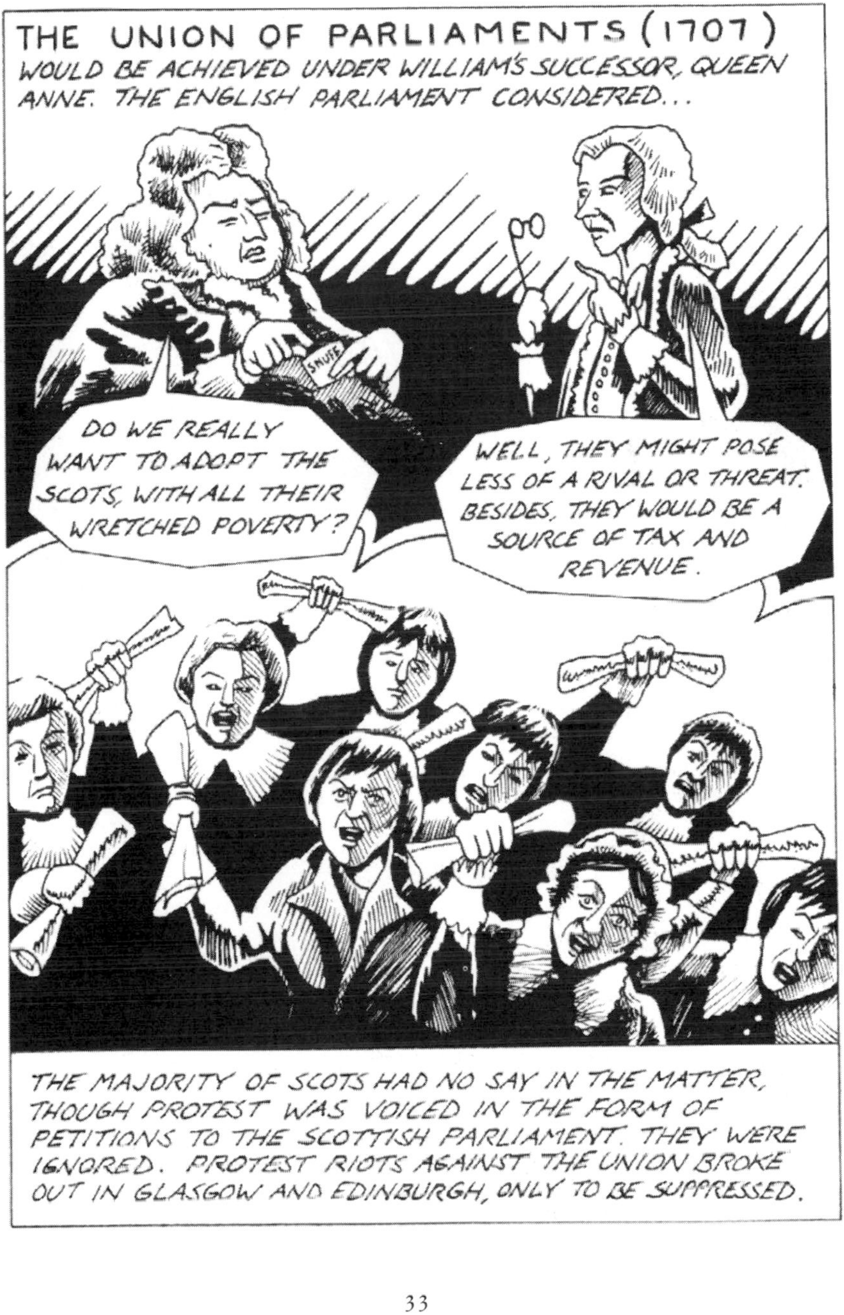
THE UNION OF PARLIAMENTS (1707)
WOULD BE ACHIEVED UNDER WILLIAM'S SUCCESSOR, QUEEN ANNE. THE ENGLISH PARLIAMENT CONSIDERED...
SNUFF
DO WE REALLY WANT TO ADOPT THE SCOTS, WITH ALL THEIR WRETCHED POVERTY?
WELL, THEY MIGHT POSE LESS OF A RIVAL OR THREAT. BESIDES, THEY WOULD BE A SOURCE OF TAX AND REVENUE.
THE MAJORITY OF SCOTS HAD NO SAY IN THE MATTER, THOUGH PROTEST WAS VOICED IN THE FORM OF PETITIONS TO THE SCOTTISH PARLIAMENT. THEY WERE IGNORED. PROTEST RIOTS AGAINST THE UNION BROKE OUT IN GLASGOW AND EDINBURGH, ONLY TO BE SUPPRESSED.

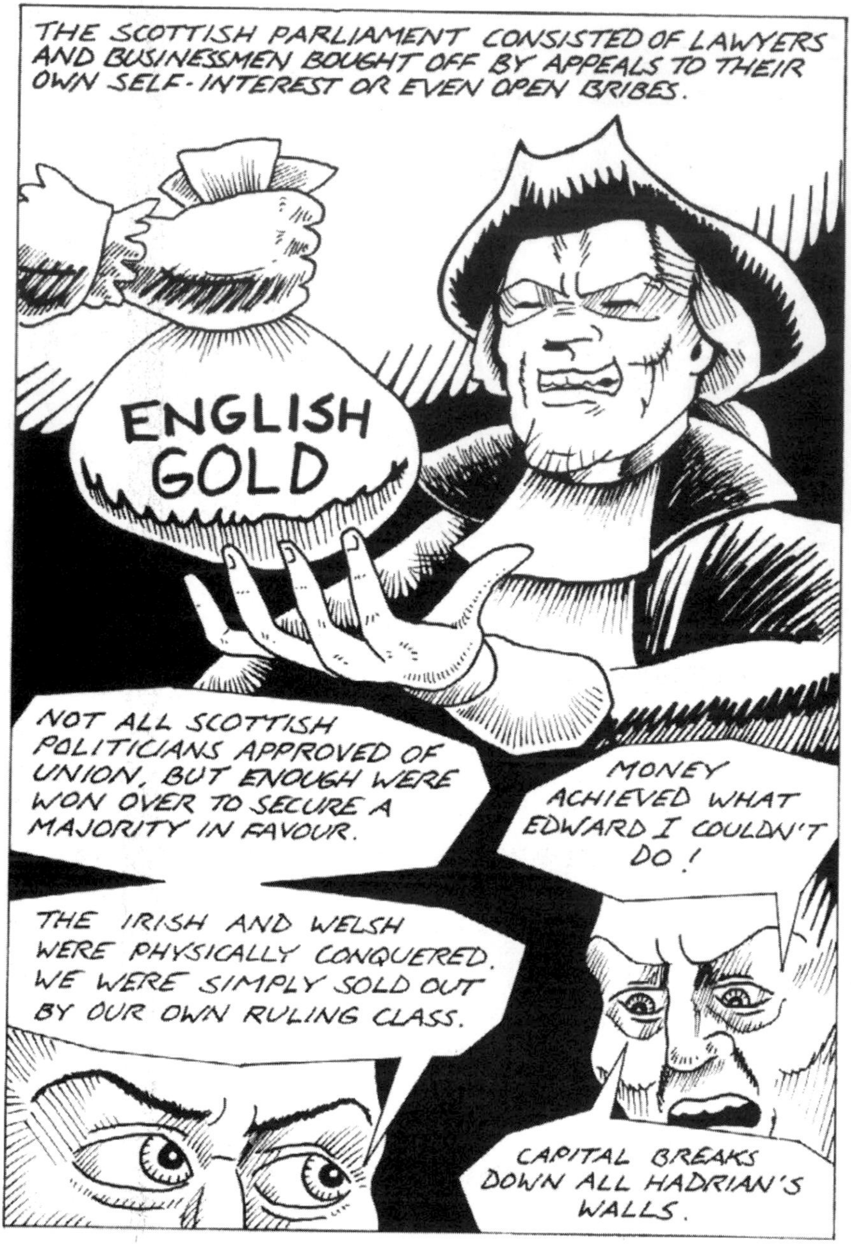
THE SCOTTISH PARLIAMENT CONSISTED OF LAWYERS AND BUSINESSMEN BOUGHT OFF BY APPEALS TO THEIR OWN SELF-INTEREST OR EVEN OPEN BRIBES.
ENGLISH GOLD
NOT ALL SCOTTISH POLITICIANS APPROVED OF UNION, BUT ENOUGH WERE WON OVER TO SECURE A MAJORITY IN FAVOUR.
MONEY ACHIEVED WHAT EDWARD I COULDN'T DO!
THE IRISH AND WELSH WERE PHYSICALLY CONQUERED. WE WERE SIMPLY SOLD OUT BY OUR OWN RULING CLASS.
CAPITAL BREAKS DOWN ALL HADRIAN'S WALLS.

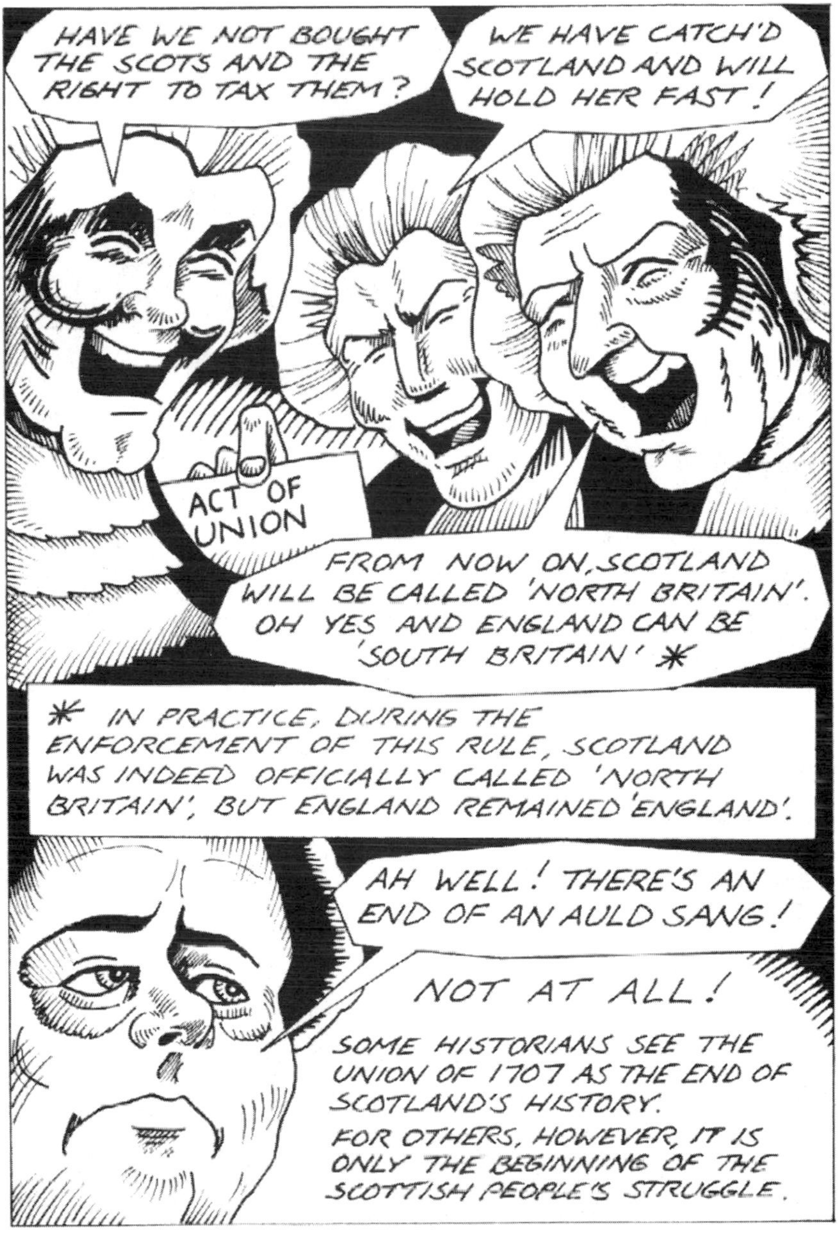
HAVE WE NOT BOUGHT THE SCOTS AND THE RIGHT TO TAX THEM?
WE HAVE CATCH'D SCOTLAND AND WILL HOLD HER FAST!
ACT OF UNION
FROM NOW ON, SCOTLAND WILL BE CALLED 'NORTH BRITAIN'. OH YES AND ENGLAND CAN BE 'SOUTH BRITAIN' *
* IN PRACTICE, DURING THE ENFORCEMENT OF THIS RULE, SCOTLAND WAS INDEED OFFICIALLY CALLED 'NORTH BRITAIN', BUT ENGLAND REMAINED 'ENGLAND'.
AH WELL! THERE'S AN END OF AN AULD SANG!
NOT AT ALL!
SOME HISTORIANS SEE THE UNION OF 1707 AS THE END OF SCOTLAND'S HISTORY.
FOR OTHERS, HOWEVER, IT IS ONLY THE BEGINNING OF THE SCOTTISH PEOPLE'S STRUGGLE.

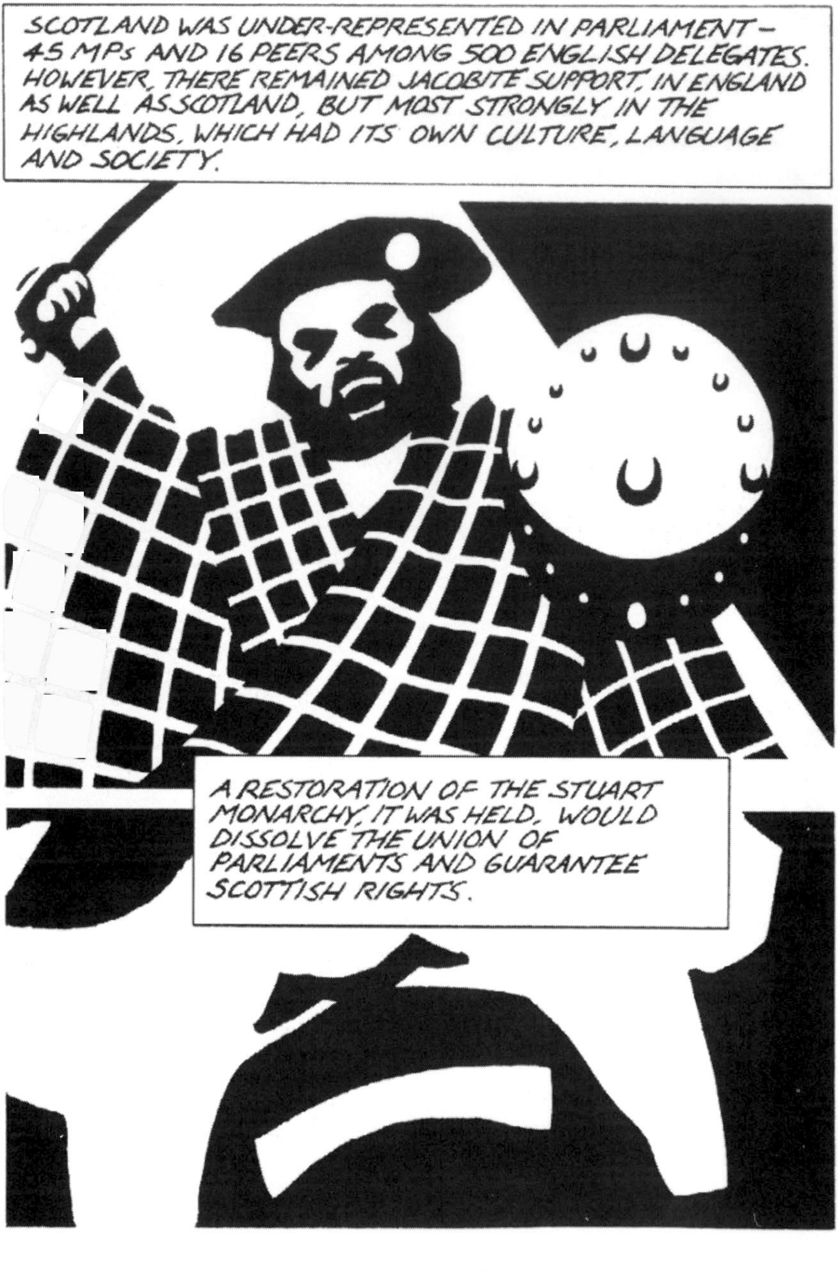
SCOTLAND WAS UNDER-REPRESENTED IN PARLIAMENT – 45 MPs AND 16 PEERS AMONG 500 ENGLISH DELEGATES. HOWEVER, THERE REMAINED JACOBITE SUPPORT, IN ENGLAND AS WELL AS SCOTLAND, BUT MOST STRONGLY IN THE HIGHLANDS, WHICH HAD ITS OWN CULTURE, LANGUAGE AND SOCIETY.
A RESTORATION OF THE STUART MONARCHY, IT WAS HELD, WOULD DISSOLVE THE UNION OF PARLIAMENTS AND GUARANTEE SCOTTISH RIGHTS.

THE JACOBITE PRETENDER JAMES VIII (& III) RETURNED FROM EXILE IN AN ATTEMPTED UPRISING IN 1715. IT FAILED AND HE FLED, BUT HIS SON CHARLES EDWARD STUART ('BONNIE PRINCE CHARLIE') TRIED AGAIN IN 1745...

AT FIRST THE '45 REBELLION WAS SUCCESSFUL.

THE JACOBITES, ADVANCING FROM SCOTLAND, REACHED AS FAR SOUTH AS DERBY.

GRADUALLY THE CAMPAIGN FELL, THE REBELS WITHDRAWING TO THE HIGHLANDS.

THEN CAME THE FINAL BLOW:

CHARLES EDWARD STUART

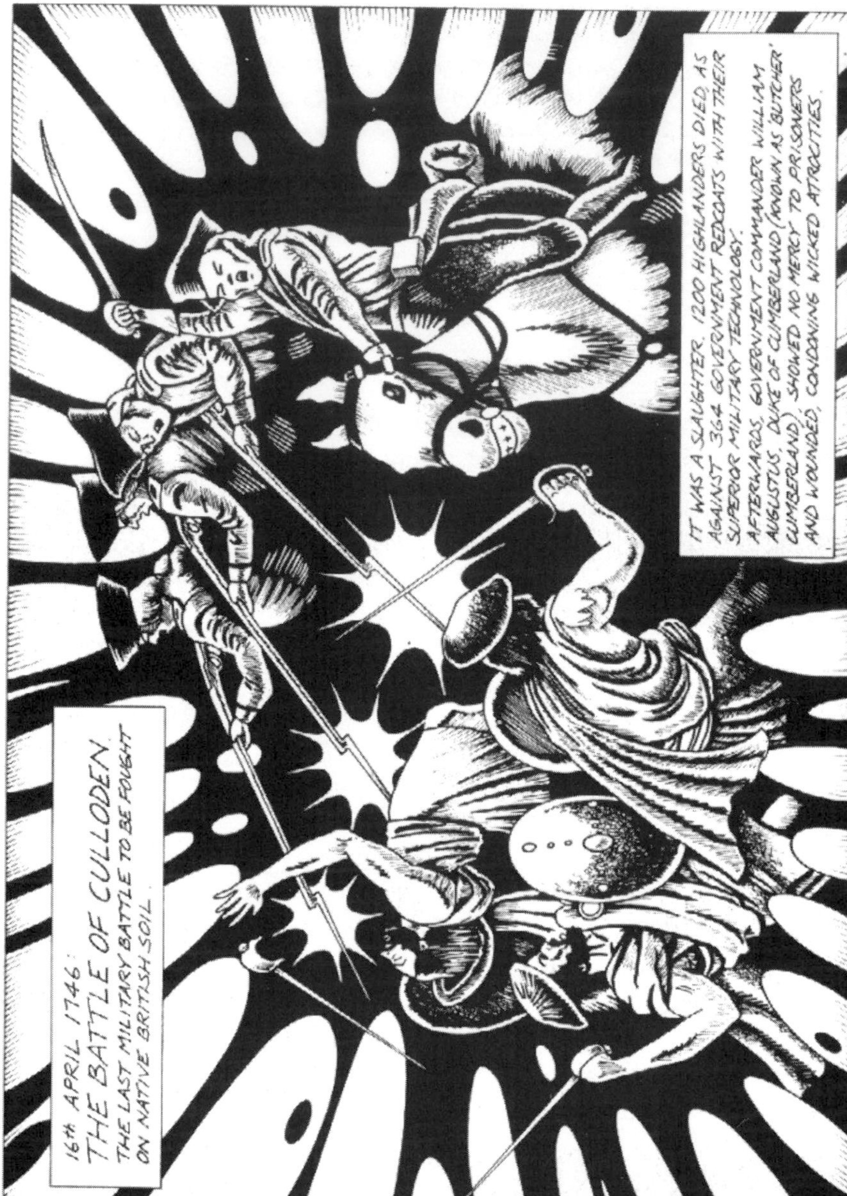
16th APRIL 1746:
THE BATTLE OF CULLODEN.
THE LAST MILITARY BATTLE TO BE FOUGHT ON NATIVE BRITISH SOIL.
IT WAS A SLAUGHTER. 1200 HIGHLANDERS DIED, AS AGAINST 364 GOVERNMENT REDCOATS WITH THEIR SUPERIOR MILITARY TECHNOLOGY.
AFTERWARDS, GOVERNMENT COMMANDER WILLIAM AUGUSTUS, DUKE OF CUMBERLAND (KNOWN AS 'BUTCHER' CUMBERLAND), SHOWED NO MERCY TO PRISONERS AND WOUNDED, CONDONING WICKED ATROCITIES.

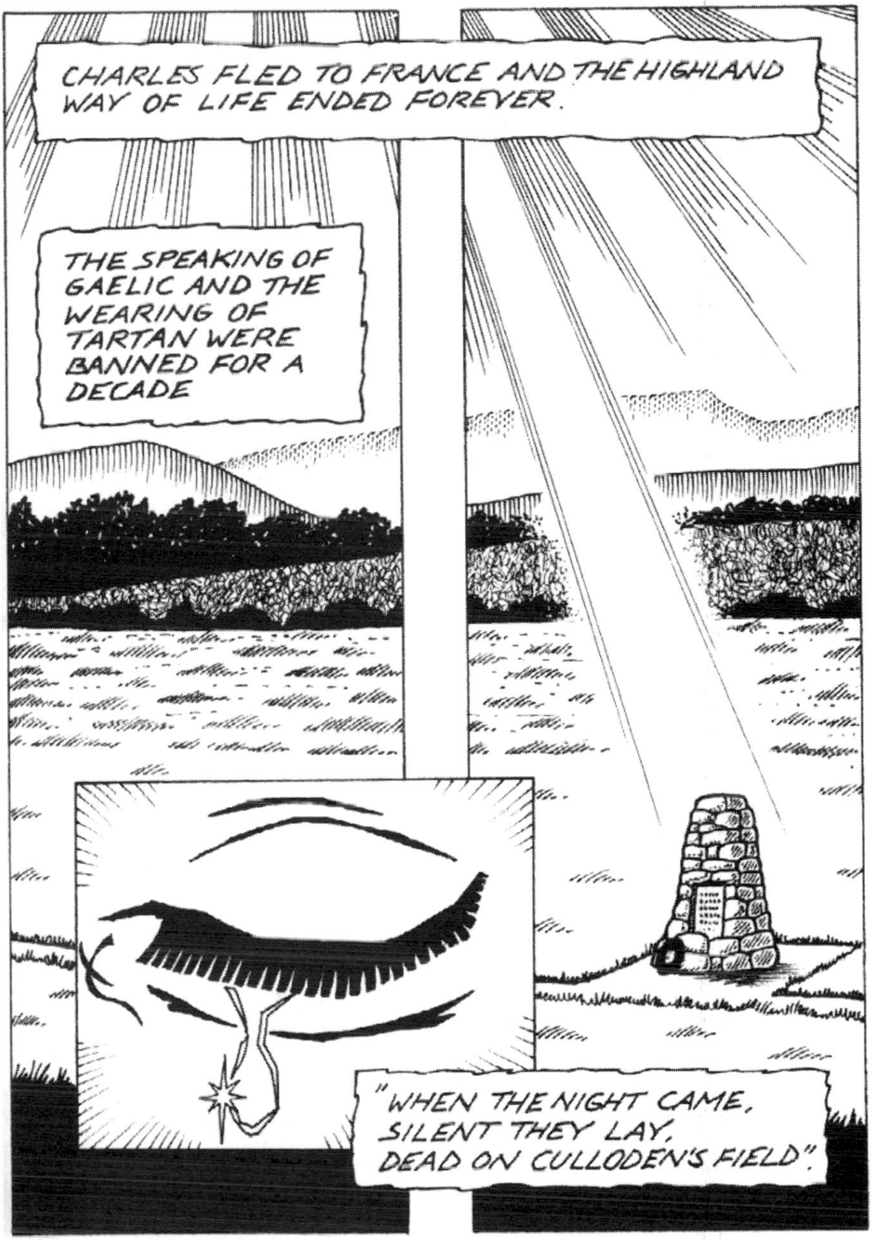
CHARLES FLED TO FRANCE AND THE HIGHLAND WAY OF LIFE ENDED FOREVER.
THE SPEAKING OF GAELIC AND THE WEARING OF TARTAN WERE BANNED FOR A DECADE
"WHEN THE NIGHT CAME, SILENT THEY LAY, DEAD ON CULLODEN'S FIELD".

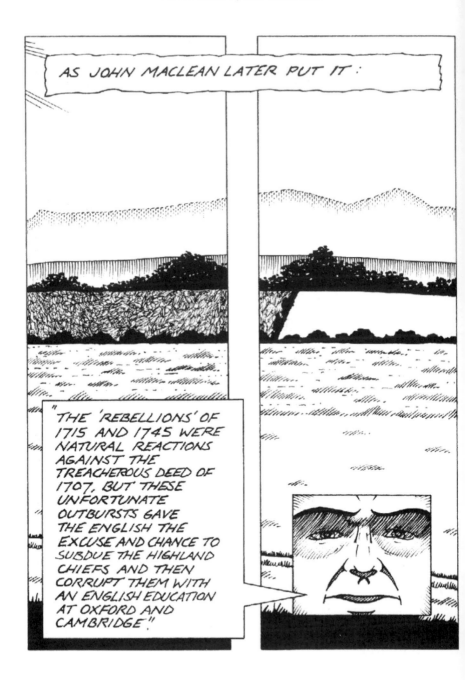

AS JOHN MACLEAN LATER PUT IT :

"THE 'REBELLIONS' OF 1715 AND 1745 WERE NATURAL REACTIONS AGAINST THE TREACHEROUS DEED OF 1707, BUT THESE UNFORTUNATE OUTBURSTS GAVE THE ENGLISH THE EXCUSE AND CHANCE TO SUBDUE THE HIGHLAND CHIEFS AND THEN CORRUPT THEM WITH AN ENGLISH EDUCATION AT OXFORD AND CAMBRIDGE."

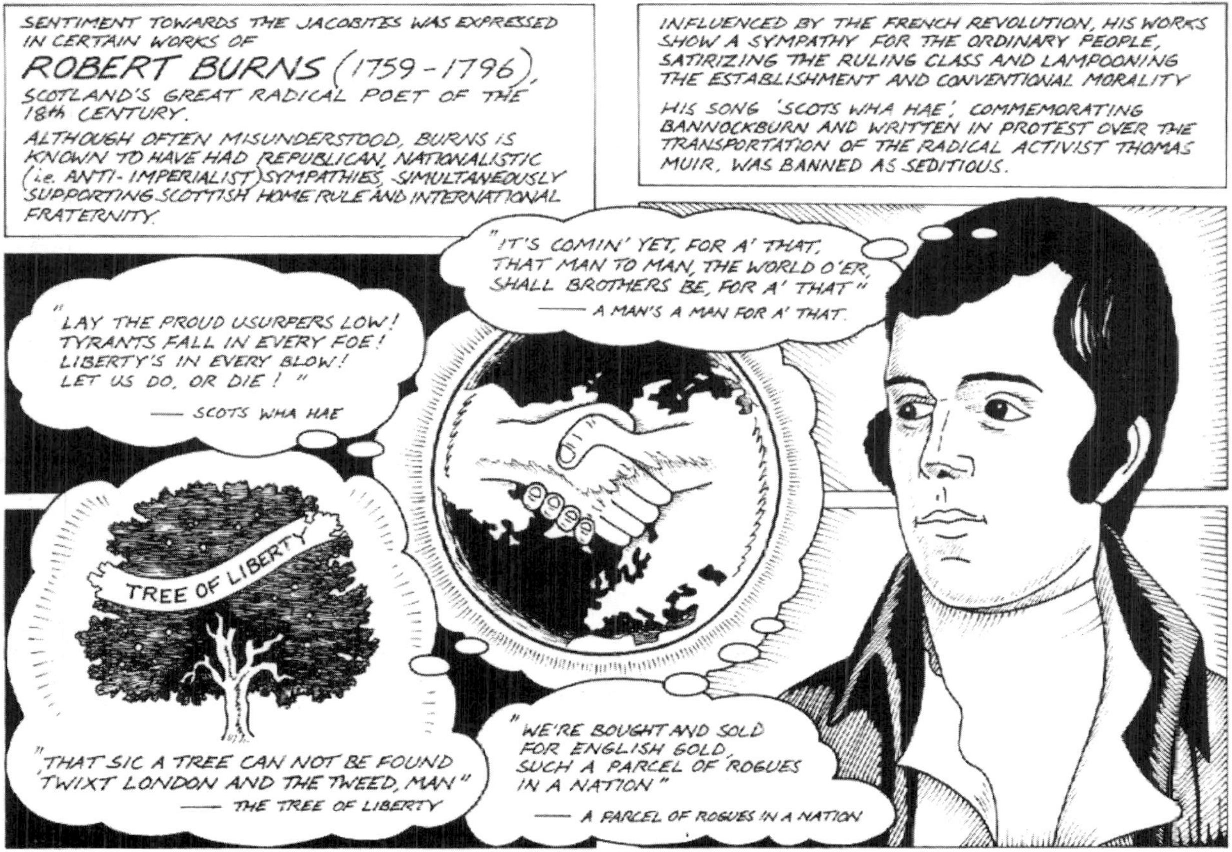
SENTIMENT TOWARDS THE JACOBITES WAS EXPRESSED IN CERTAIN WORKS OF
ROBERT BURNS (1759-1796),
SCOTLAND'S GREAT RADICAL POET OF THE 18th CENTURY.
ALTHOUGH OFTEN MISUNDERSTOOD, BURNS IS KNOWN TO HAVE HAD REPUBLICAN, NATIONALISTIC (i.e. ANTI-IMPERIALIST) SYMPATHIES, SIMULTANEOUSLY SUPPORTING SCOTTISH HOME RULE AND INTERNATIONAL FRATERNITY.
INFLUENCED BY THE FRENCH REVOLUTION, HIS WORKS SHOW A SYMPATHY FOR THE ORDINARY PEOPLE, SATIRIZING THE RULING CLASS AND LAMPOONING THE ESTABLISHMENT AND CONVENTIONAL MORALITY
HIS SONG 'SCOTS WHA HAE', COMMEMORATING BANNOCKBURN AND WRITTEN IN PROTEST OVER THE TRANSPORTATION OF THE RADICAL ACTIVIST THOMAS MUIR, WAS BANNED AS SEDITIOUS.
"LAY THE PROUD USURPERS LOW! TYRANTS FALL IN EVERY FOE! LIBERTY'S IN EVERY BLOW! LET US DO, OR DIE!"
— SCOTS WHA HAE
"IT'S COMIN' YET, FOR A' THAT, THAT MAN TO MAN, THE WORLD O'ER, SHALL BROTHERS BE, FOR A' THAT"
— A MAN'S A MAN FOR A' THAT.
TREE OF LIBERTY
"THAT SIC A TREE CAN NOT BE FOUND 'TWIXT LONDON AND THE TWEED, MAN"
— THE TREE OF LIBERTY
"WE'RE BOUGHT AND SOLD FOR ENGLISH GOLD, SUCH A PARCEL OF ROGUES IN A NATION"
— A PARCEL OF ROGUES IN A NATION

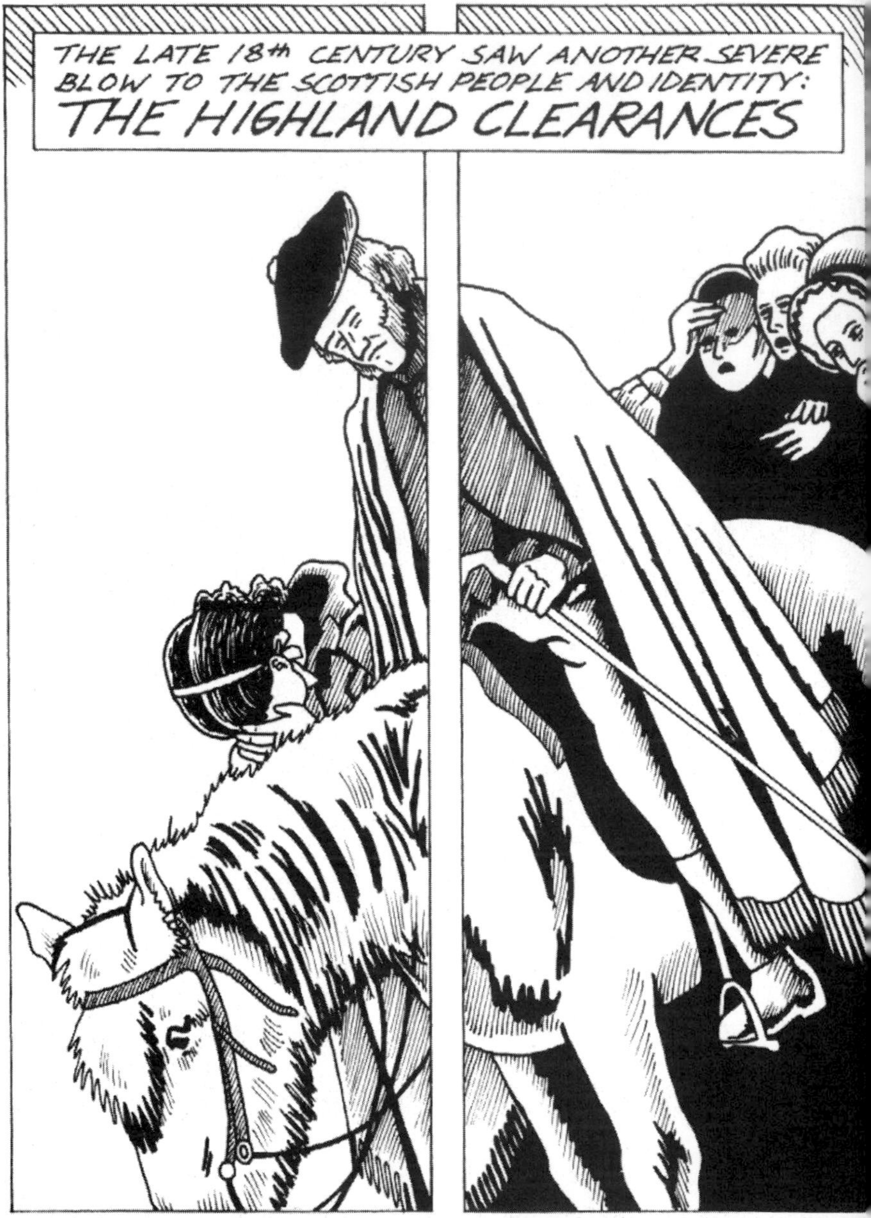
THE LATE 18th CENTURY SAW ANOTHER SEVERE BLOW TO THE SCOTTISH PEOPLE AND IDENTITY:
THE HIGHLAND CLEARANCES

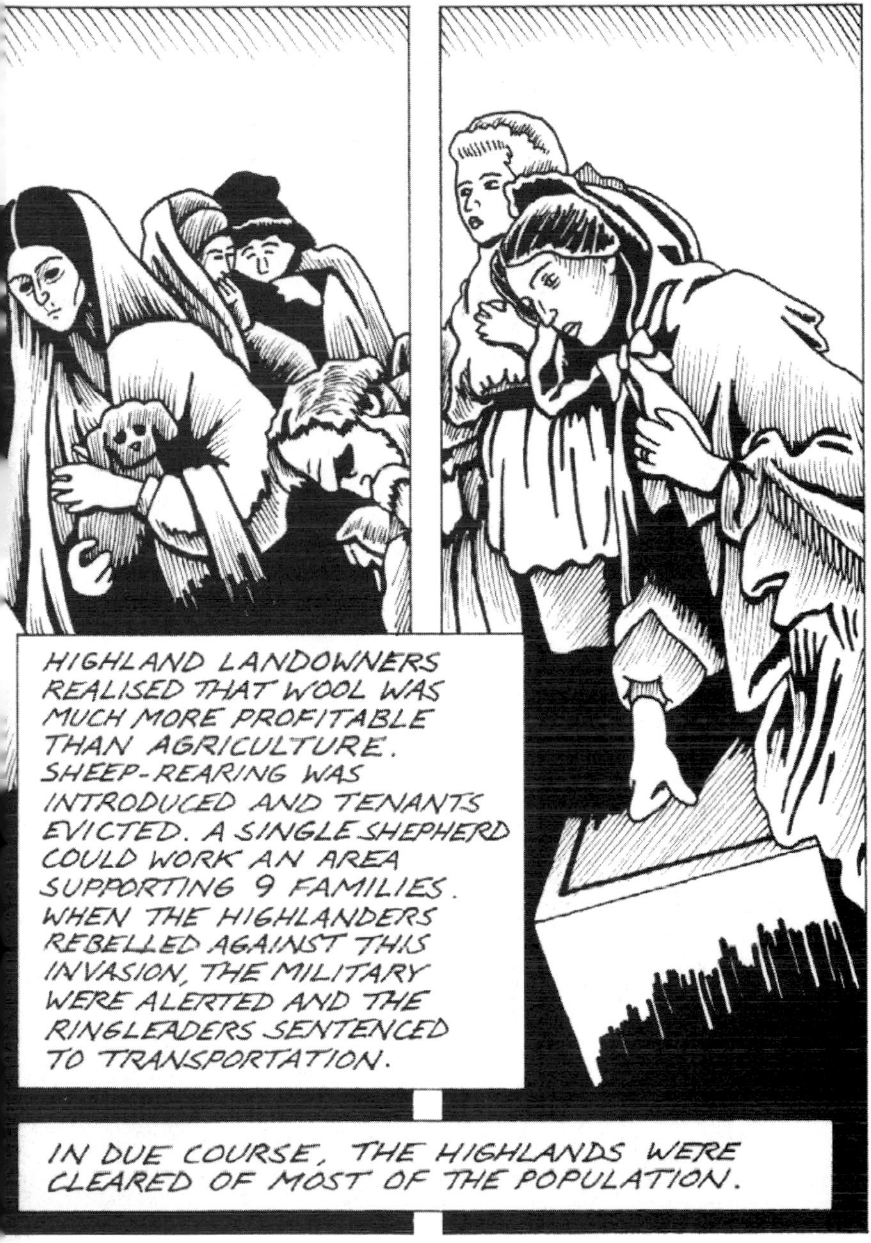
HIGHLAND LANDOWNERS REALISED THAT WOOL WAS MUCH MORE PROFITABLE THAN AGRICULTURE. SHEEP-REARING WAS INTRODUCED AND TENANTS EVICTED. A SINGLE SHEPHERD COULD WORK AN AREA SUPPORTING 9 FAMILIES. WHEN THE HIGHLANDERS REBELLED AGAINST THIS INVASION, THE MILITARY WERE ALERTED AND THE RINGLEADERS SENTENCED TO TRANSPORTATION.
IN DUE COURSE, THE HIGHLANDS WERE CLEARED OF MOST OF THE POPULATION.

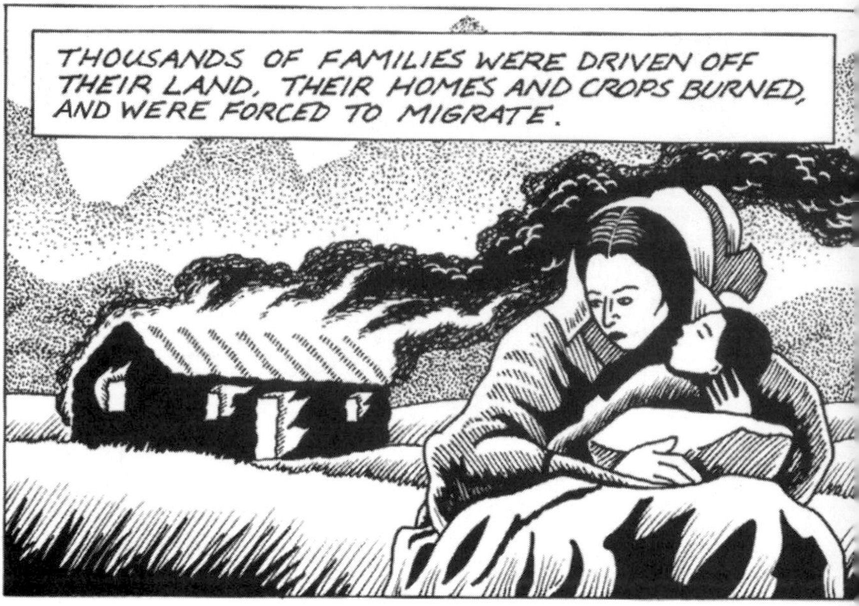
THOUSANDS OF FAMILIES WERE DRIVEN OFF THEIR LAND, THEIR HOMES AND CROPS BURNED, AND WERE FORCED TO MIGRATE.

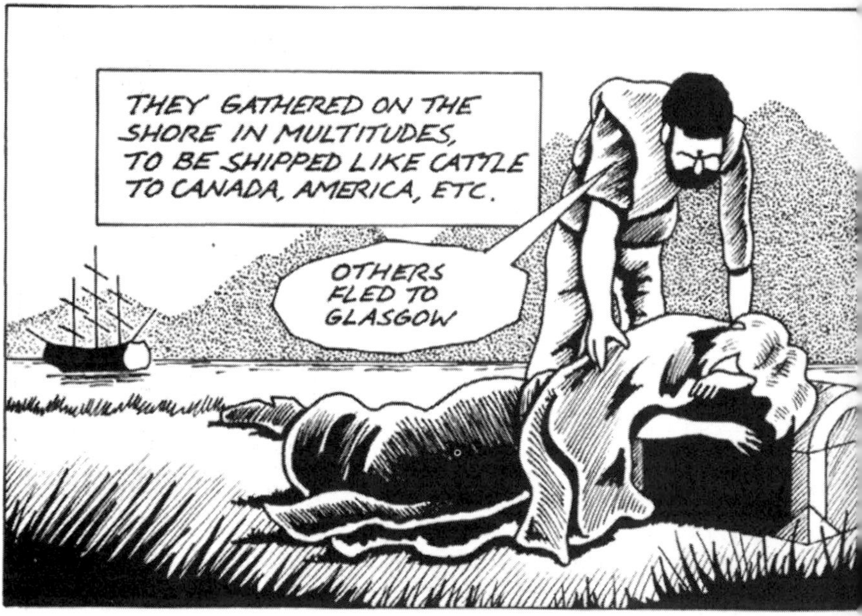
THEY GATHERED ON THE SHORE IN MULTITUDES, TO BE SHIPPED LIKE CATTLE TO CANADA, AMERICA, ETC.
OTHERS FLED TO GLASGOW

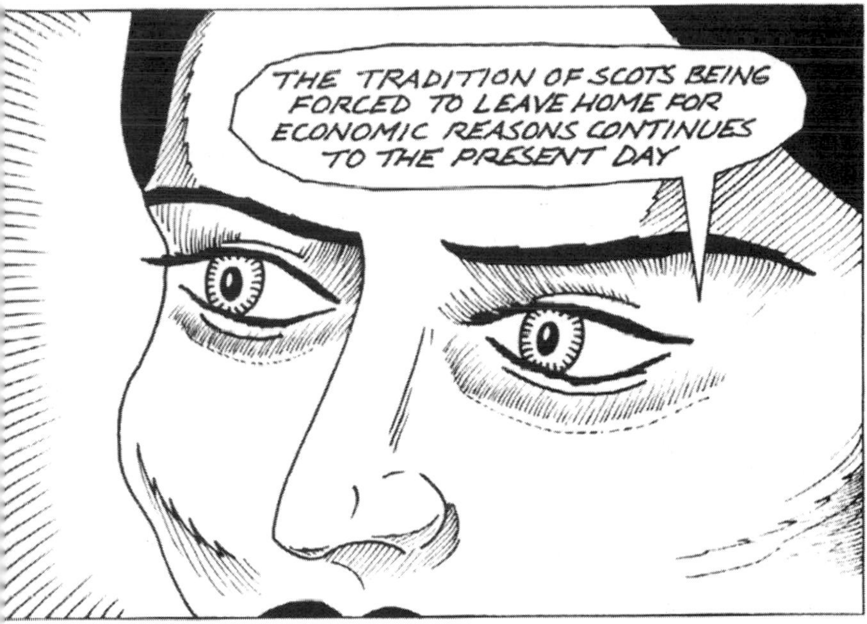
THE TRADITION OF SCOTS BEING FORCED TO LEAVE HOME FOR ECONOMIC REASONS CONTINUES TO THE PRESENT DAY

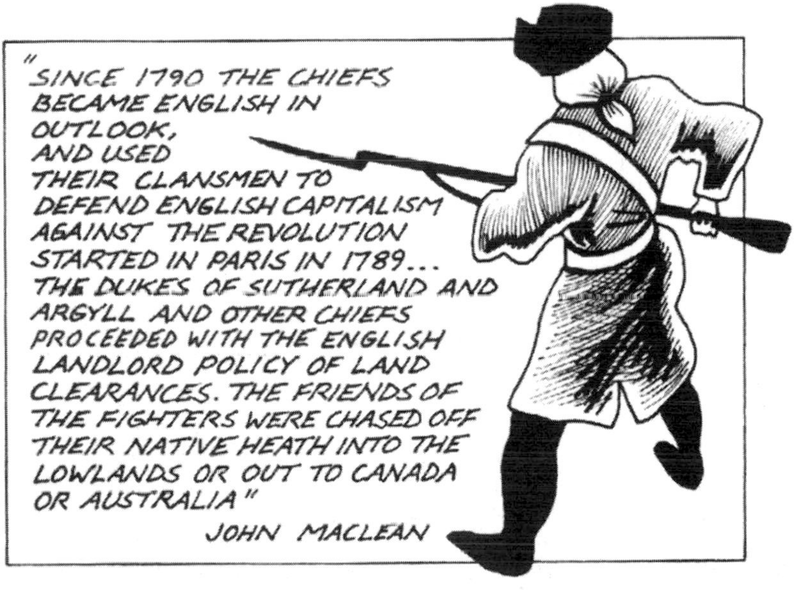
"SINCE 1790 THE CHIEFS BECAME ENGLISH IN OUTLOOK, AND USED THEIR CLANSMEN TO DEFEND ENGLISH CAPITALISM AGAINST THE REVOLUTION STARTED IN PARIS IN 1789... THE DUKES OF SUTHERLAND AND ARGYLL AND OTHER CHIEFS PROCEEDED WITH THE ENGLISH LANDLORD POLICY OF LAND CLEARANCES. THE FRIENDS OF THE FIGHTERS WERE CHASED OFF THEIR NATIVE HEATH INTO THE LOWLANDS OR OUT TO CANADA OR AUSTRALIA"
JOHN MACLEAN

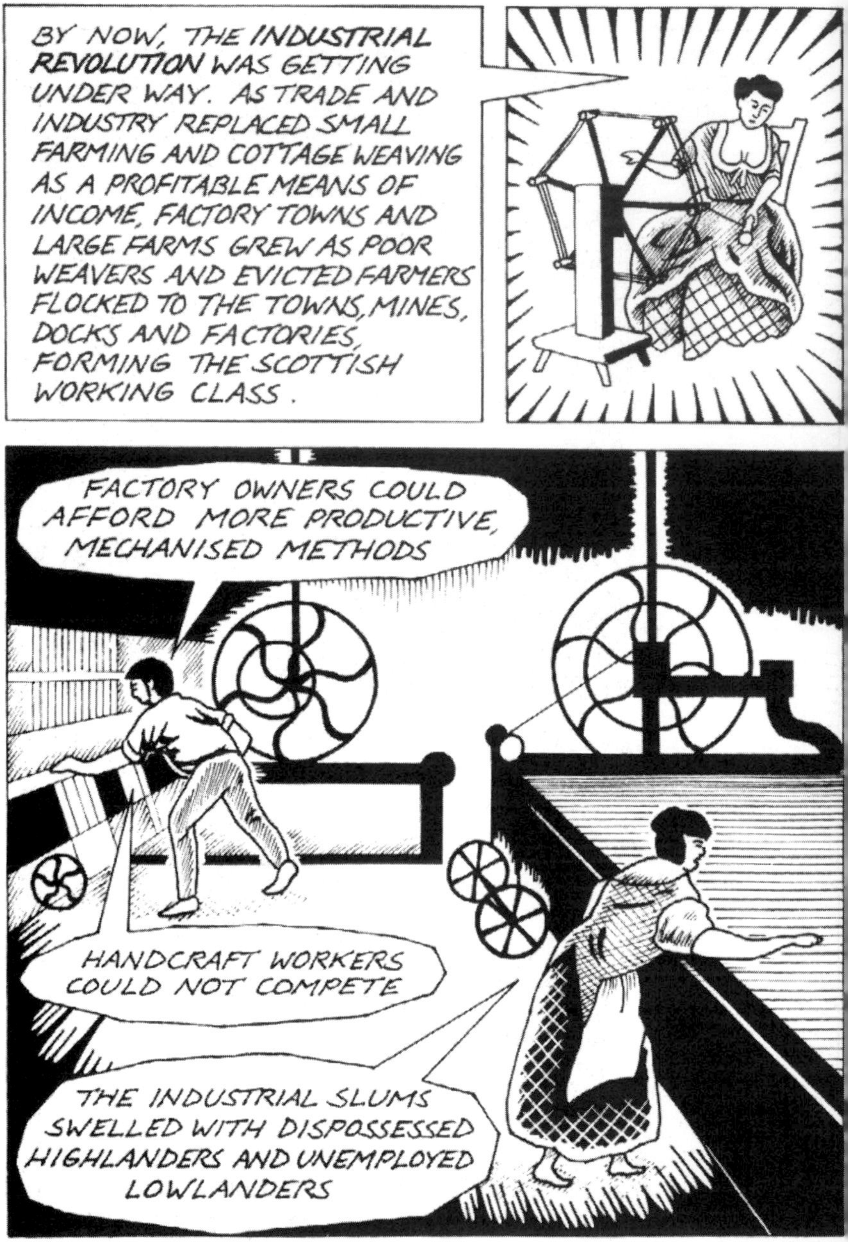
BY NOW, THE **INDUSTRIAL REVOLUTION** WAS GETTING UNDER WAY. AS TRADE AND INDUSTRY REPLACED SMALL FARMING AND COTTAGE WEAVING AS A PROFITABLE MEANS OF INCOME, FACTORY TOWNS AND LARGE FARMS GREW AS POOR WEAVERS AND EVICTED FARMERS FLOCKED TO THE TOWNS, MINES, DOCKS AND FACTORIES, FORMING THE SCOTTISH WORKING CLASS.
FACTORY OWNERS COULD AFFORD MORE PRODUCTIVE, MECHANISED METHODS
HANDCRAFT WORKERS COULD NOT COMPETE
THE INDUSTRIAL SLUMS SWELLED WITH DISPOSSESSED HIGHLANDERS AND UNEMPLOYED LOWLANDERS

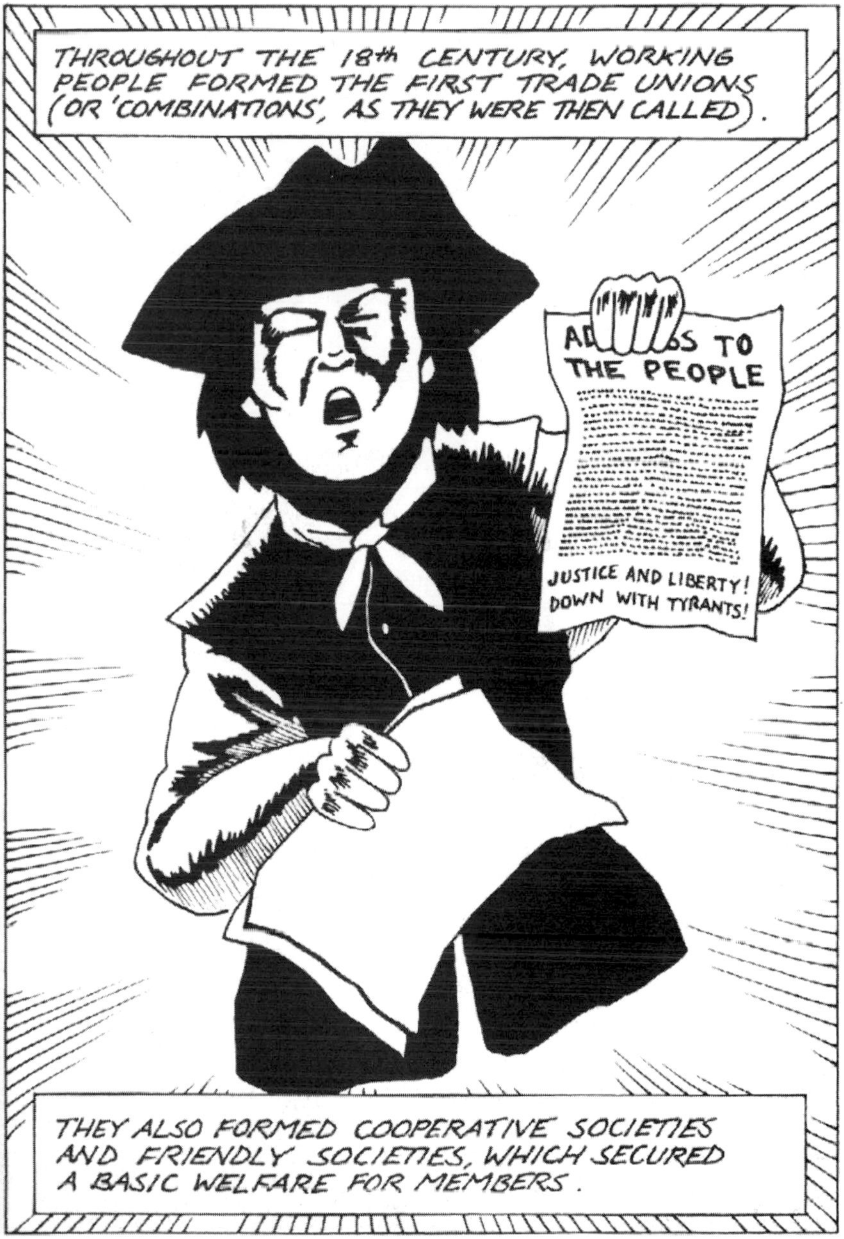
THROUGHOUT THE 18th CENTURY, WORKING PEOPLE FORMED THE FIRST TRADE UNIONS (OR 'COMBINATIONS', AS THEY WERE THEN CALLED).
THE PEOPLE
JUSTICE AND LIBERTY! DOWN WITH TYRANTS!
THEY ALSO FORMED COOPERATIVE SOCIETIES AND FRIENDLY SOCIETIES, WHICH SECURED A BASIC WELFARE FOR MEMBERS.

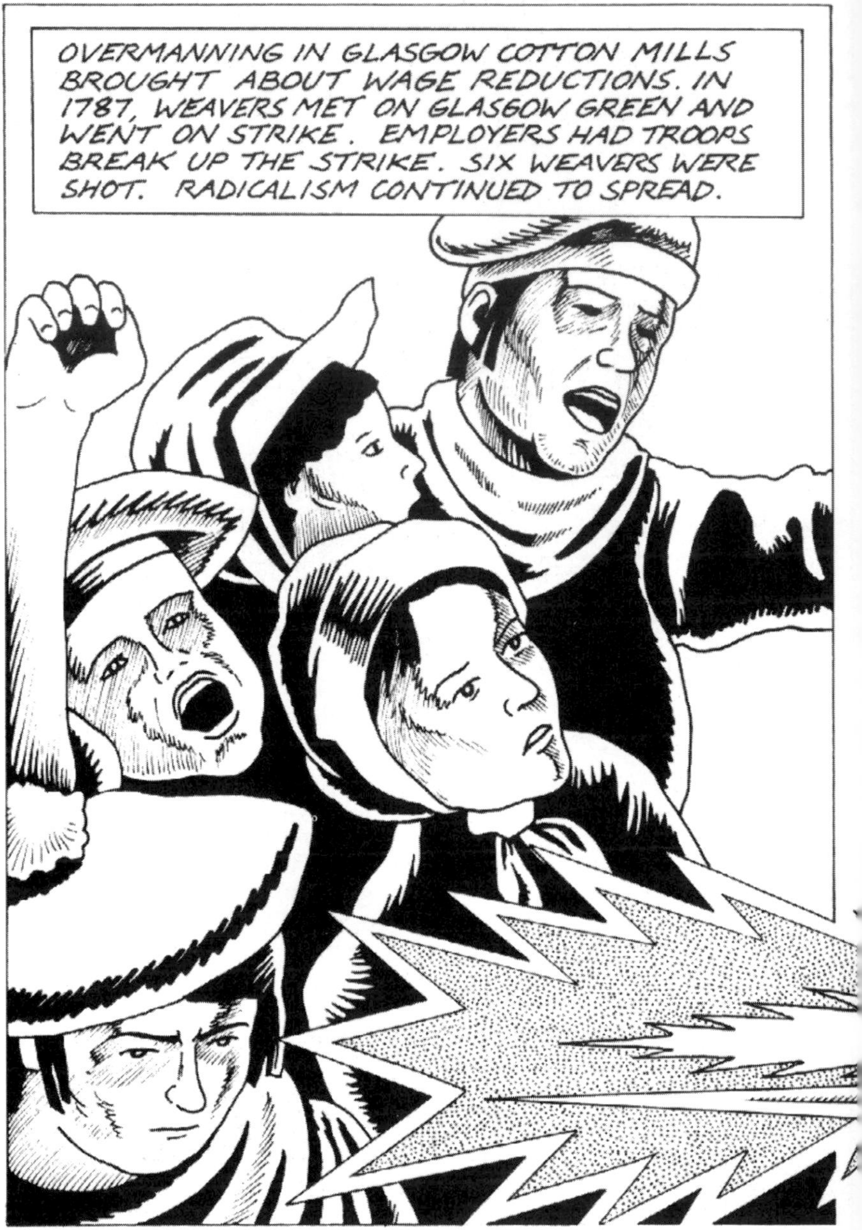
OVERMANNING IN GLASGOW COTTON MILLS BROUGHT ABOUT WAGE REDUCTIONS. IN 1787, WEAVERS MET ON GLASGOW GREEN AND WENT ON STRIKE. EMPLOYERS HAD TROOPS BREAK UP THE STRIKE. SIX WEAVERS WERE SHOT. RADICALISM CONTINUED TO SPREAD.

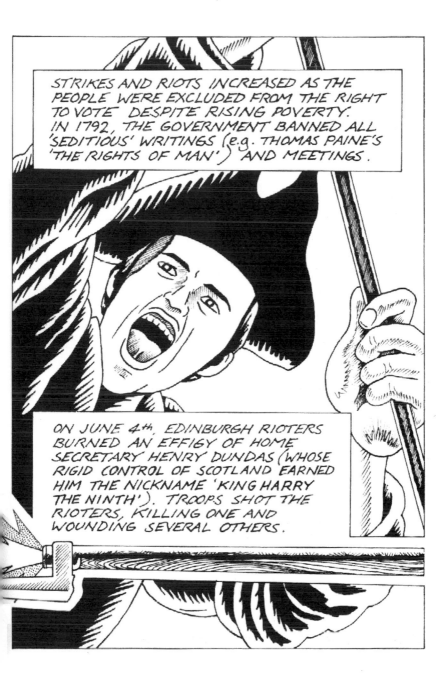

STRIKES AND RIOTS INCREASED AS THE PEOPLE WERE EXCLUDED FROM THE RIGHT TO VOTE DESPITE RISING POVERTY. IN 1792, THE GOVERNMENT BANNED ALL 'SEDITIOUS' WRITINGS (e.g. THOMAS PAINE'S 'THE RIGHTS OF MAN') AND MEETINGS.

ON JUNE 4th, EDINBURGH RIOTERS BURNED AN EFFIGY OF HOME SECRETARY HENRY DUNDAS (WHOSE RIGID CONTROL OF SCOTLAND EARNED HIM THE NICKNAME 'KING HARRY THE NINTH'). TROOPS SHOT THE RIOTERS, KILLING ONE AND WOUNDING SEVERAL OTHERS.

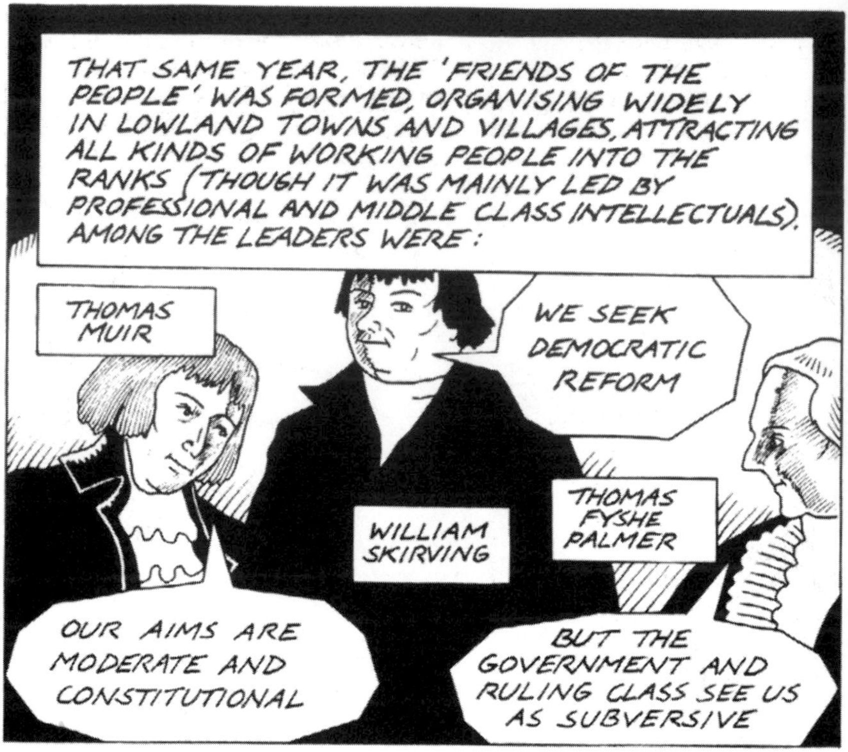
THAT SAME YEAR, THE 'FRIENDS OF THE PEOPLE' WAS FORMED, ORGANISING WIDELY IN LOWLAND TOWNS AND VILLAGES, ATTRACTING ALL KINDS OF WORKING PEOPLE INTO THE RANKS (THOUGH IT WAS MAINLY LED BY PROFESSIONAL AND MIDDLE CLASS INTELLECTUALS). AMONG THE LEADERS WERE:
THOMAS MUIR
WE SEEK DEMOCRATIC REFORM
WILLIAM SKIRVING
THOMAS FYSHE PALMER
OUR AIMS ARE MODERATE AND CONSTITUTIONAL
BUT THE GOVERNMENT AND RULING CLASS SEE US AS SUBVERSIVE

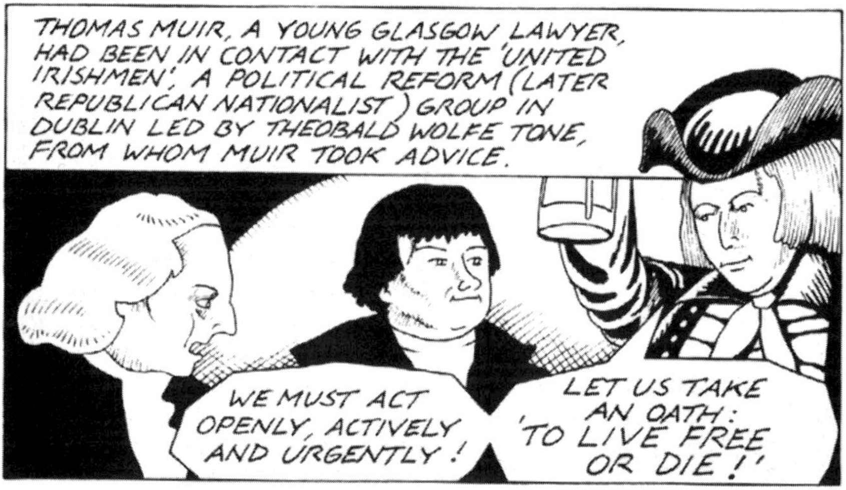
THOMAS MUIR, A YOUNG GLASGOW LAWYER, HAD BEEN IN CONTACT WITH THE 'UNITED IRISHMEN', A POLITICAL REFORM (LATER REPUBLICAN NATIONALIST) GROUP IN DUBLIN LED BY THEOBALD WOLFE TONE, FROM WHOM MUIR TOOK ADVICE.
WE MUST ACT OPENLY, ACTIVELY AND URGENTLY!
LET US TAKE AN OATH: 'TO LIVE FREE OR DIE!'

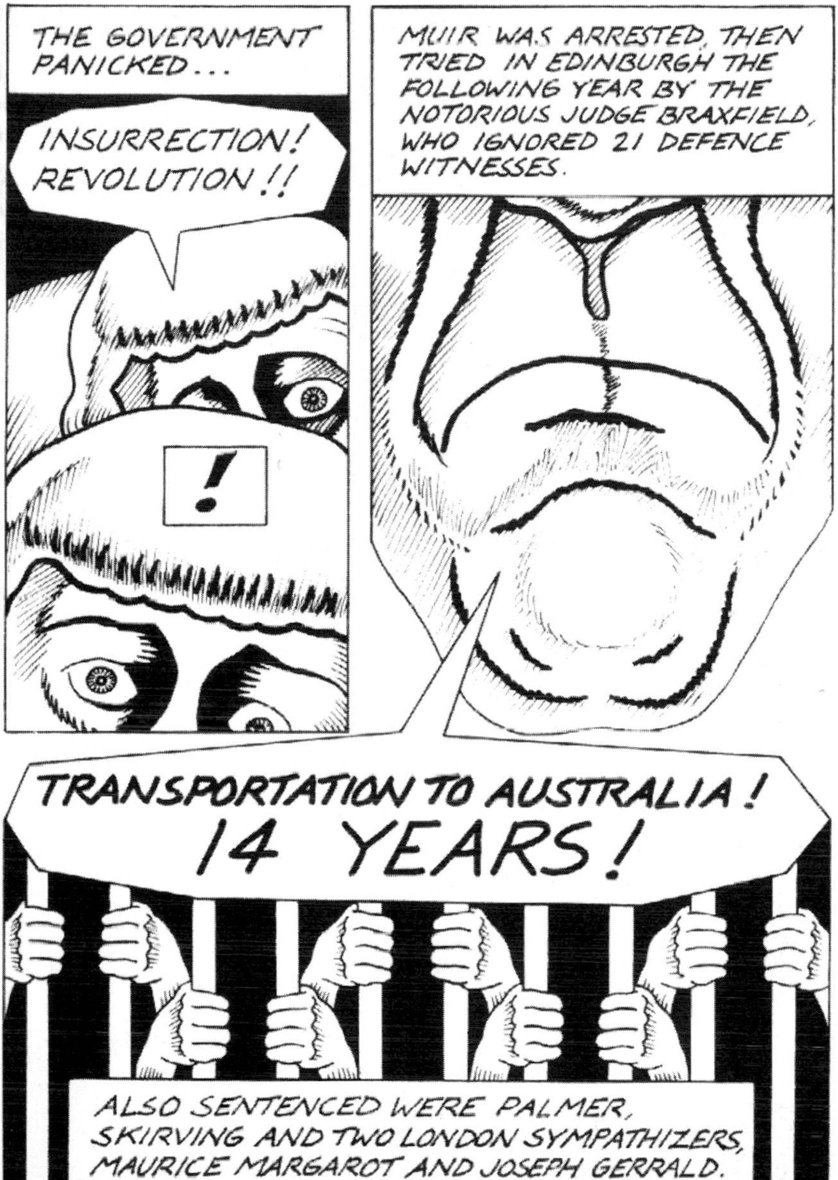
THE GOVERNMENT PANICKED...
INSURRECTION! REVOLUTION!!
!
MUIR WAS ARRESTED, THEN TRIED IN EDINBURGH THE FOLLOWING YEAR BY THE NOTORIOUS JUDGE BRAXFIELD, WHO IGNORED 21 DEFENCE WITNESSES.
TRANSPORTATION TO AUSTRALIA! 14 YEARS!
ALSO SENTENCED WERE PALMER, SKIRVING AND TWO LONDON SYMPATHIZERS, MAURICE MARGAROT AND JOSEPH GERRALD.

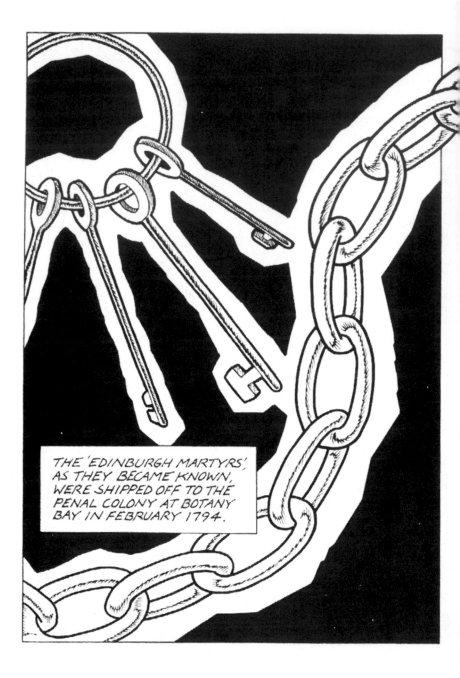

THE 'EDINBURGH MARTYRS', AS THEY BECAME KNOWN, WERE SHIPPED OFF TO THE PENAL COLONY AT BOTANY BAY IN FEBRUARY 1794.

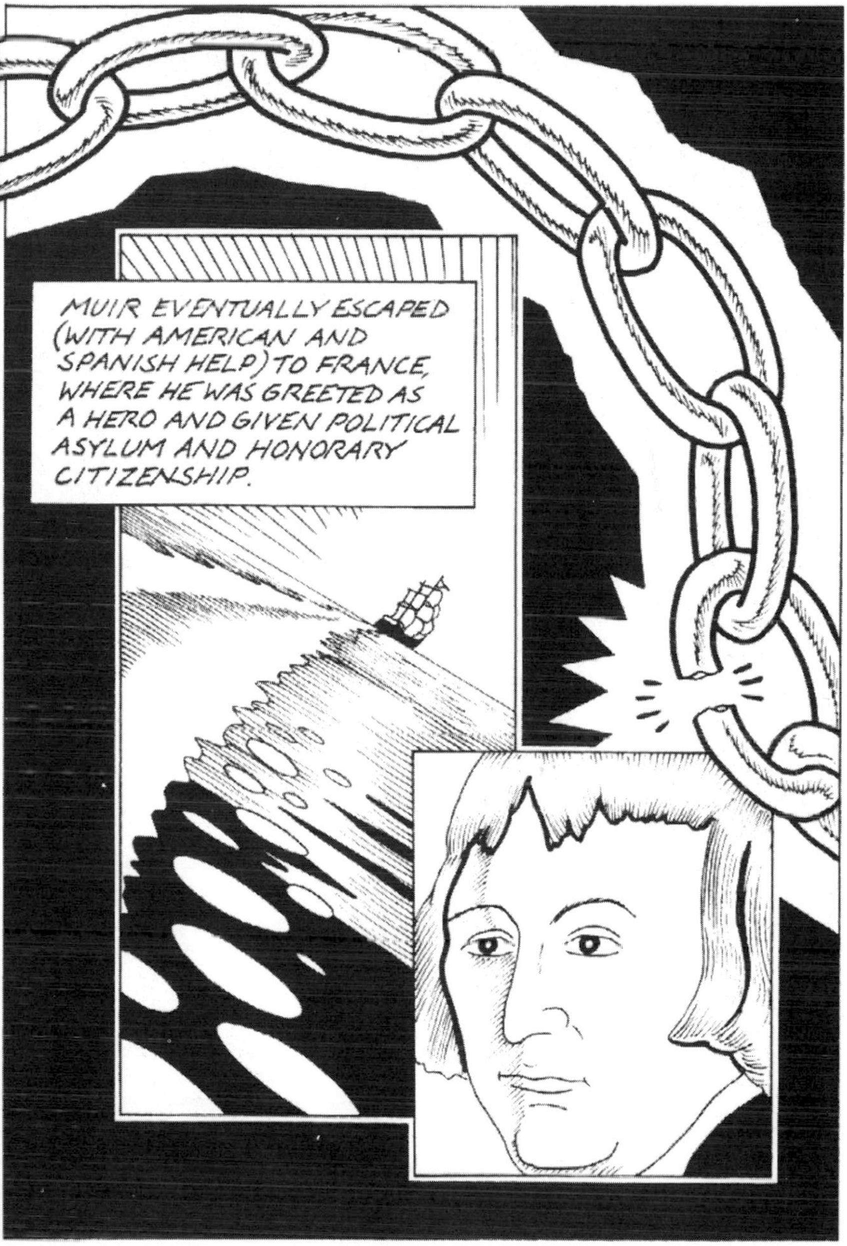
MUIR EVENTUALLY ESCAPED (WITH AMERICAN AND SPANISH HELP) TO FRANCE, WHERE HE WAS GREETED AS A HERO AND GIVEN POLITICAL ASYLUM AND HONORARY CITIZENSHIP.

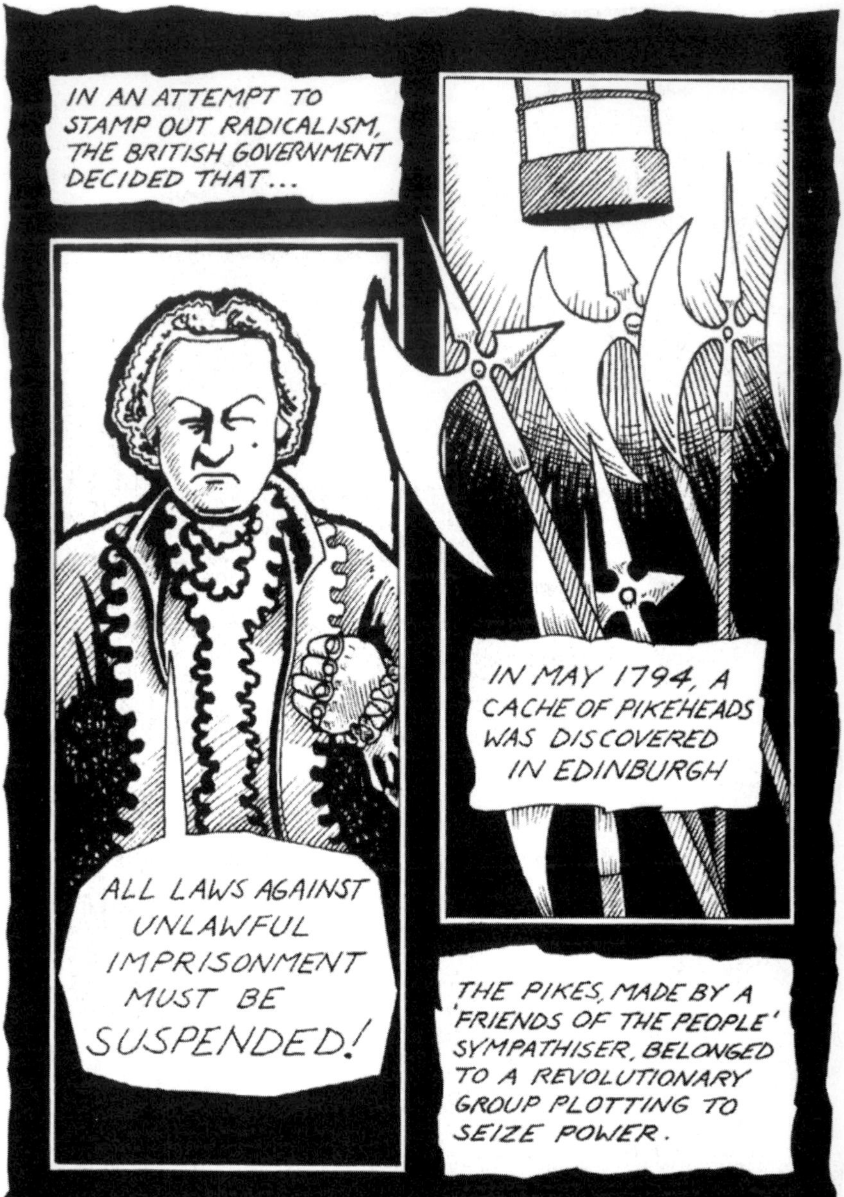
IN AN ATTEMPT TO STAMP OUT RADICALISM, THE BRITISH GOVERNMENT DECIDED THAT...
ALL LAWS AGAINST UNLAWFUL IMPRISONMENT MUST BE SUSPENDED!
IN MAY 1794, A CACHE OF PIKEHEADS WAS DISCOVERED IN EDINBURGH
THE PIKES, MADE BY A 'FRIENDS OF THE PEOPLE' SYMPATHISER, BELONGED TO A REVOLUTIONARY GROUP PLOTTING TO SEIZE POWER.

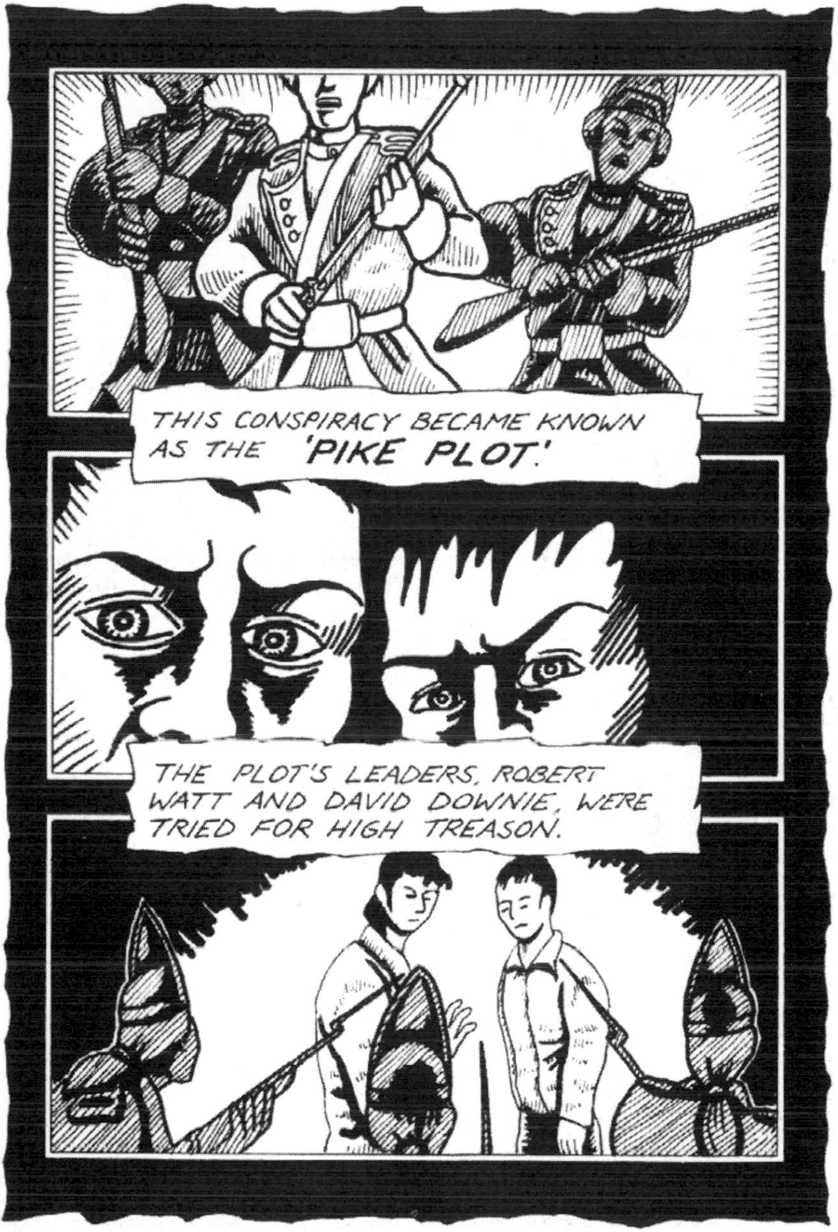
THIS CONSPIRACY BECAME KNOWN AS THE 'PIKE PLOT.'
THE PLOT'S LEADERS, ROBERT WATT AND DAVID DOWNIE, WERE TRIED FOR HIGH TREASON.

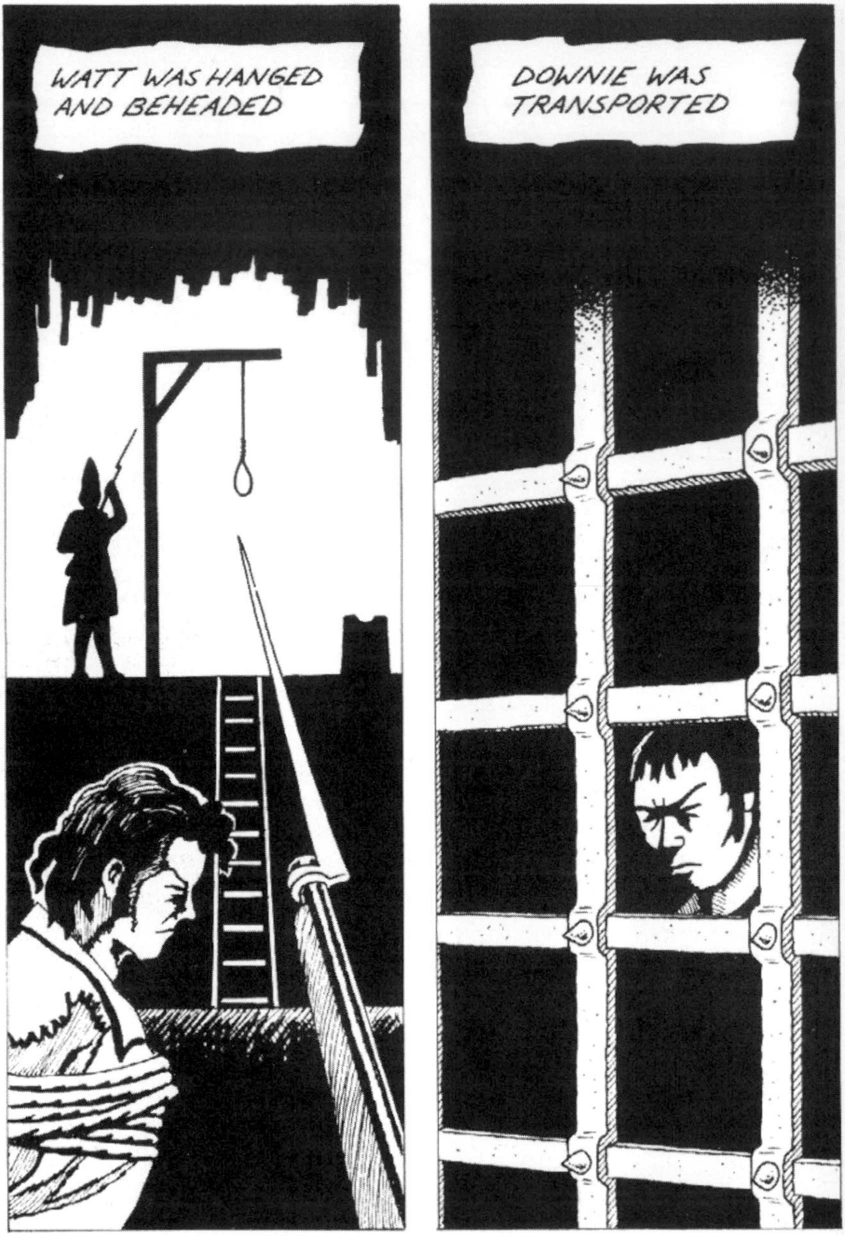
WATT WAS HANGED AND BEHEADED
DOWNIE WAS TRANSPORTED

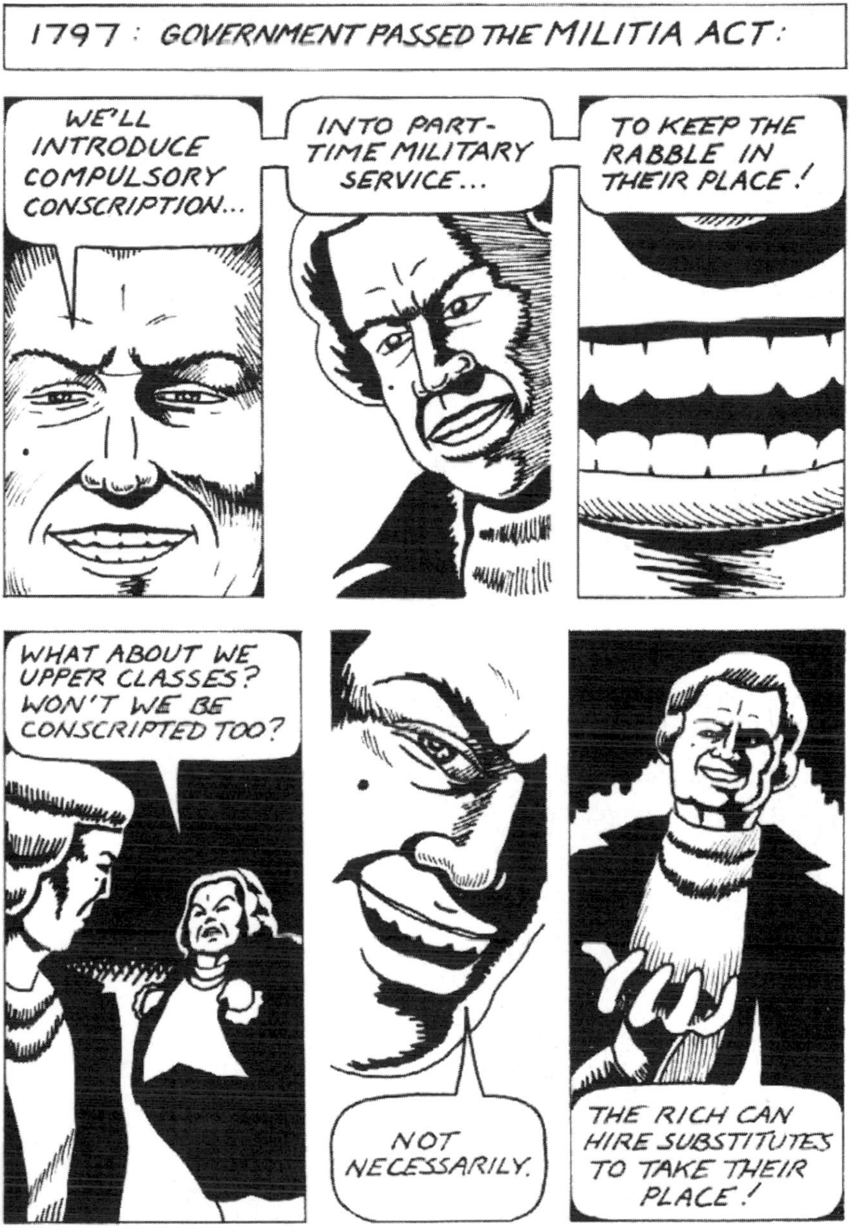
1797: GOVERNMENT PASSED THE MILITIA ACT:
WE'LL INTRODUCE COMPULSORY CONSCRIPTION...
INTO PART-TIME MILITARY SERVICE...
TO KEEP THE RABBLE IN THEIR PLACE!
WHAT ABOUT WE UPPER CLASSES? WON'T WE BE CONSCRIPTED TOO?
NOT NECESSARILY.
THE RICH CAN HIRE SUBSTITUTES TO TAKE THEIR PLACE!

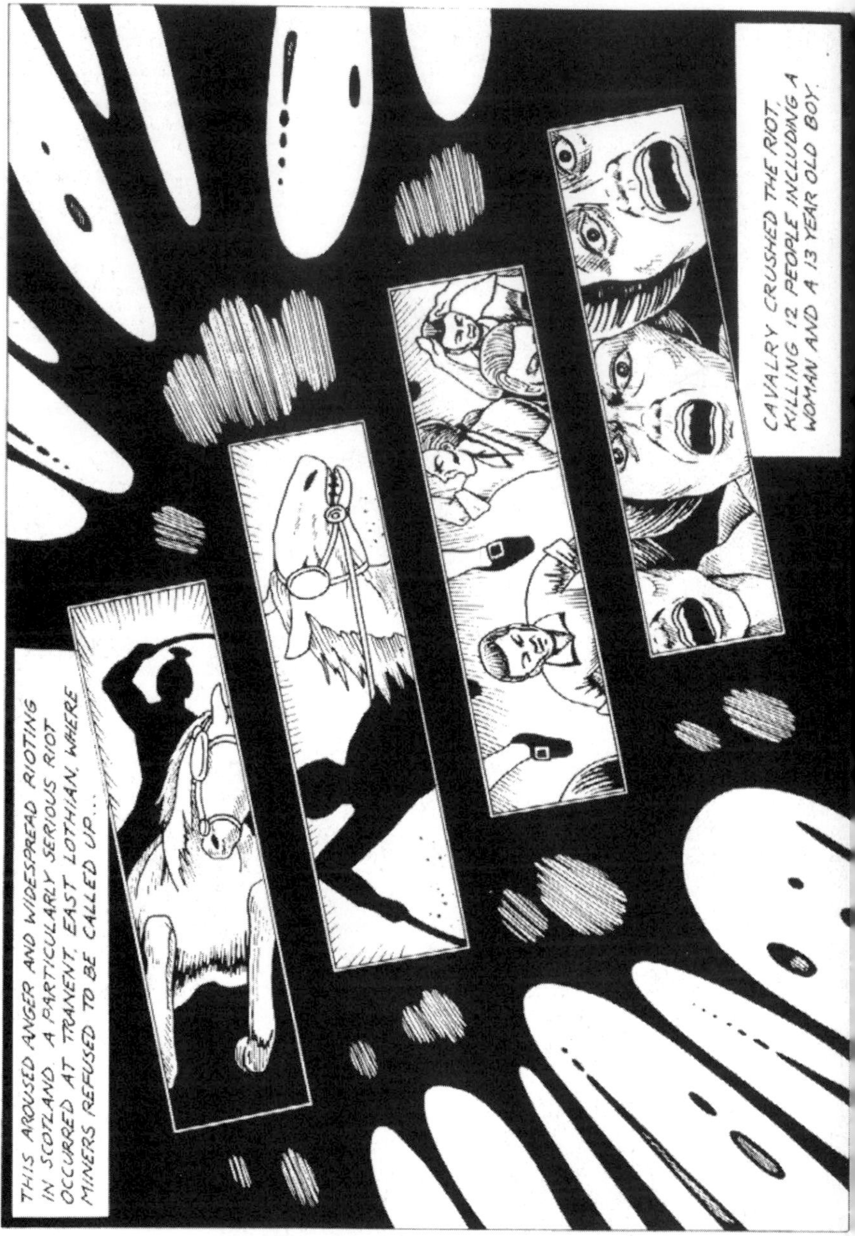
THIS AROUSED ANGER AND WIDESPREAD RIOTING IN SCOTLAND. A PARTICULARLY SERIOUS RIOT OCCURRED AT TRANENT, EAST LOTHIAN, WHERE MINERS REFUSED TO BE CALLED UP...
CAVALRY CRUSHED THE RIOT, KILLING 12 PEOPLE INCLUDING A WOMAN AND A 13 YEAR OLD BOY.

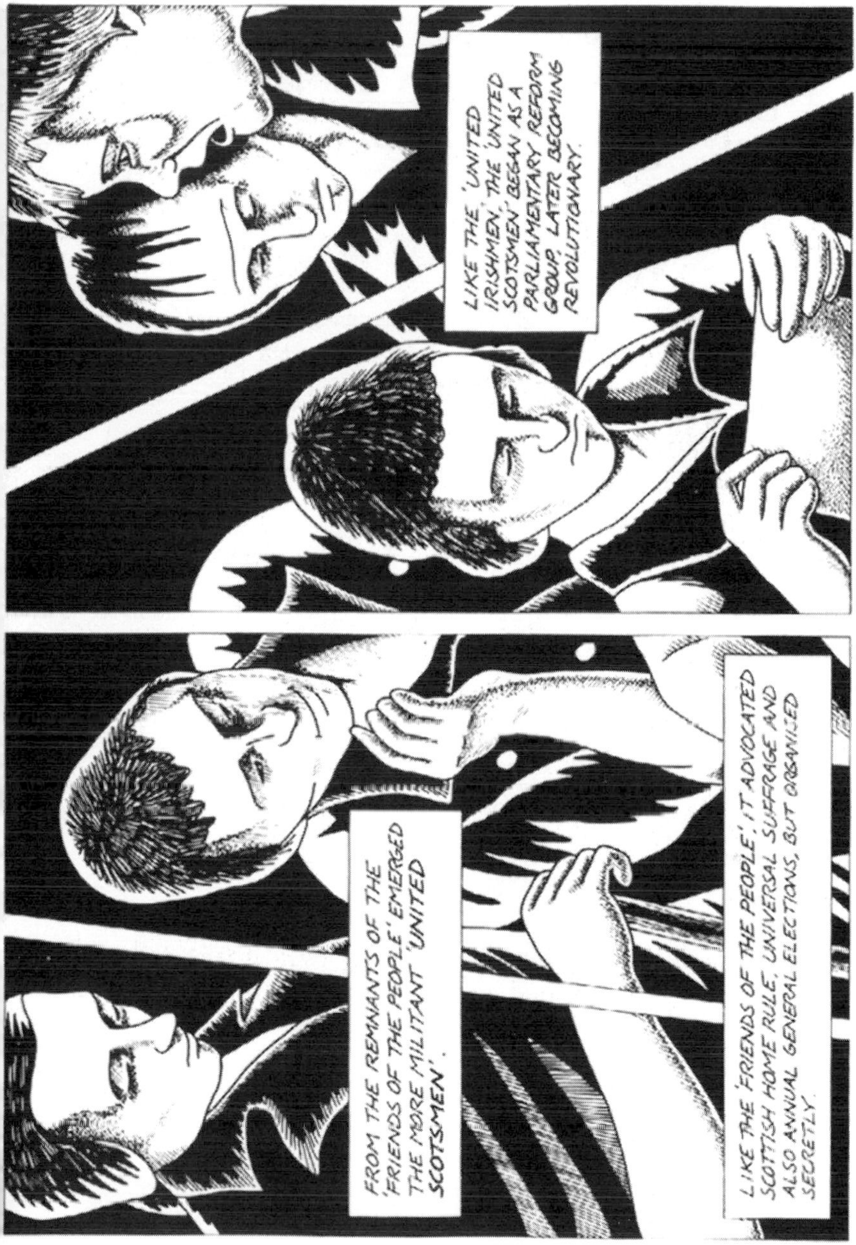
FROM THE REMNANTS OF THE 'FRIENDS OF THE PEOPLE' EMERGED THE MORE MILITANT 'UNITED SCOTSMEN'.
LIKE THE 'FRIENDS OF THE PEOPLE', IT ADVOCATED SCOTTISH HOME RULE, UNIVERSAL SUFFRAGE AND ALSO ANNUAL GENERAL ELECTIONS, BUT ORGANISED SECRETLY.
LIKE THE 'UNITED IRISHMEN', THE 'UNITED SCOTSMEN' BEGAN AS A PARLIAMENTARY REFORM GROUP, LATER BECOMING REVOLUTIONARY.

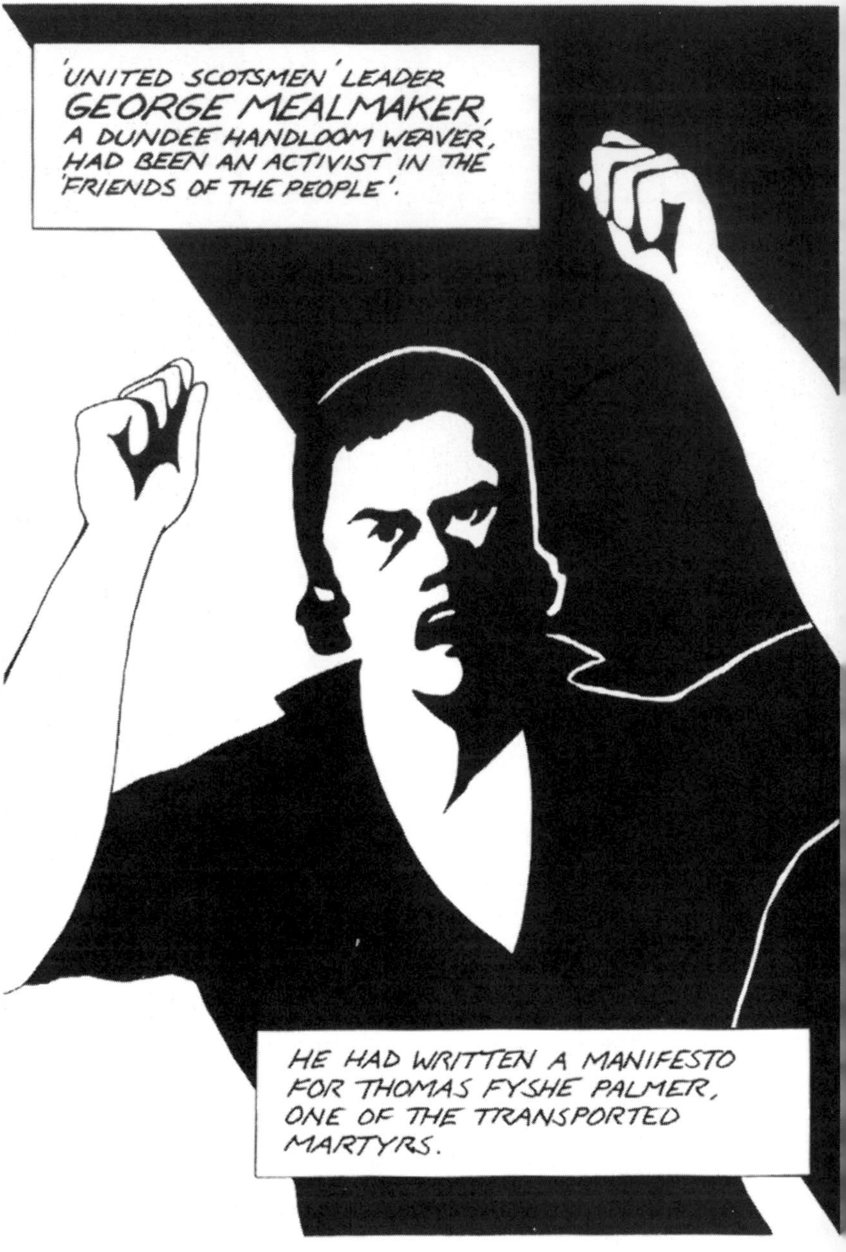
'UNITED SCOTSMEN' LEADER
GEORGE MEALMAKER,
A DUNDEE HANDLOOM WEAVER,
HAD BEEN AN ACTIVIST IN THE
'FRIENDS OF THE PEOPLE'.
HE HAD WRITTEN A MANIFESTO
FOR THOMAS FYSHE PALMER,
ONE OF THE TRANSPORTED
MARTYRS.

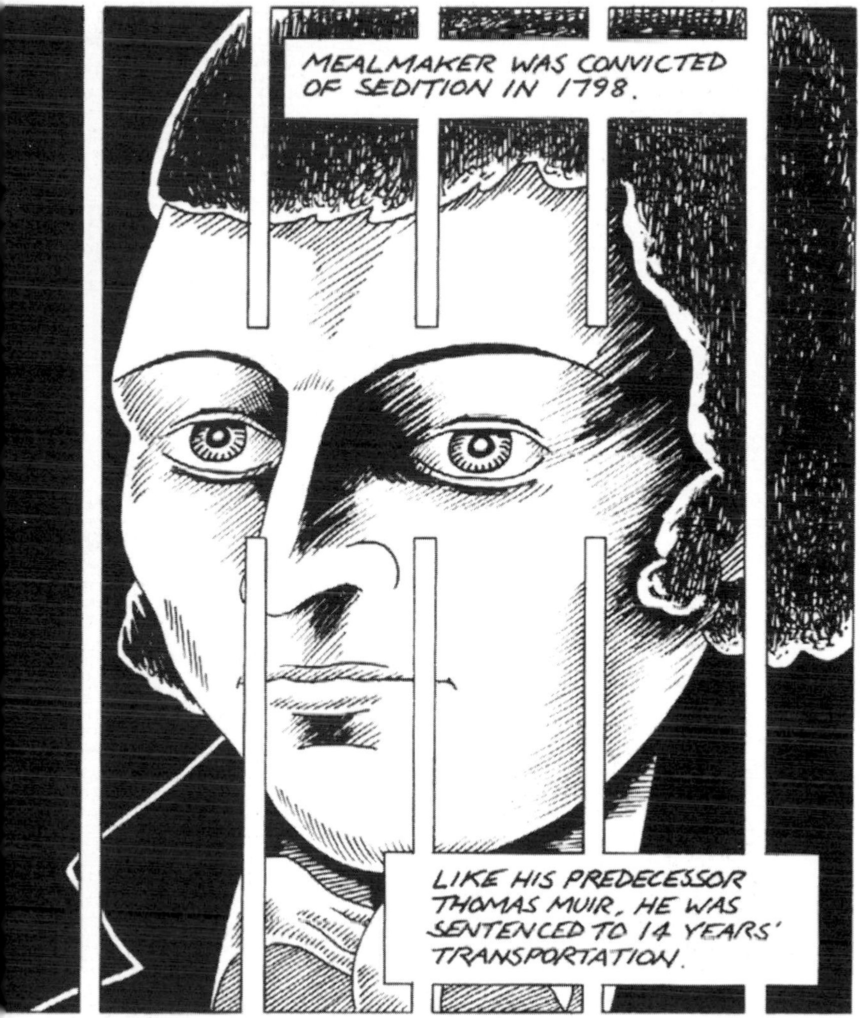
MEALMAKER WAS CONVICTED OF SEDITION IN 1798.
LIKE HIS PREDECESSOR THOMAS MUIR, HE WAS SENTENCED TO 14 YEARS' TRANSPORTATION.

THE RISING TIDE OF 'SEDITION' CAUSED CONCERN AMONG THE UPPER ECHELONS OF SOCIETY. SCOTTISH JACOBITISM HAD BEEN BAD ENOUGH, BUT POPULAR SCOTTISH REPUBLICANISM POSED AN EVEN GREATER THREAT TO THE EXISTING ORDER. MANY SCOTS HAD PARTICIPATED IN BOTH THE AMERICAN AND FRENCH REVOLUTIONS AND THE SEEDS OF REBELLION WERE BEING CARRIED HOME.

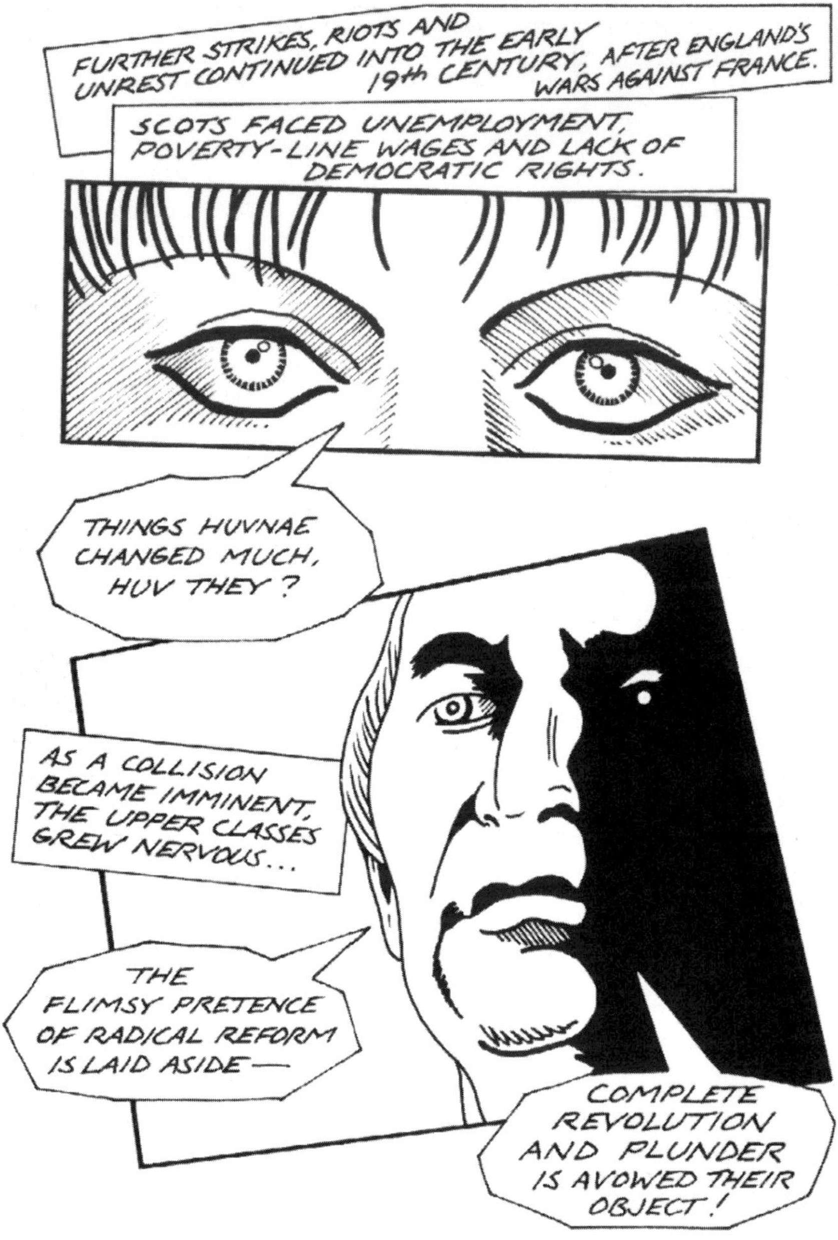
FURTHER STRIKES, RIOTS AND UNREST CONTINUED INTO THE EARLY 19th CENTURY, AFTER ENGLAND'S WARS AGAINST FRANCE.
SCOTS FACED UNEMPLOYMENT, POVERTY-LINE WAGES AND LACK OF DEMOCRATIC RIGHTS.
THINGS HUVNAE CHANGED MUCH, HUV THEY?
AS A COLLISION BECAME IMMINENT, THE UPPER CLASSES GREW NERVOUS...
THE FLIMSY PRETENCE OF RADICAL REFORM IS LAID ASIDE—
COMPLETE REVOLUTION AND PLUNDER IS AVOWED THEIR OBJECT!

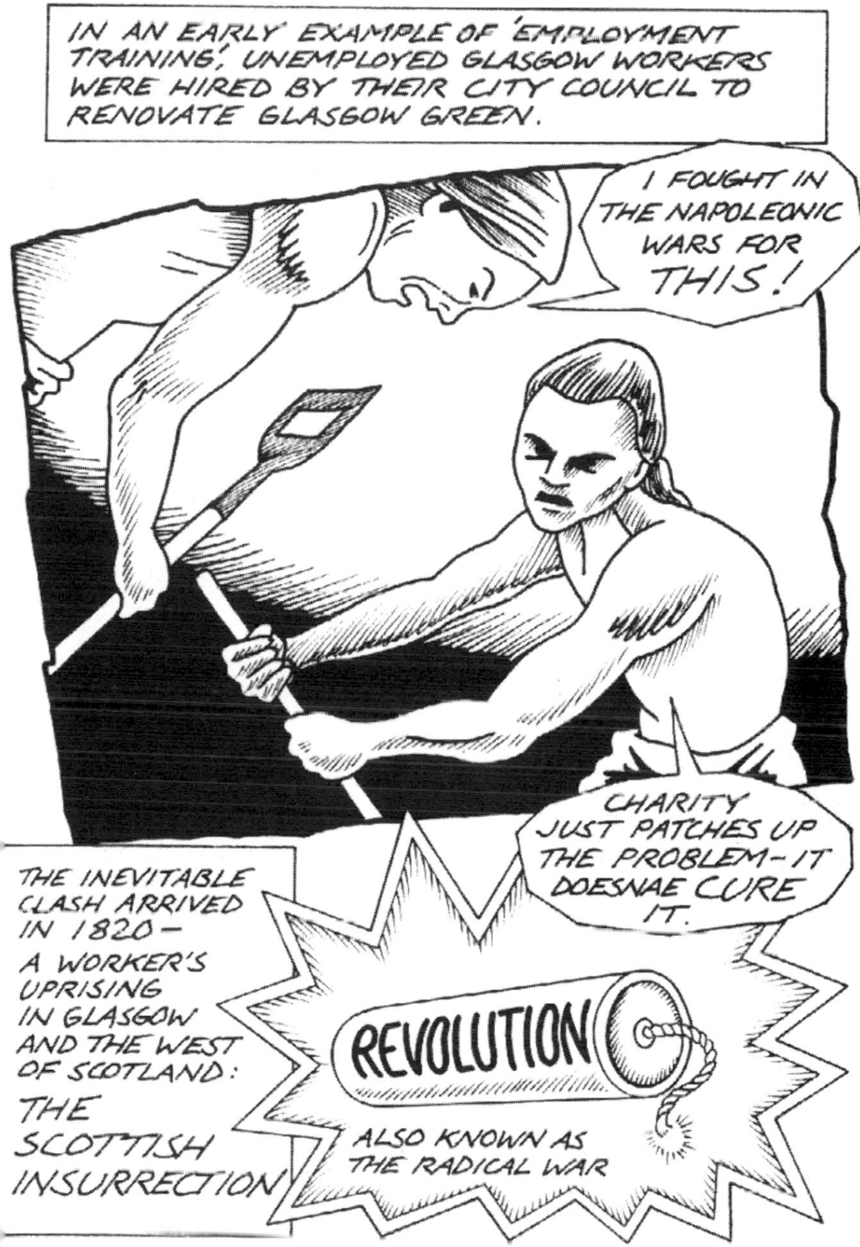

IN AN EARLY EXAMPLE OF 'EMPLOYMENT TRAINING', UNEMPLOYED GLASGOW WORKERS WERE HIRED BY THEIR CITY COUNCIL TO RENOVATE GLASGOW GREEN.
I FOUGHT IN THE NAPOLEONIC WARS FOR THIS!
CHARITY JUST PATCHES UP THE PROBLEM – IT DOESNAE CURE IT.
THE INEVITABLE CLASH ARRIVED IN 1820 – A WORKER'S UPRISING IN GLASGOW AND THE WEST OF SCOTLAND: THE SCOTTISH INSURRECTION
REVOLUTION
ALSO KNOWN AS THE RADICAL WAR

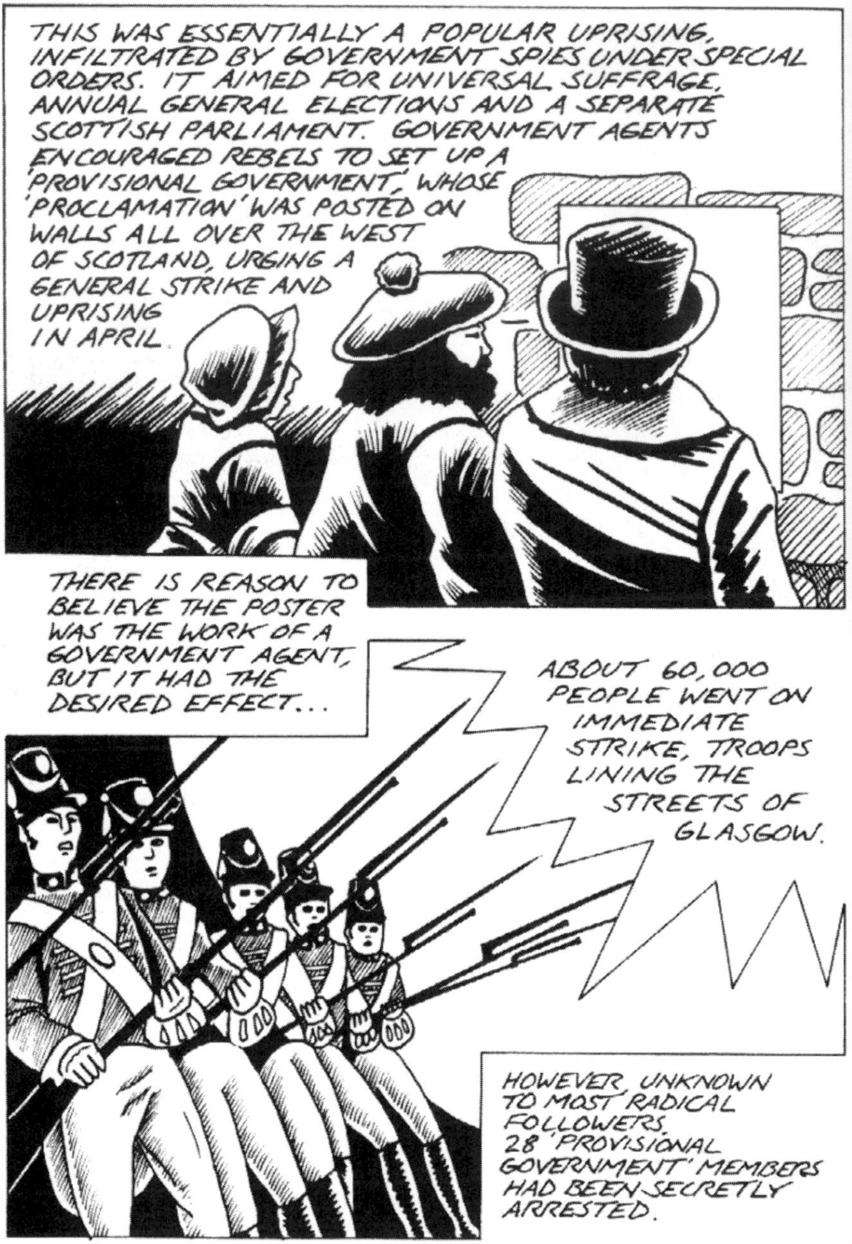
THIS WAS ESSENTIALLY A POPULAR UPRISING, INFILTRATED BY GOVERNMENT SPIES UNDER SPECIAL ORDERS. IT AIMED FOR UNIVERSAL SUFFRAGE, ANNUAL GENERAL ELECTIONS AND A SEPARATE SCOTTISH PARLIAMENT. GOVERNMENT AGENTS ENCOURAGED REBELS TO SET UP A 'PROVISIONAL GOVERNMENT', WHOSE 'PROCLAMATION' WAS POSTED ON WALLS ALL OVER THE WEST OF SCOTLAND, URGING A GENERAL STRIKE AND UPRISING IN APRIL.
THERE IS REASON TO BELIEVE THE POSTER WAS THE WORK OF A GOVERNMENT AGENT, BUT IT HAD THE DESIRED EFFECT...
ABOUT 60,000 PEOPLE WENT ON IMMEDIATE STRIKE, TROOPS LINING THE STREETS OF GLASGOW.
HOWEVER, UNKNOWN TO MOST RADICAL FOLLOWERS, 28 'PROVISIONAL GOVERNMENT' MEMBERS HAD BEEN SECRETLY ARRESTED.

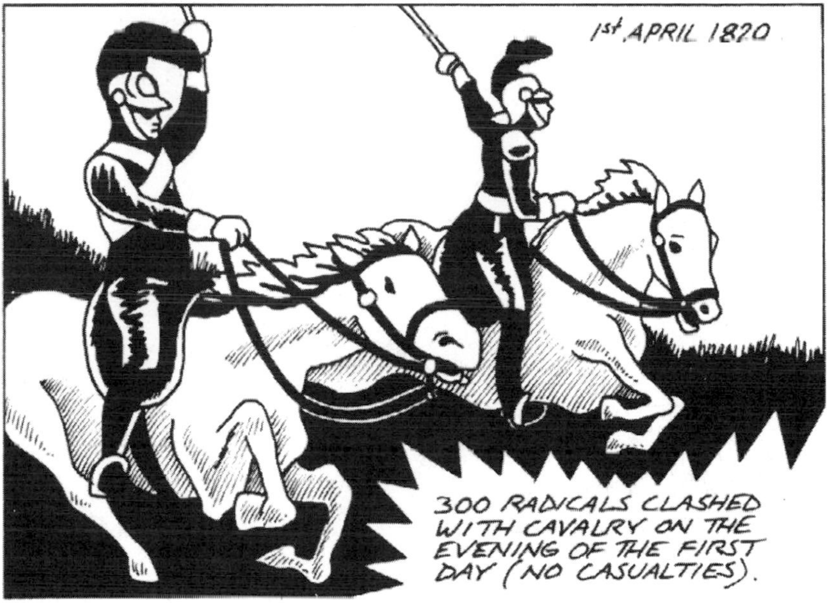
1st APRIL 1820
300 RADICALS CLASHED WITH CAVALRY ON THE EVENING OF THE FIRST DAY (NO CASUALTIES).

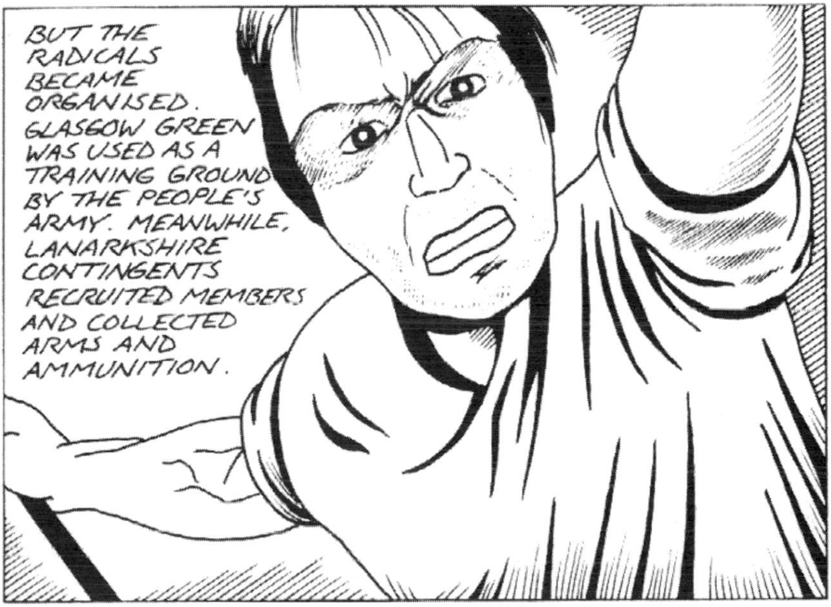
BUT THE RADICALS BECAME ORGANISED. GLASGOW GREEN WAS USED AS A TRAINING GROUND BY THE PEOPLE'S ARMY. MEANWHILE, LANARKSHIRE CONTINGENTS RECRUITED MEMBERS AND COLLECTED ARMS AND AMMUNITION.

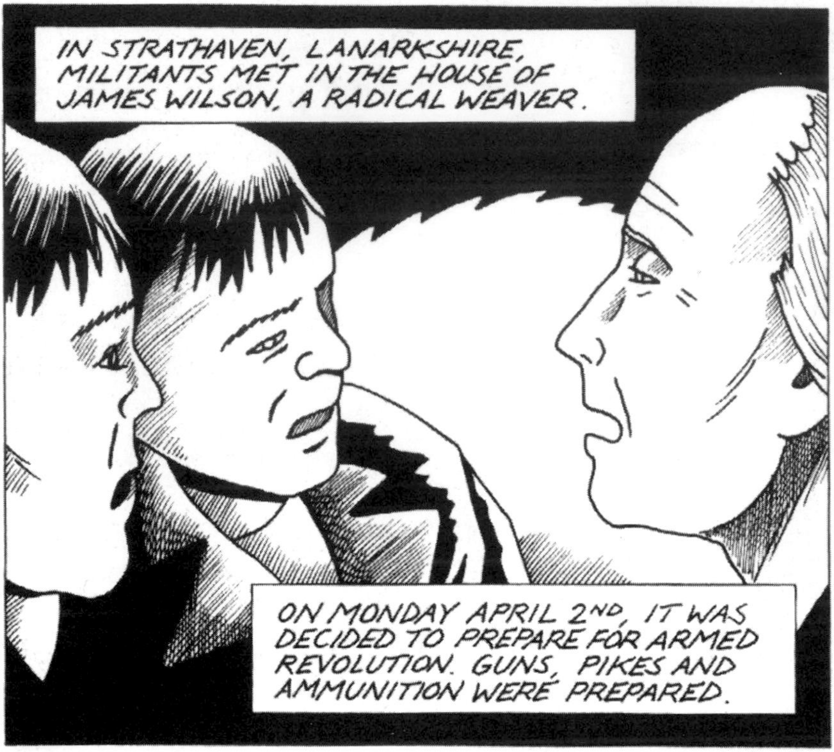
IN STRATHAVEN, LANARKSHIRE, MILITANTS MET IN THE HOUSE OF JAMES WILSON, A RADICAL WEAVER.
ON MONDAY APRIL 2ND, IT WAS DECIDED TO PREPARE FOR ARMED REVOLUTION. GUNS, PIKES AND AMMUNITION WERE PREPARED.

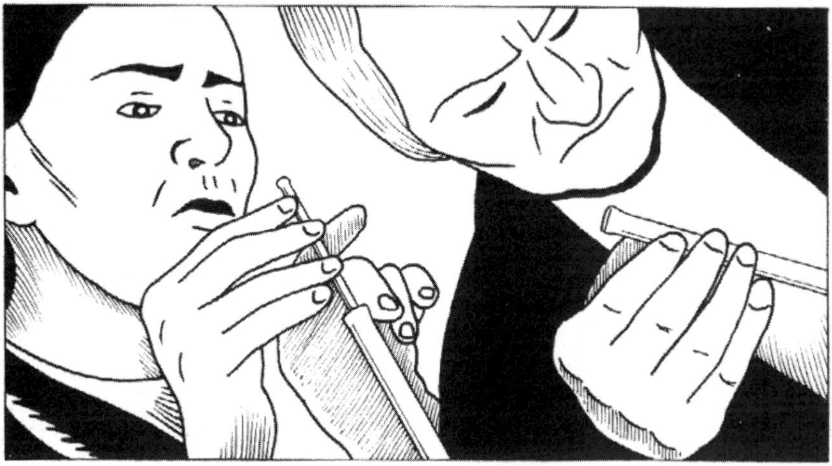

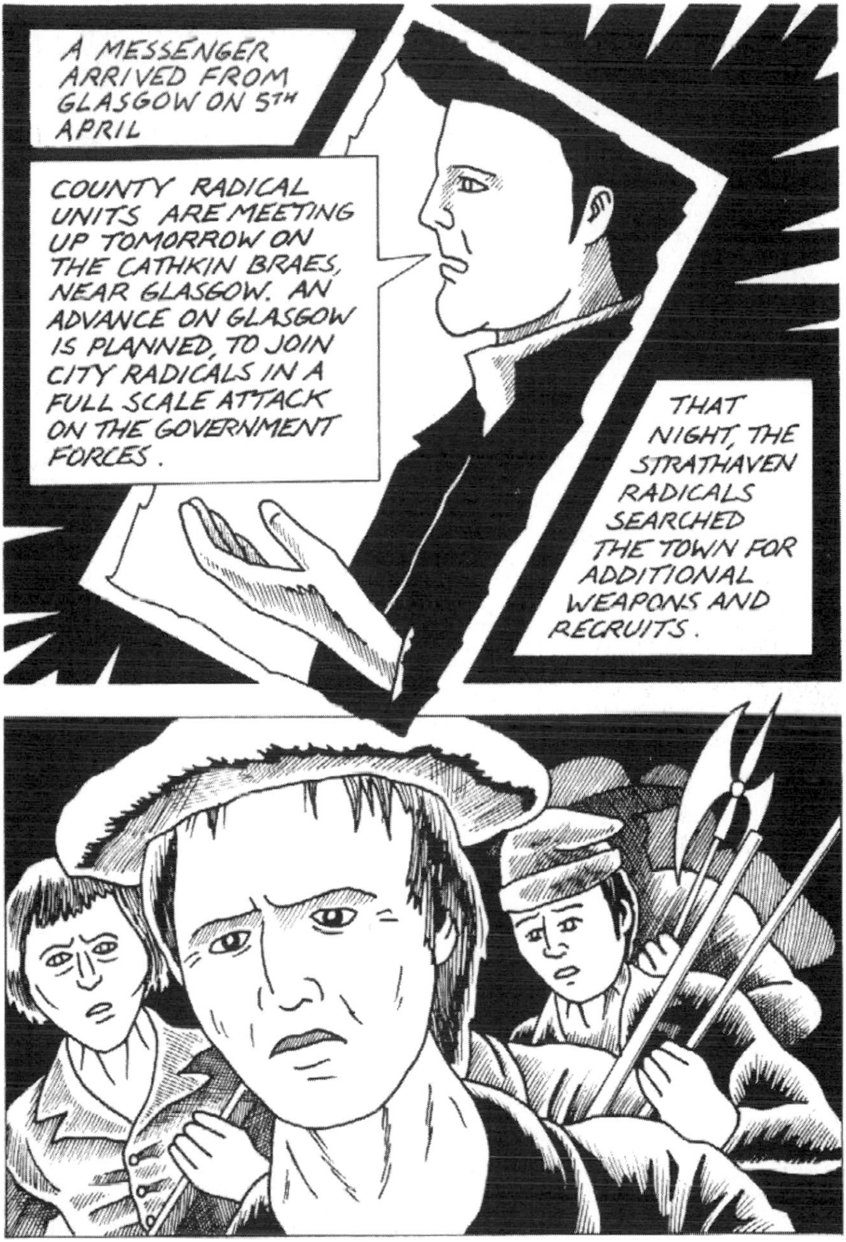
A MESSENGER ARRIVED FROM GLASGOW ON 5TH APRIL
COUNTY RADICAL UNITS ARE MEETING UP TOMORROW ON THE CATHKIN BRAES, NEAR GLASGOW. AN ADVANCE ON GLASGOW IS PLANNED, TO JOIN CITY RADICALS IN A FULL SCALE ATTACK ON THE GOVERNMENT FORCES.
THAT NIGHT, THE STRATHAVEN RADICALS SEARCHED THE TOWN FOR ADDITIONAL WEAPONS AND RECRUITS.

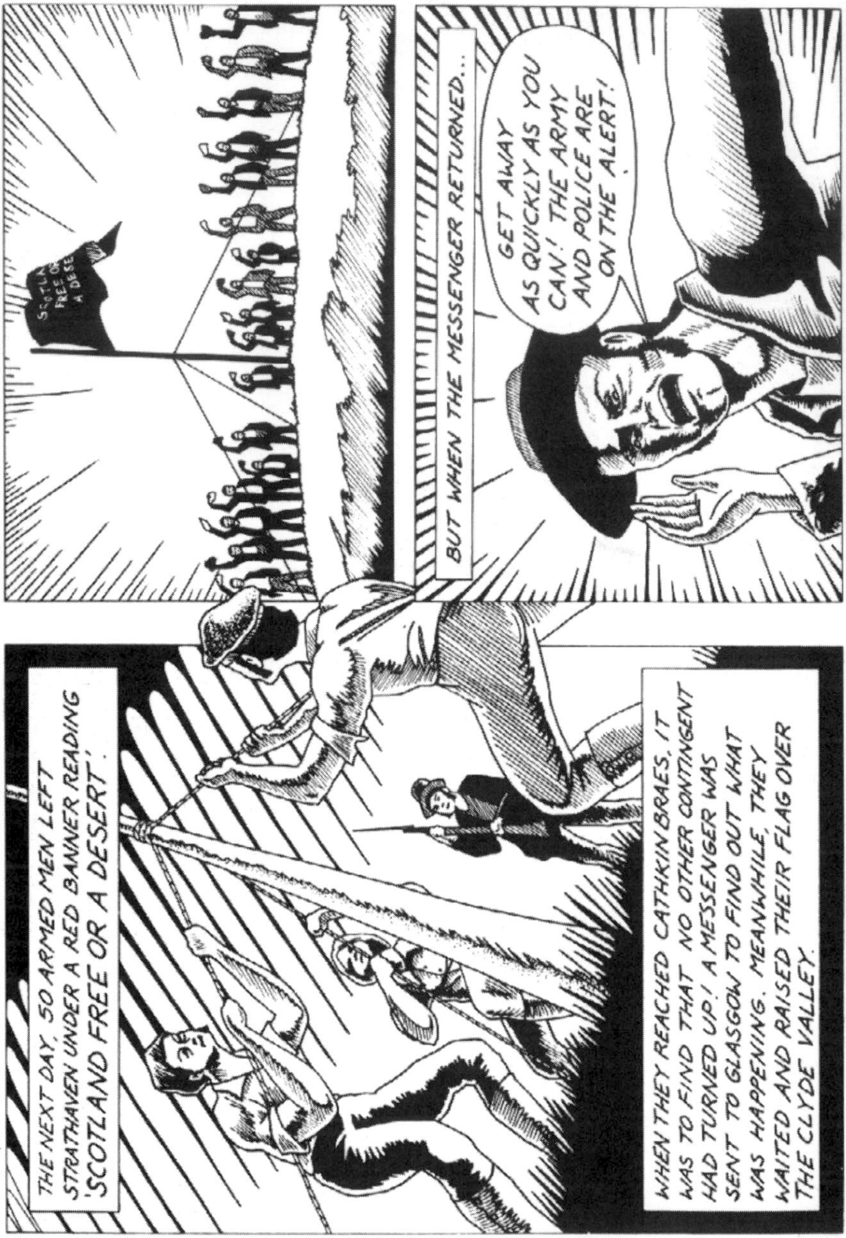
THE NEXT DAY, 50 ARMED MEN LEFT STRATHAVEN UNDER A RED BANNER READING 'SCOTLAND FREE OR A DESERT'.
WHEN THEY REACHED CATHKIN BRAES, IT WAS TO FIND THAT NO OTHER CONTINGENT HAD TURNED UP! A MESSENGER WAS SENT TO GLASGOW TO FIND OUT WHAT WAS HAPPENING. MEANWHILE, THEY WAITED AND RAISED THEIR FLAG OVER THE CLYDE VALLEY.
BUT WHEN THE MESSENGER RETURNED...
GET AWAY AS QUICKLY AS YOU CAN! THE ARMY AND POLICE ARE ON THE ALERT!

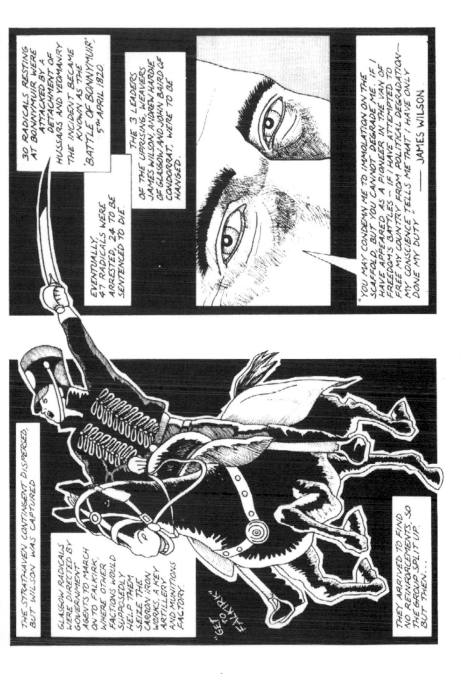

30 RADICALS RESTING AT BONNYMUIR WERE ATTACKED BY A DETACHMENT OF HUSSARS AND YEOMANRY. THE INCIDENT BECAME KNOWN AS THE 'BATTLE OF BONNYMUIR' 5TH APRIL 1820

EVENTUALLY, 47 RADICALS WERE ARRESTED, 24 TO BE SENTENCED TO DIE.

THE 3 LEADERS OF THE UPRISING, WEAVERS JAMES WILSON, ANDREW HARDIE OF GLASGOW, AND JOHN BAIRD OF CONDORRAT, WERE TO BE HANGED.

"YOU MAY CONDEMN ME TO IMMOLATION ON THE SCAFFOLD, BUT YOU CANNOT DEGRADE ME. IF I HAVE APPEARED AS A PIONEER IN THE VAN OF FREEDOM'S BATTLES — IF I HAVE ATTEMPTED TO FREE MY COUNTRY FROM POLITICAL DEGRADATION — MY CONSCIENCE TELLS ME THAT I HAVE ONLY DONE MY DUTY." —— JAMES WILSON

THE STRATHAVEN CONTINGENT DISPERSED, BUT WILSON WAS CAPTURED

GLASGOW RADICALS WERE DIRECTED BY GOVERNMENT AGENTS TO MARCH ON TO FALKIRK, WHERE OTHER FACTIONS WOULD SUPPOSEDLY HELP THEM SEIZE THE CARRON IRON WORKS, A KEY ARTILLERY AND MUNITIONS FACTORY.

"GET FORK" FALLA

THEY ARRIVED TO FIND NO REINFORCEMENTS, SO THE GROUP SPLIT UP. BUT THEN...

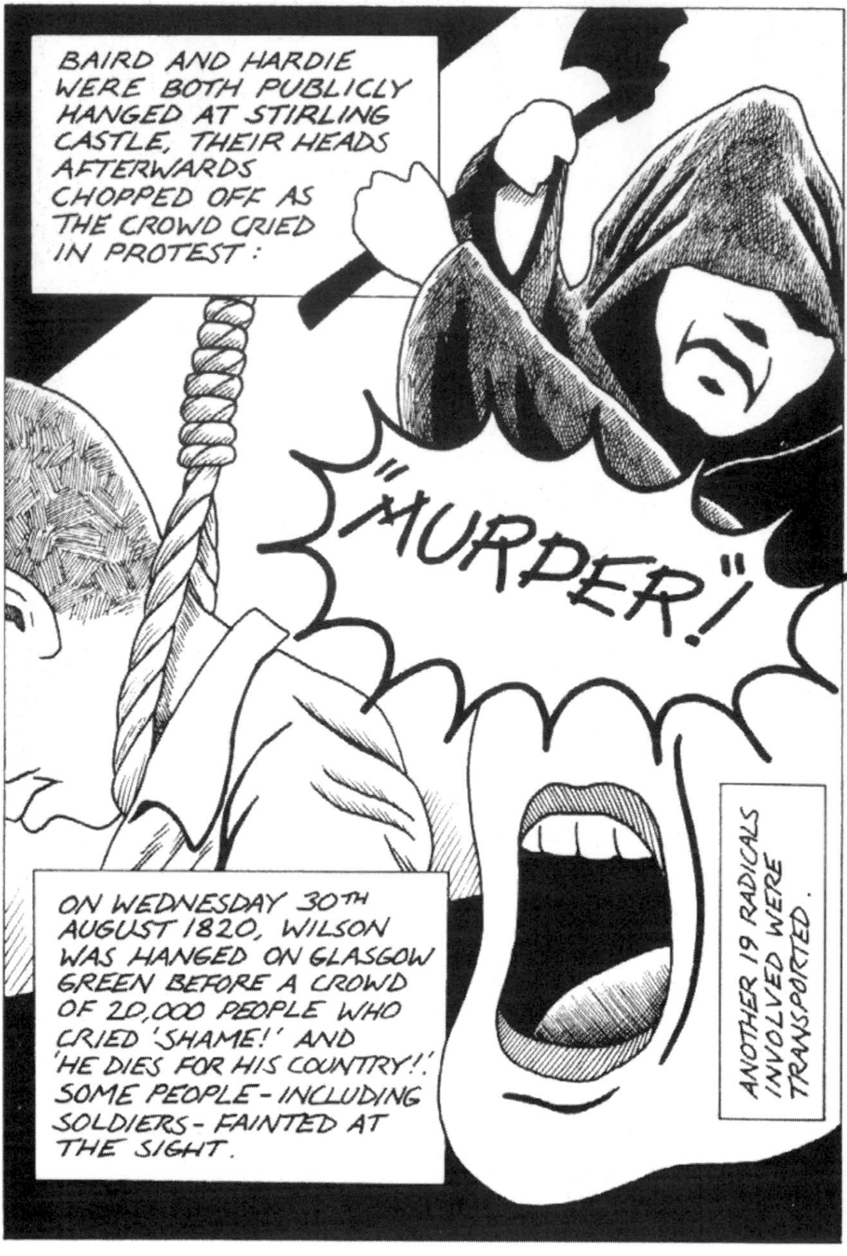
BAIRD AND HARDIE WERE BOTH PUBLICLY HANGED AT STIRLING CASTLE, THEIR HEADS AFTERWARDS CHOPPED OFF AS THE CROWD CRIED IN PROTEST:
"MURDER!"
ON WEDNESDAY 30TH AUGUST 1820, WILSON WAS HANGED ON GLASGOW GREEN BEFORE A CROWD OF 20,000 PEOPLE WHO CRIED 'SHAME!' AND 'HE DIES FOR HIS COUNTRY!'. SOME PEOPLE - INCLUDING SOLDIERS - FAINTED AT THE SIGHT.
ANOTHER 19 RADICALS INVOLVED WERE TRANSPORTED.

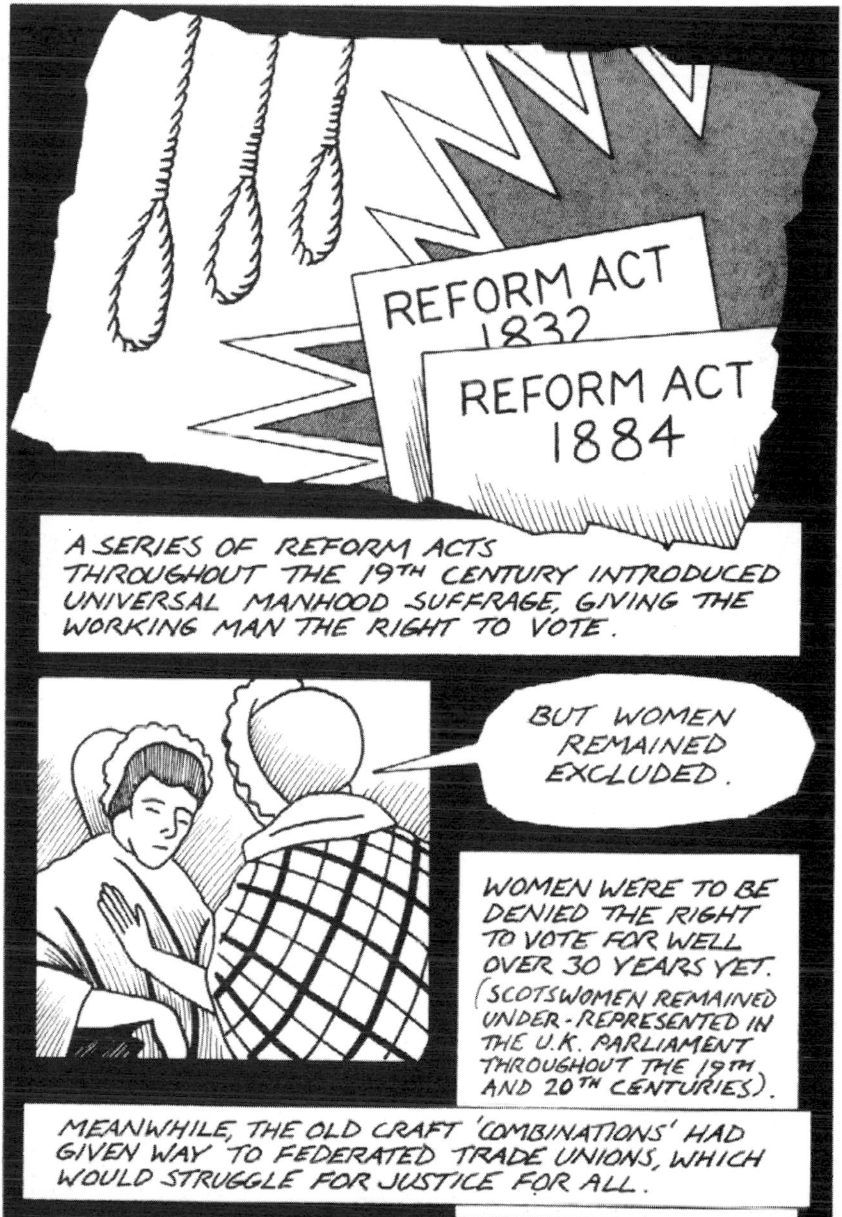
REFORM ACT 1832
REFORM ACT 1884
A SERIES OF REFORM ACTS THROUGHOUT THE 19TH CENTURY INTRODUCED UNIVERSAL MANHOOD SUFFRAGE, GIVING THE WORKING MAN THE RIGHT TO VOTE.
BUT WOMEN REMAINED EXCLUDED.
WOMEN WERE TO BE DENIED THE RIGHT TO VOTE FOR WELL OVER 30 YEARS YET. (SCOTSWOMEN REMAINED UNDER-REPRESENTED IN THE U.K. PARLIAMENT THROUGHOUT THE 19TH AND 20TH CENTURIES).
MEANWHILE, THE OLD CRAFT 'COMBINATIONS' HAD GIVEN WAY TO FEDERATED TRADE UNIONS, WHICH WOULD STRUGGLE FOR JUSTICE FOR ALL.

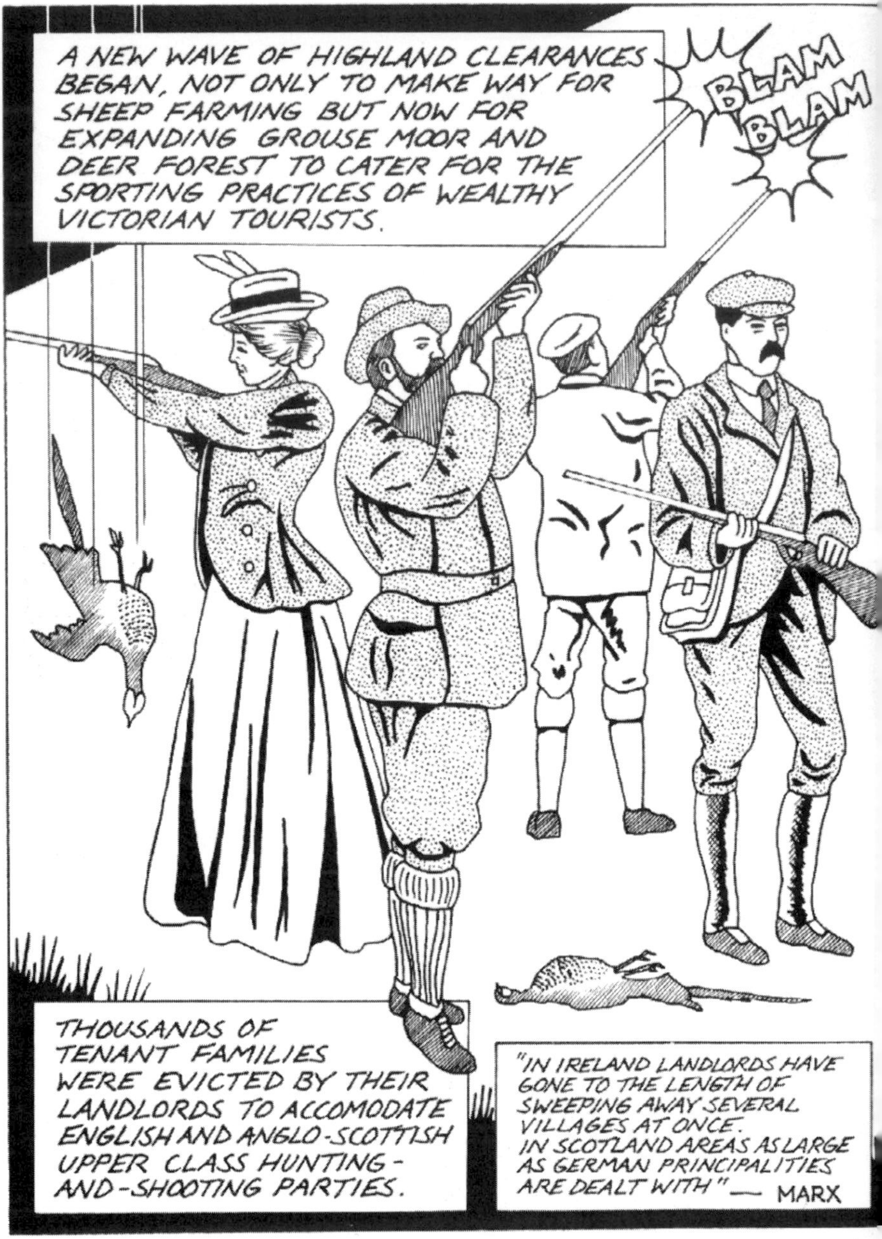

A NEW WAVE OF HIGHLAND CLEARANCES BEGAN, NOT ONLY TO MAKE WAY FOR SHEEP FARMING BUT NOW FOR EXPANDING GROUSE MOOR AND DEER FOREST TO CATER FOR THE SPORTING PRACTICES OF WEALTHY VICTORIAN TOURISTS.
BLAM
BLAM
THOUSANDS OF TENANT FAMILIES WERE EVICTED BY THEIR LANDLORDS TO ACCOMODATE ENGLISH AND ANGLO-SCOTTISH UPPER CLASS HUNTING-AND-SHOOTING PARTIES.
"IN IRELAND LANDLORDS HAVE GONE TO THE LENGTH OF SWEEPING AWAY SEVERAL VILLAGES AT ONCE. IN SCOTLAND AREAS AS LARGE AS GERMAN PRINCIPALITIES ARE DEALT WITH" — MARX

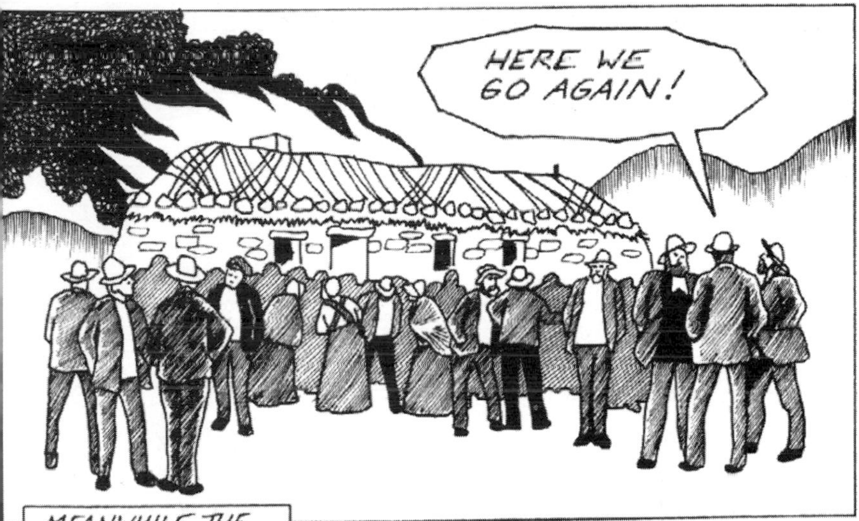
HERE WE GO AGAIN!

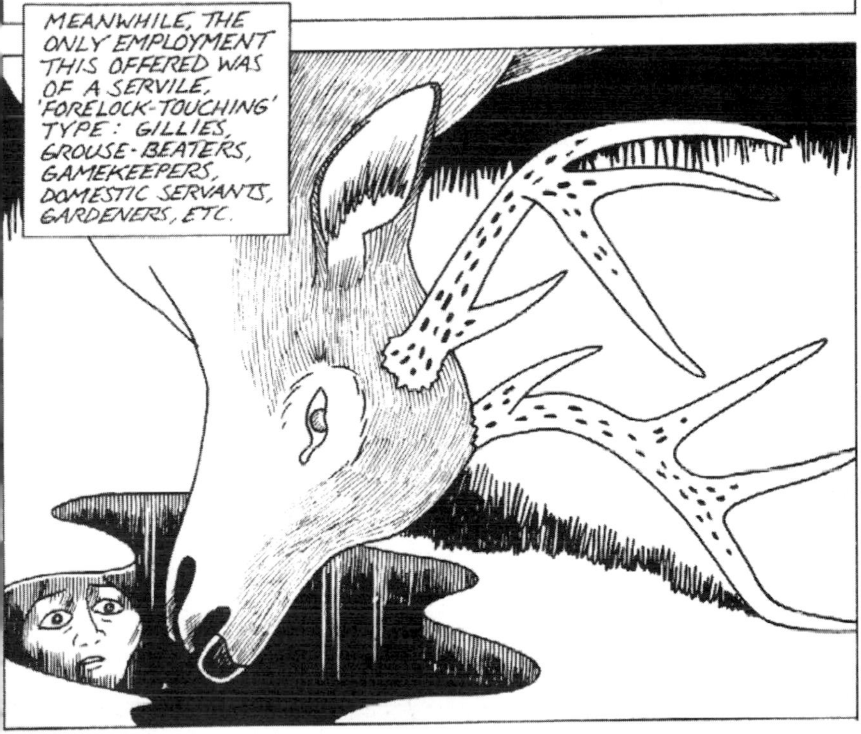
MEANWHILE, THE ONLY EMPLOYMENT THIS OFFERED WAS OF A SERVILE, 'FORELOCK-TOUCHING' TYPE: GILLIES, GROUSE-BEATERS, GAMEKEEPERS, DOMESTIC SERVANTS, GARDENERS, ETC.

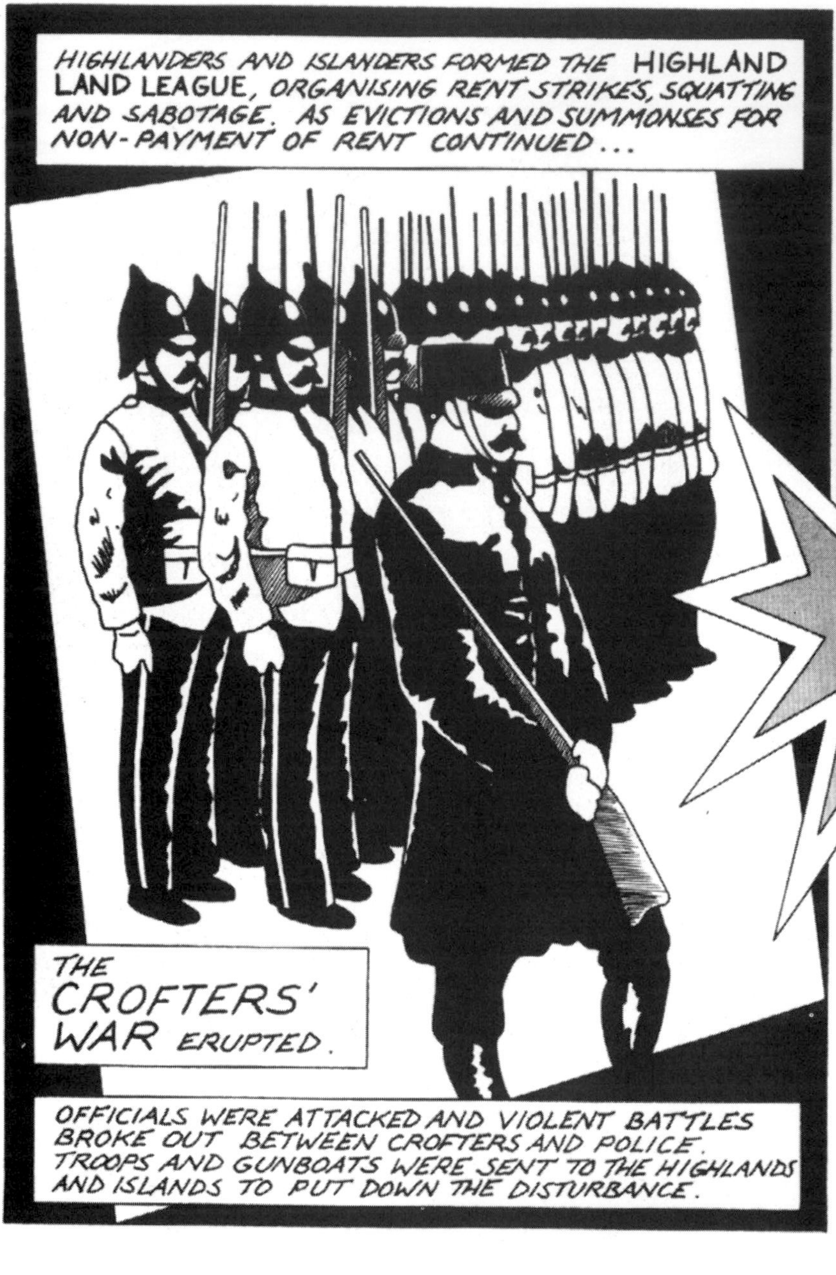
HIGHLANDERS AND ISLANDERS FORMED THE HIGHLAND LAND LEAGUE, ORGANISING RENT STRIKES, SQUATTING AND SABOTAGE. AS EVICTIONS AND SUMMONSES FOR NON-PAYMENT OF RENT CONTINUED...
THE CROFTERS' WAR ERUPTED.
OFFICIALS WERE ATTACKED AND VIOLENT BATTLES BROKE OUT BETWEEN CROFTERS AND POLICE. TROOPS AND GUNBOATS WERE SENT TO THE HIGHLANDS AND ISLANDS TO PUT DOWN THE DISTURBANCE.

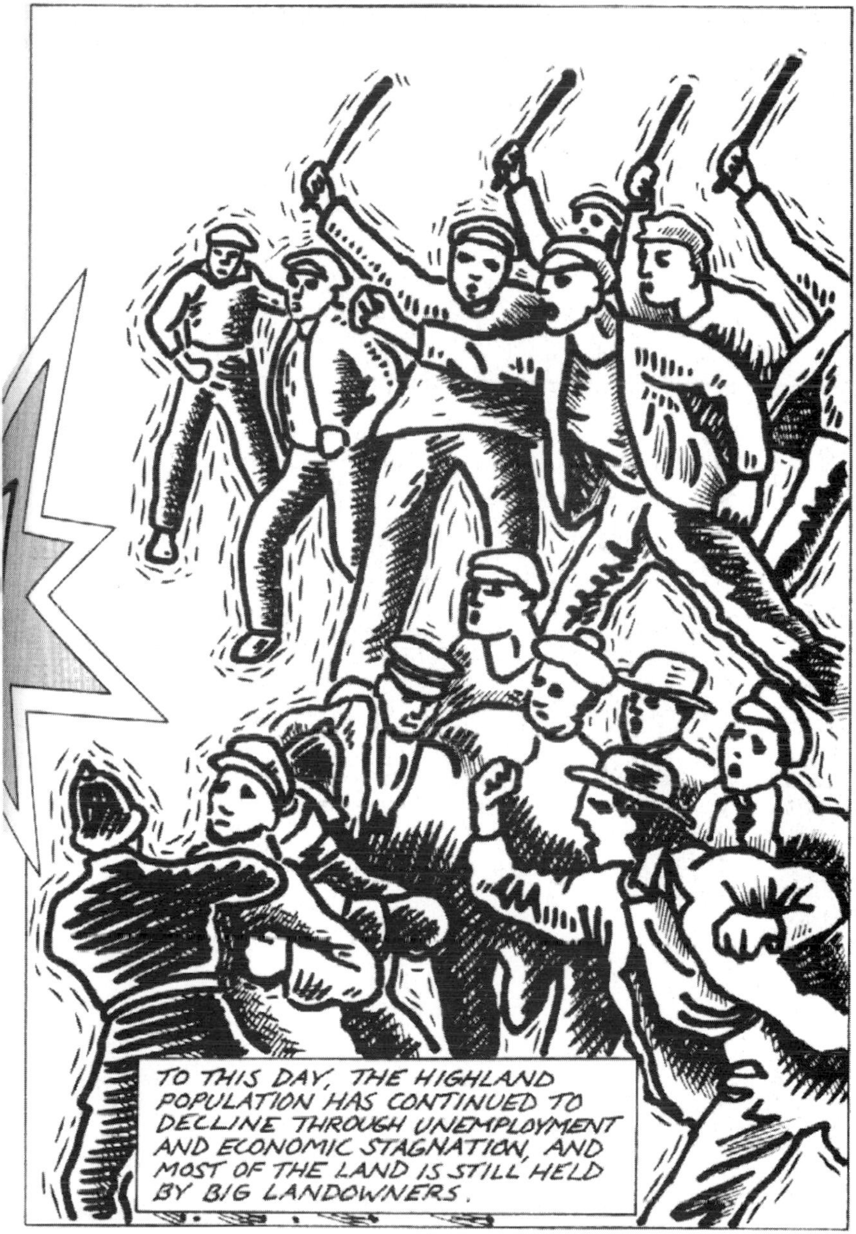
TO THIS DAY, THE HIGHLAND POPULATION HAS CONTINUED TO DECLINE THROUGH UNEMPLOYMENT AND ECONOMIC STAGNATION, AND MOST OF THE LAND IS STILL HELD BY BIG LANDOWNERS.

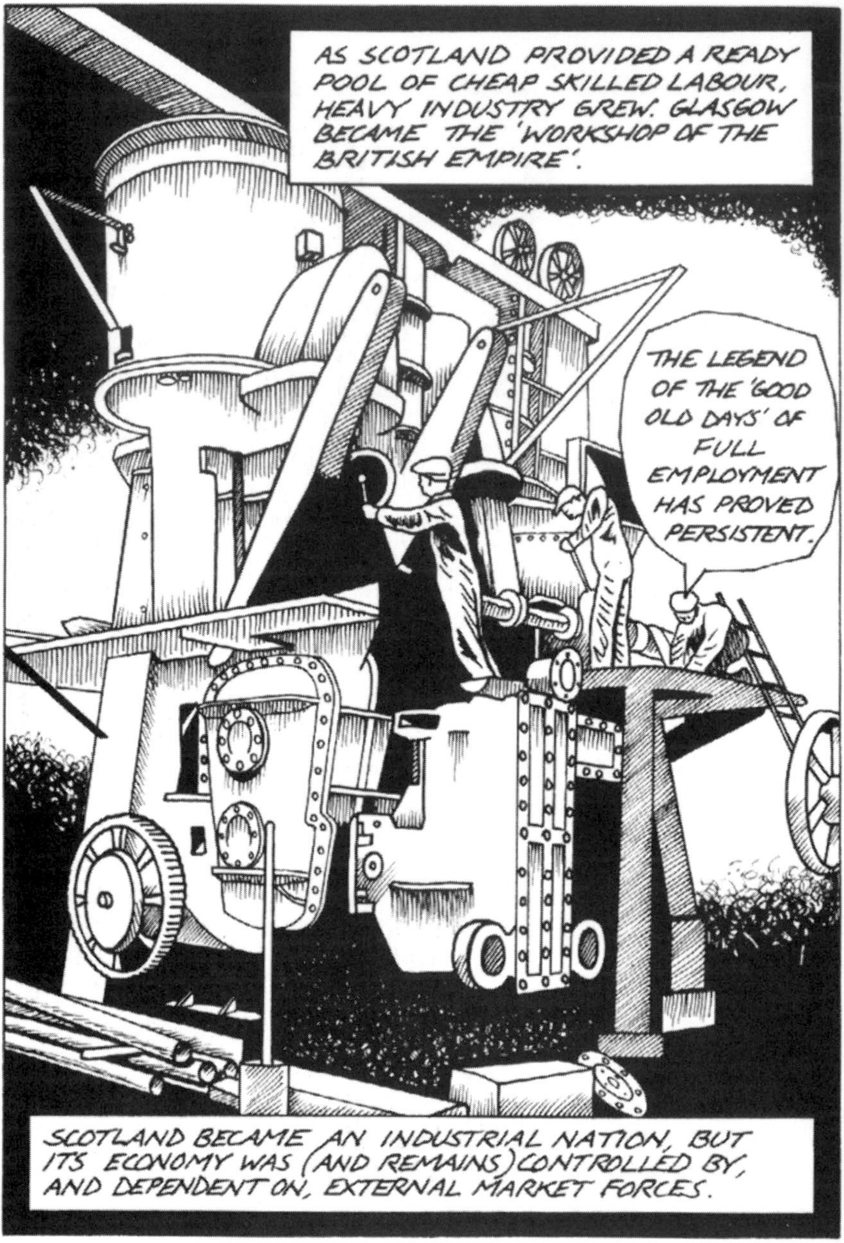
AS SCOTLAND PROVIDED A READY POOL OF CHEAP SKILLED LABOUR, HEAVY INDUSTRY GREW. GLASGOW BECAME THE 'WORKSHOP OF THE BRITISH EMPIRE'.
THE LEGEND OF THE 'GOOD OLD DAYS' OF FULL EMPLOYMENT HAS PROVED PERSISTENT.
SCOTLAND BECAME AN INDUSTRIAL NATION, BUT ITS ECONOMY WAS (AND REMAINS) CONTROLLED BY, AND DEPENDENT ON, EXTERNAL MARKET FORCES.

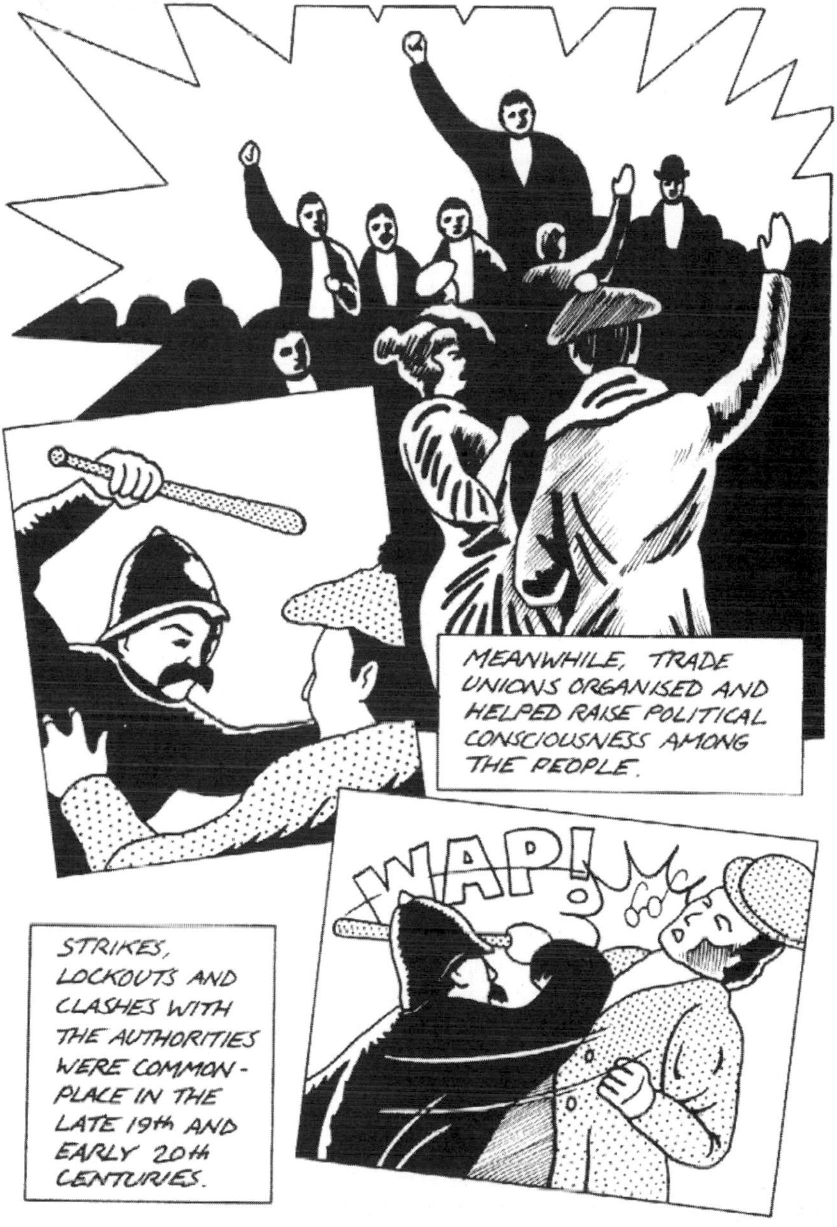
MEANWHILE, TRADE UNIONS ORGANISED AND HELPED RAISE POLITICAL CONSCIOUSNESS AMONG THE PEOPLE.
WAP!
STRIKES, LOCKOUTS AND CLASHES WITH THE AUTHORITIES WERE COMMON-PLACE IN THE LATE 19th AND EARLY 20th CENTURIES.

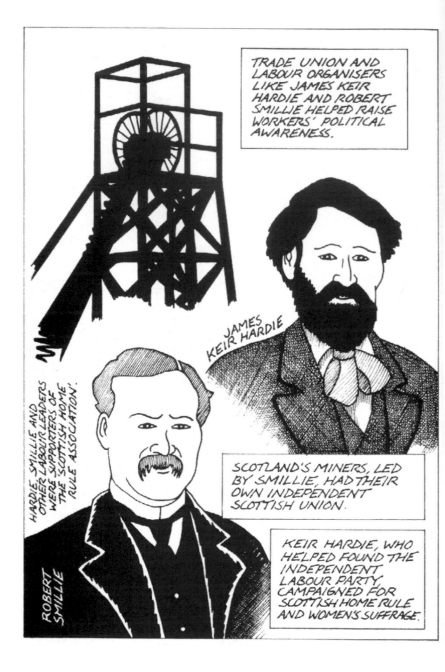

TRADE UNION AND LABOUR ORGANISERS LIKE JAMES KEIR HARDIE AND ROBERT SMILLIE HELPED RAISE WORKERS' POLITICAL AWARENESS.

JAMES KEIR HARDIE

HARDIE, SMILLIE AND OTHER LABOUR LEADERS WERE SUPPORTERS OF THE 'SCOTTISH HOME RULE ASSOCIATION'.

SCOTLAND'S MINERS, LED BY SMILLIE, HAD THEIR OWN INDEPENDENT SCOTTISH UNION.

KEIR HARDIE, WHO HELPED FOUND THE INDEPENDENT LABOUR PARTY, CAMPAIGNED FOR SCOTTISH HOME RULE AND WOMEN'S SUFFRAGE.

ROBERT SMILLIE

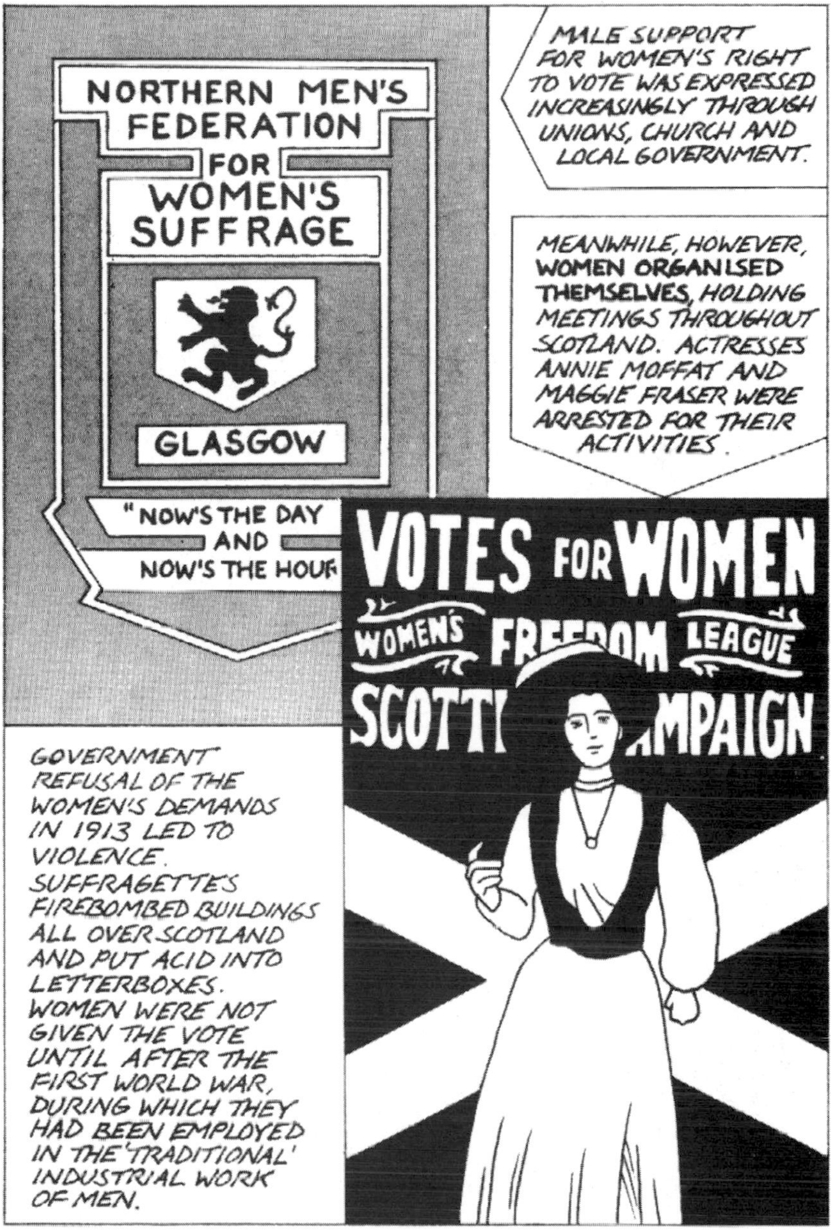
NORTHERN MEN'S FEDERATION FOR WOMEN'S SUFFRAGE
GLASGOW
"NOW'S THE DAY AND NOW'S THE HOUR
MALE SUPPORT FOR WOMEN'S RIGHT TO VOTE WAS EXPRESSED INCREASINGLY THROUGH UNIONS, CHURCH AND LOCAL GOVERNMENT.
MEANWHILE, HOWEVER, WOMEN ORGANISED THEMSELVES, HOLDING MEETINGS THROUGHOUT SCOTLAND. ACTRESSES ANNIE MOFFAT AND MAGGIE FRASER WERE ARRESTED FOR THEIR ACTIVITIES.
VOTES FOR WOMEN
WOMEN'S FREEDOM LEAGUE
SCOTTI MPAIGN
GOVERNMENT REFUSAL OF THE WOMEN'S DEMANDS IN 1913 LED TO VIOLENCE. SUFFRAGETTES FIREBOMBED BUILDINGS ALL OVER SCOTLAND AND PUT ACID INTO LETTERBOXES. WOMEN WERE NOT GIVEN THE VOTE UNTIL AFTER THE FIRST WORLD WAR, DURING WHICH THEY HAD BEEN EMPLOYED IN THE 'TRADITIONAL' INDUSTRIAL WORK OF MEN.

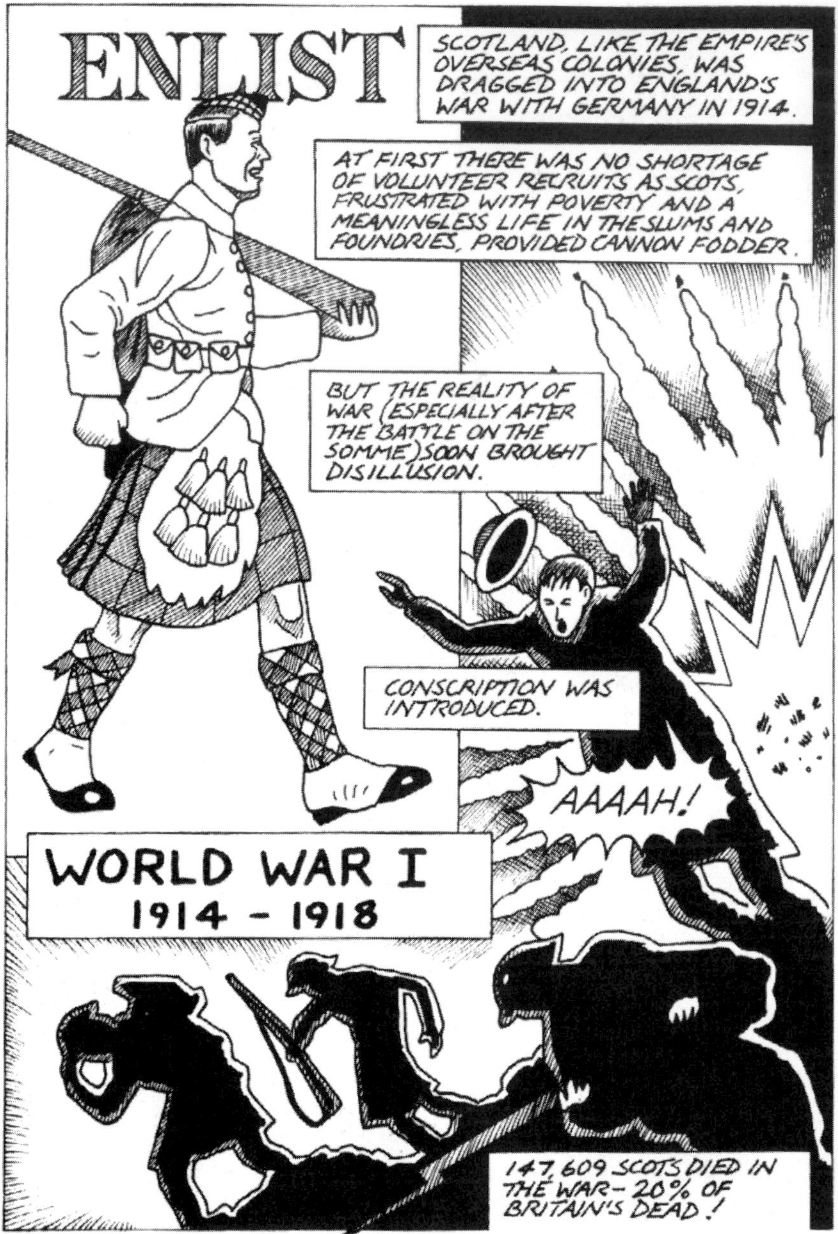
ENLIST
SCOTLAND, LIKE THE EMPIRE'S OVERSEAS COLONIES, WAS DRAGGED INTO ENGLAND'S WAR WITH GERMANY IN 1914.
AT FIRST THERE WAS NO SHORTAGE OF VOLUNTEER RECRUITS AS SCOTS, FRUSTRATED WITH POVERTY AND A MEANINGLESS LIFE IN THE SLUMS AND FOUNDRIES, PROVIDED CANNON FODDER.
BUT THE REALITY OF WAR (ESPECIALLY AFTER THE BATTLE ON THE SOMME) SOON BROUGHT DISILLUSION.
CONSCRIPTION WAS INTRODUCED.
AAAAH!
WORLD WAR I
1914 - 1918
147,609 SCOTS DIED IN THE WAR – 20% OF BRITAIN'S DEAD!

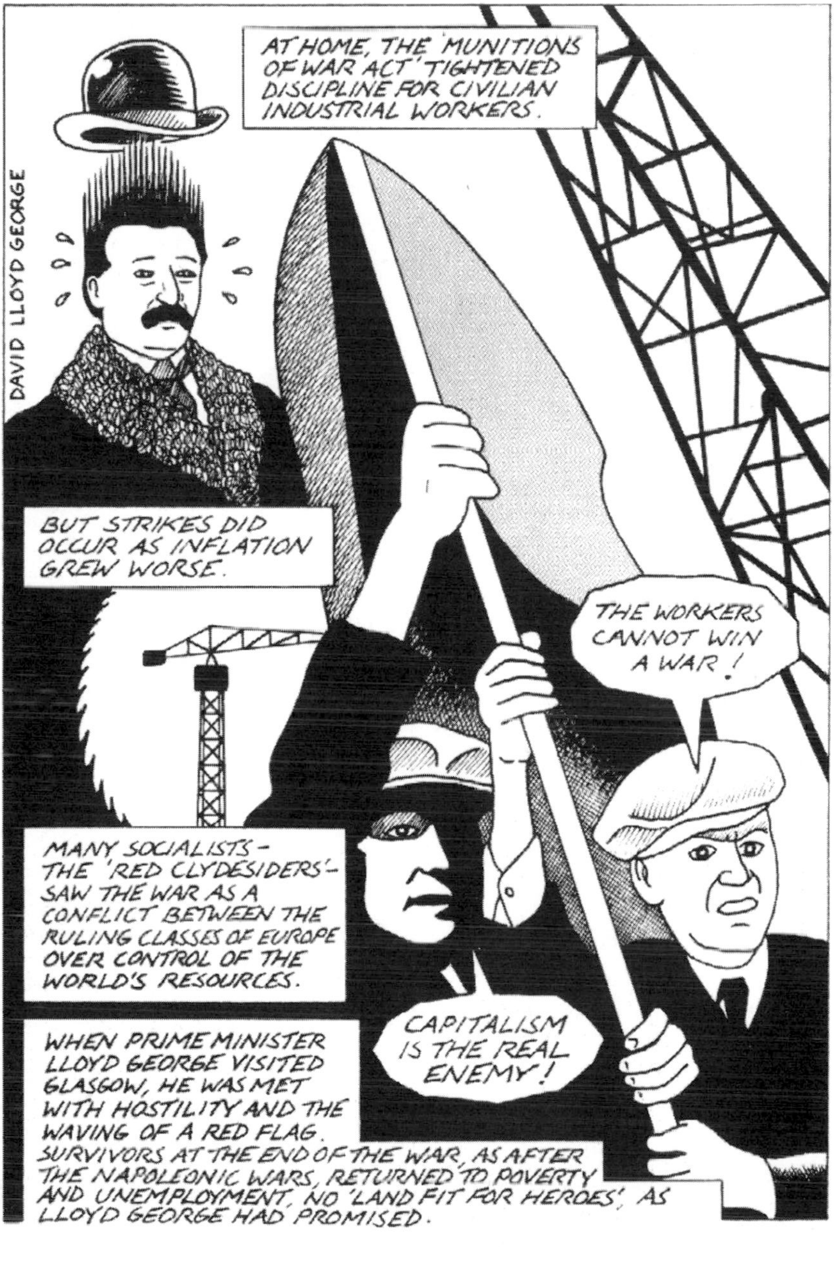
AT HOME, THE 'MUNITIONS OF WAR ACT' TIGHTENED DISCIPLINE FOR CIVILIAN INDUSTRIAL WORKERS.
DAVID LLOYD GEORGE
BUT STRIKES DID OCCUR AS INFLATION GREW WORSE.
THE WORKERS CANNOT WIN A WAR!
MANY SOCIALISTS - THE 'RED CLYDESIDERS' - SAW THE WAR AS A CONFLICT BETWEEN THE RULING CLASSES OF EUROPE OVER CONTROL OF THE WORLD'S RESOURCES.
CAPITALISM IS THE REAL ENEMY!
WHEN PRIME MINISTER LLOYD GEORGE VISITED GLASGOW, HE WAS MET WITH HOSTILITY AND THE WAVING OF A RED FLAG.
SURVIVORS AT THE END OF THE WAR, AS AFTER THE NAPOLEONIC WARS, RETURNED TO POVERTY AND UNEMPLOYMENT, NO 'LAND FIT FOR HEROES' AS LLOYD GEORGE HAD PROMISED.

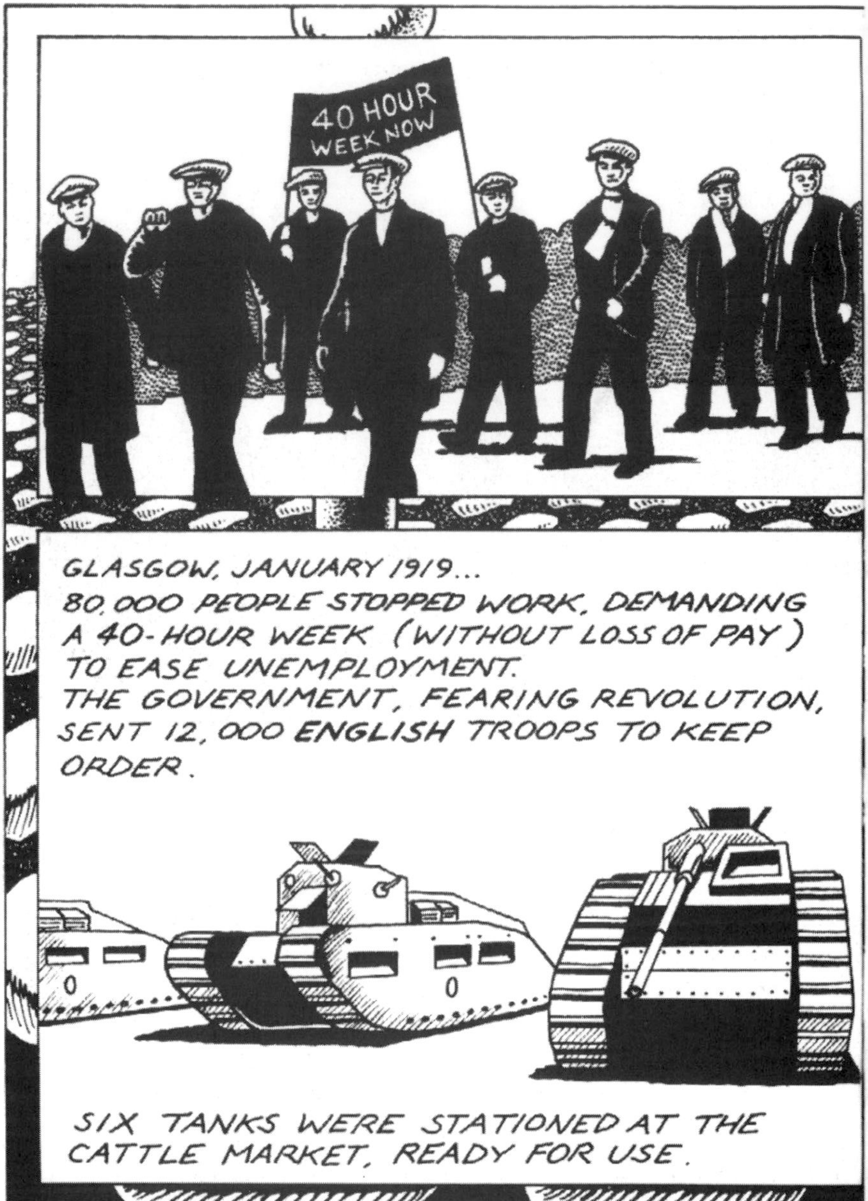
40 HOUR WEEK NOW
GLASGOW, JANUARY 1919...
80,000 PEOPLE STOPPED WORK, DEMANDING A 40-HOUR WEEK (WITHOUT LOSS OF PAY) TO EASE UNEMPLOYMENT.
THE GOVERNMENT, FEARING REVOLUTION, SENT 12,000 ENGLISH TROOPS TO KEEP ORDER.
SIX TANKS WERE STATIONED AT THE CATTLE MARKET, READY FOR USE.

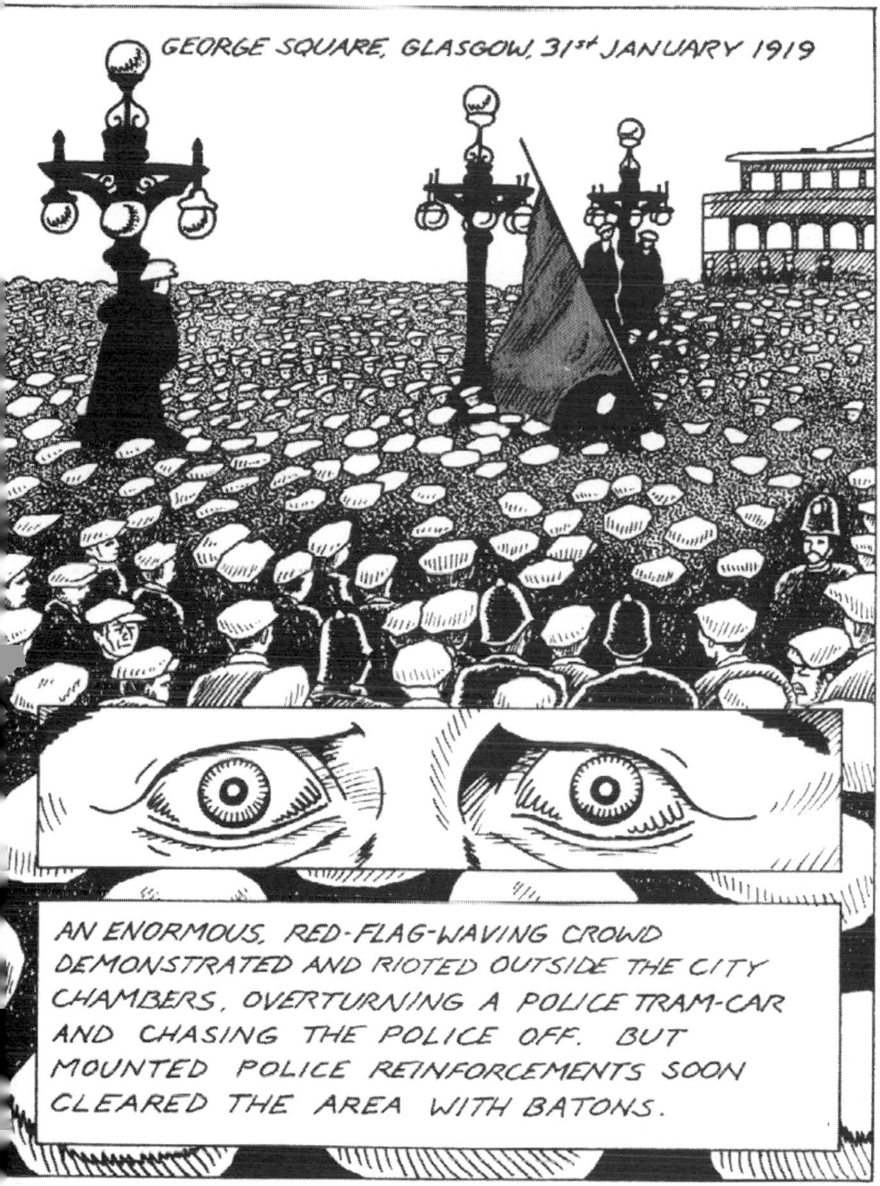
GEORGE SQUARE, GLASGOW, 31st JANUARY 1919
AN ENORMOUS, RED-FLAG-WAVING CROWD DEMONSTRATED AND RIOTED OUTSIDE THE CITY CHAMBERS, OVERTURNING A POLICE TRAM-CAR AND CHASING THE POLICE OFF. BUT MOUNTED POLICE REINFORCEMENTS SOON CLEARED THE AREA WITH BATONS.

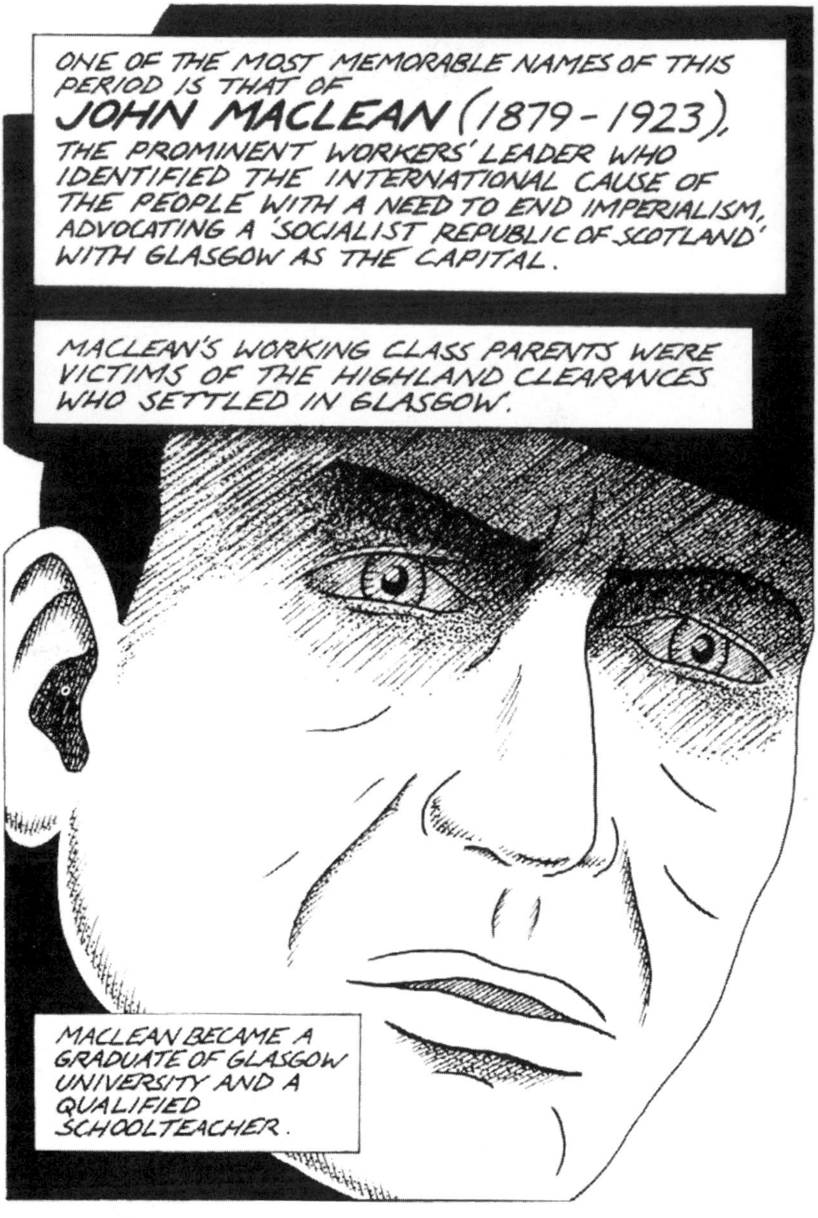
ONE OF THE MOST MEMORABLE NAMES OF THIS PERIOD IS THAT OF JOHN MACLEAN (1879 - 1923), THE PROMINENT WORKERS' LEADER WHO IDENTIFIED THE INTERNATIONAL CAUSE OF THE PEOPLE WITH A NEED TO END IMPERIALISM, ADVOCATING A 'SOCIALIST REPUBLIC OF SCOTLAND' WITH GLASGOW AS THE CAPITAL.
MACLEAN'S WORKING CLASS PARENTS WERE VICTIMS OF THE HIGHLAND CLEARANCES WHO SETTLED IN GLASGOW.
MACLEAN BECAME A GRADUATE OF GLASGOW UNIVERSITY AND A QUALIFIED SCHOOLTEACHER.

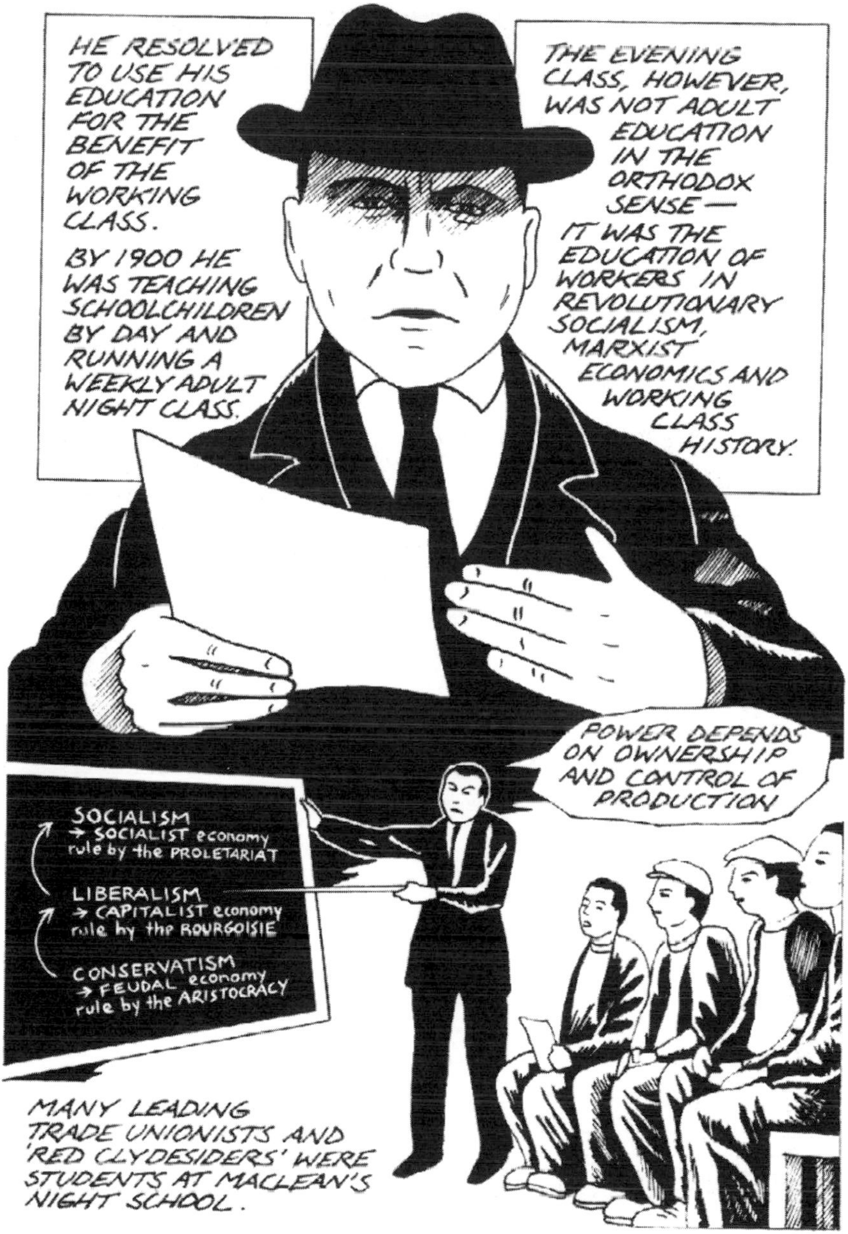
HE RESOLVED TO USE HIS EDUCATION FOR THE BENEFIT OF THE WORKING CLASS.
BY 1900 HE WAS TEACHING SCHOOLCHILDREN BY DAY AND RUNNING A WEEKLY ADULT NIGHT CLASS.
THE EVENING CLASS, HOWEVER, WAS NOT ADULT EDUCATION IN THE ORTHODOX SENSE— IT WAS THE EDUCATION OF WORKERS IN REVOLUTIONARY SOCIALISM, MARXIST ECONOMICS AND WORKING CLASS HISTORY.
POWER DEPENDS ON OWNERSHIP AND CONTROL OF PRODUCTION
SOCIALISM
→ SOCIALIST economy
rule by the PROLETARIAT
LIBERALISM
→ CAPITALIST economy
rule by the BOURGOISIE
CONSERVATISM
→ FEUDAL economy
rule by the ARISTOCRACY
MANY LEADING TRADE UNIONISTS AND 'RED CLYDESIDERS' WERE STUDENTS AT MACLEAN'S NIGHT SCHOOL.

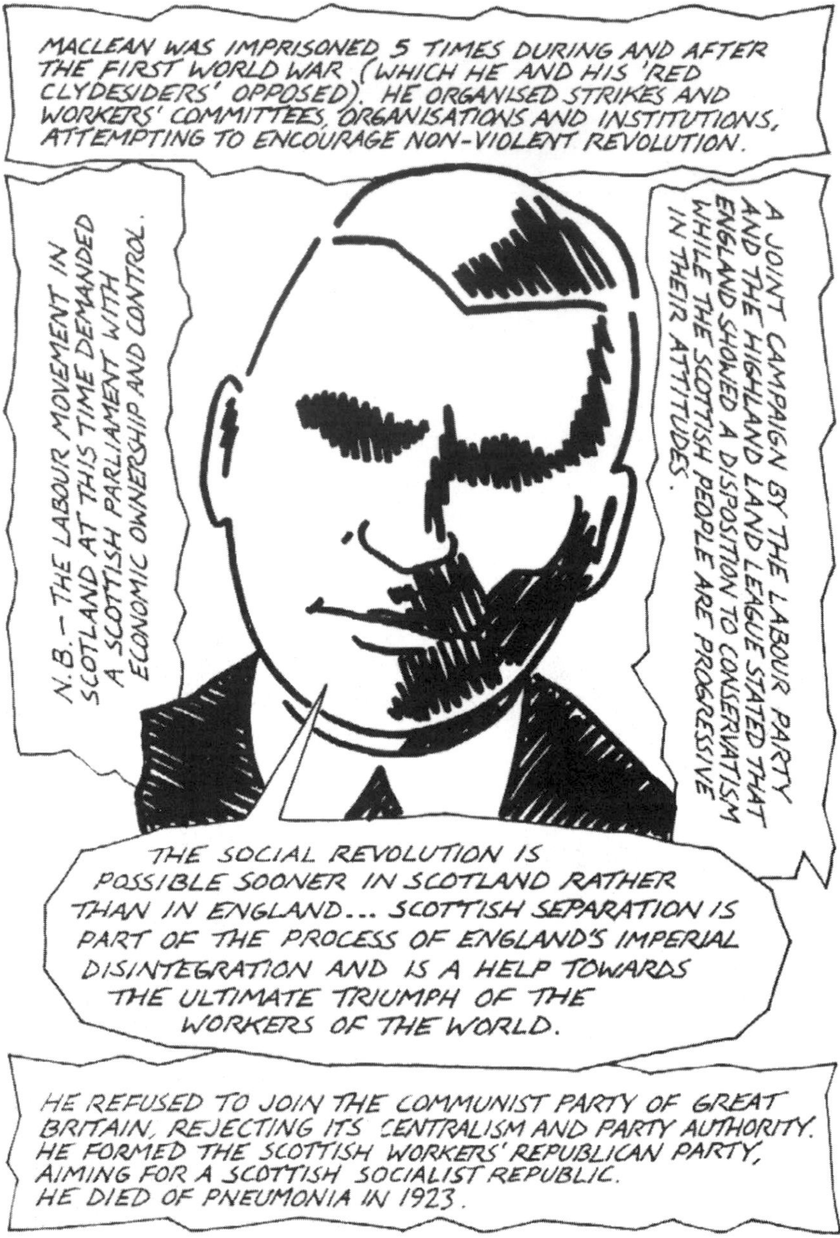
MACLEAN WAS IMPRISONED 5 TIMES DURING AND AFTER THE FIRST WORLD WAR (WHICH HE AND HIS 'RED CLYDESIDERS' OPPOSED). HE ORGANISED STRIKES AND WORKERS' COMMITTEES, ORGANISATIONS AND INSTITUTIONS, ATTEMPTING TO ENCOURAGE NON-VIOLENT REVOLUTION.
N.B. – THE LABOUR MOVEMENT IN SCOTLAND AT THIS TIME DEMANDED A SCOTTISH PARLIAMENT WITH ECONOMIC OWNERSHIP AND CONTROL.
A JOINT CAMPAIGN BY THE LABOUR PARTY AND THE HIGHLAND LAND LEAGUE STATED THAT ENGLAND SHOWED A DISPOSITION TO CONSERVATISM WHILE THE SCOTTISH PEOPLE ARE PROGRESSIVE IN THEIR ATTITUDES.
THE SOCIAL REVOLUTION IS POSSIBLE SOONER IN SCOTLAND RATHER THAN IN ENGLAND... SCOTTISH SEPARATION IS PART OF THE PROCESS OF ENGLAND'S IMPERIAL DISINTEGRATION AND IS A HELP TOWARDS THE ULTIMATE TRIUMPH OF THE WORKERS OF THE WORLD.
HE REFUSED TO JOIN THE COMMUNIST PARTY OF GREAT BRITAIN, REJECTING ITS CENTRALISM AND PARTY AUTHORITY. HE FORMED THE SCOTTISH WORKERS' REPUBLICAN PARTY, AIMING FOR A SCOTTISH SOCIALIST REPUBLIC. HE DIED OF PNEUMONIA IN 1923.

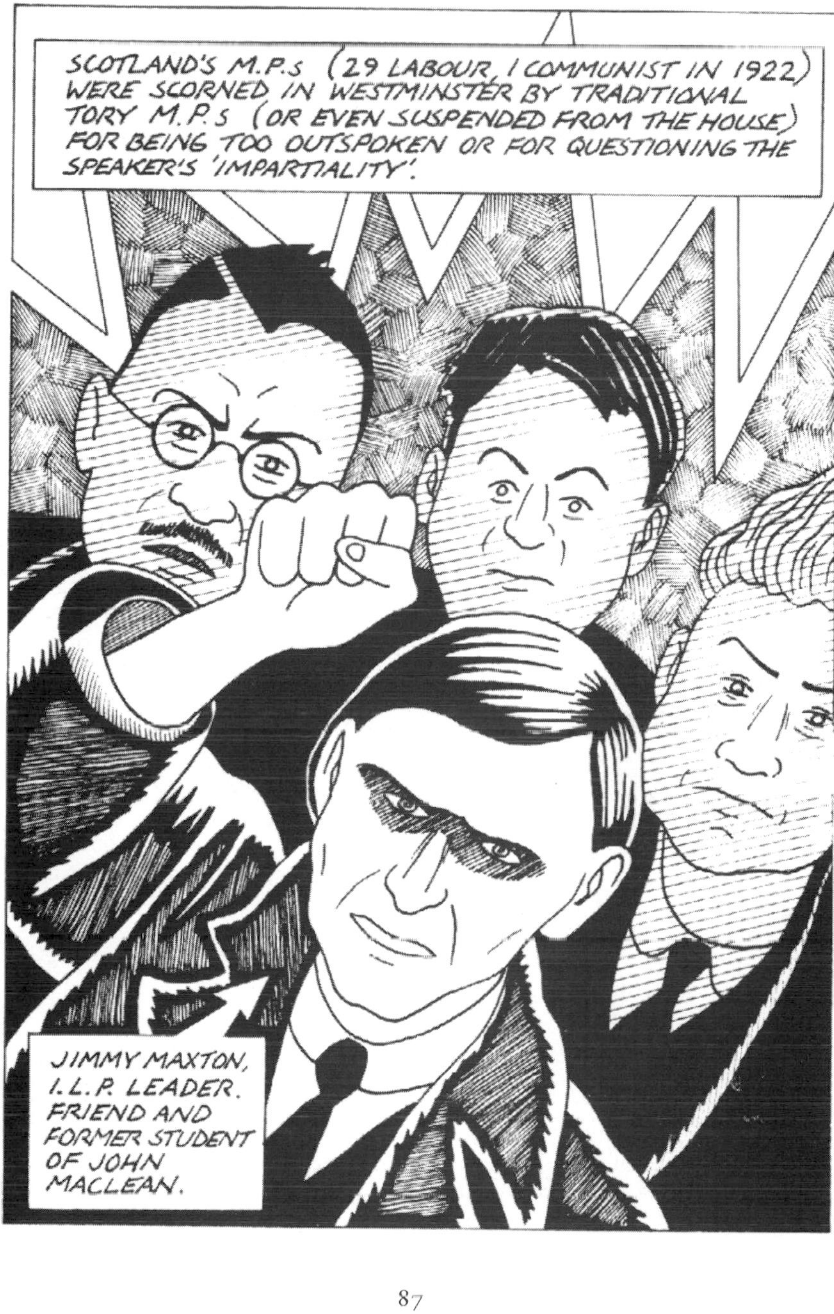
SCOTLAND'S M.P.s (29 LABOUR, 1 COMMUNIST IN 1922) WERE SCORNED IN WESTMINSTER BY TRADITIONAL TORY M.P.s (OR EVEN SUSPENDED FROM THE HOUSE) FOR BEING TOO OUTSPOKEN OR FOR QUESTIONING THE SPEAKER'S 'IMPARTIALITY'.
JIMMY MAXTON, I.L.P. LEADER. FRIEND AND FORMER STUDENT OF JOHN MACLEAN.

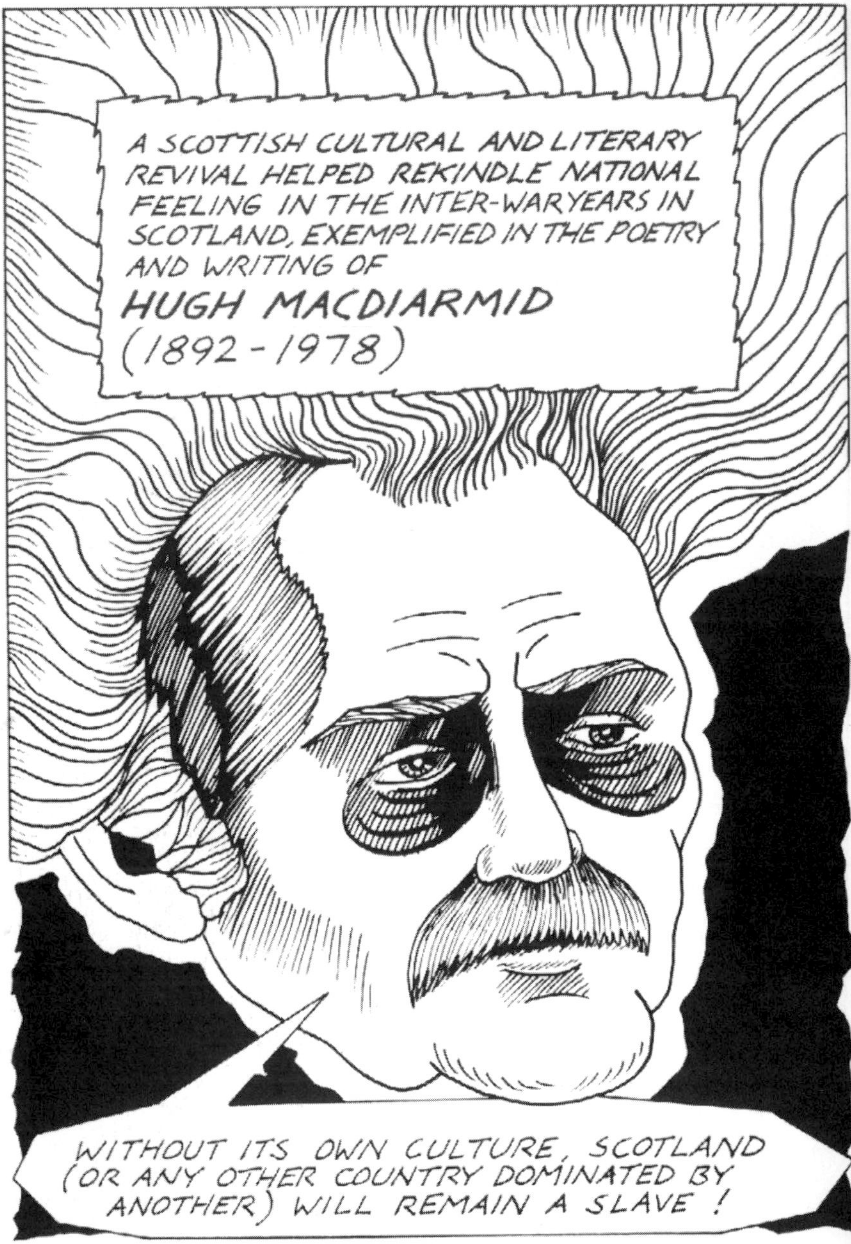
A SCOTTISH CULTURAL AND LITERARY REVIVAL HELPED REKINDLE NATIONAL FEELING IN THE INTER-WARYEARS IN SCOTLAND, EXEMPLIFIED IN THE POETRY AND WRITING OF
HUGH MACDIARMID (1892-1978)
WITHOUT ITS OWN CULTURE, SCOTLAND (OR ANY OTHER COUNTRY DOMINATED BY ANOTHER) WILL REMAIN A SLAVE!

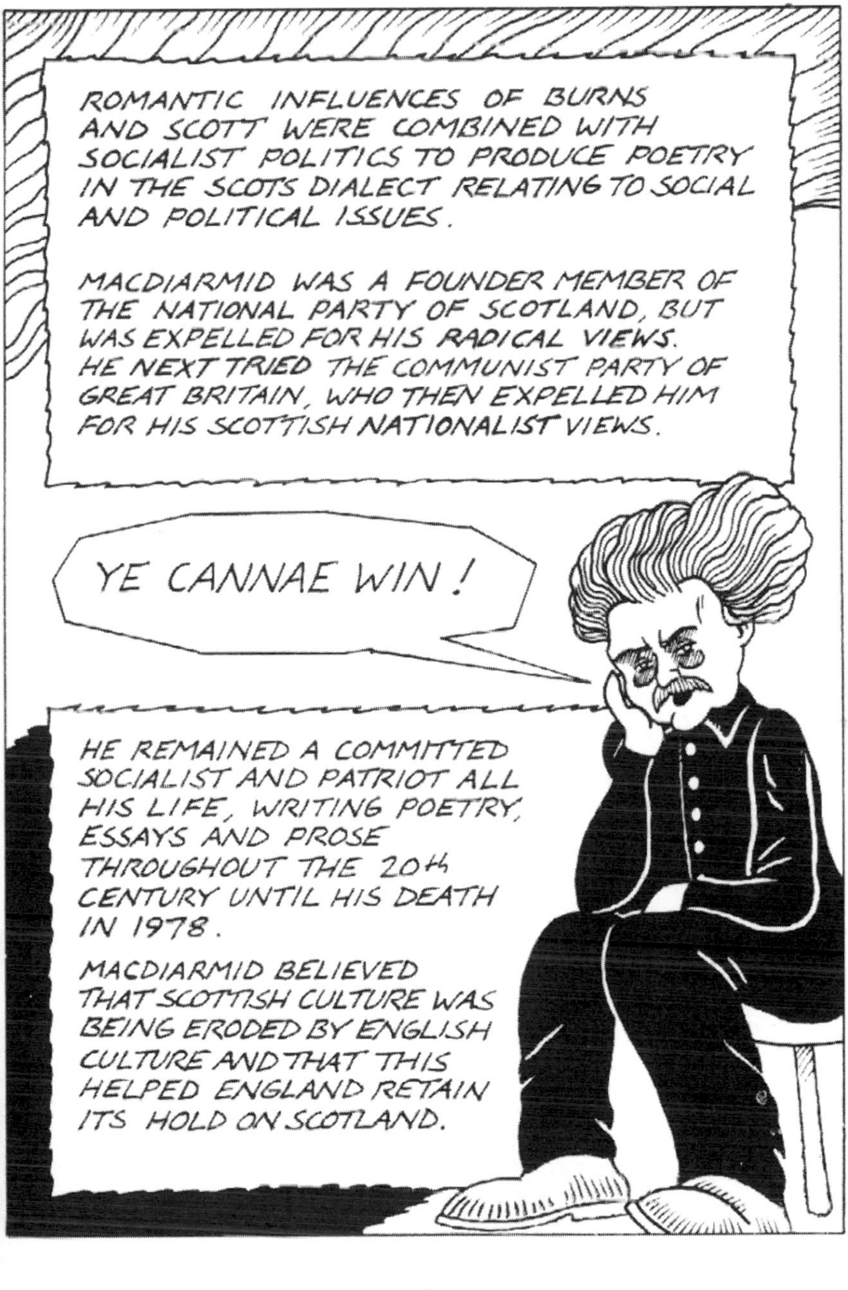
ROMANTIC INFLUENCES OF BURNS AND SCOTT WERE COMBINED WITH SOCIALIST POLITICS TO PRODUCE POETRY IN THE SCOTS DIALECT RELATING TO SOCIAL AND POLITICAL ISSUES.
MACDIARMID WAS A FOUNDER MEMBER OF THE NATIONAL PARTY OF SCOTLAND, BUT WAS EXPELLED FOR HIS RADICAL VIEWS. HE NEXT TRIED THE COMMUNIST PARTY OF GREAT BRITAIN, WHO THEN EXPELLED HIM FOR HIS SCOTTISH NATIONALIST VIEWS.
YE CANNAE WIN!
HE REMAINED A COMMITTED SOCIALIST AND PATRIOT ALL HIS LIFE, WRITING POETRY, ESSAYS AND PROSE THROUGHOUT THE 20th CENTURY UNTIL HIS DEATH IN 1978.
MACDIARMID BELIEVED THAT SCOTTISH CULTURE WAS BEING ERODED BY ENGLISH CULTURE AND THAT THIS HELPED ENGLAND RETAIN ITS HOLD ON SCOTLAND.

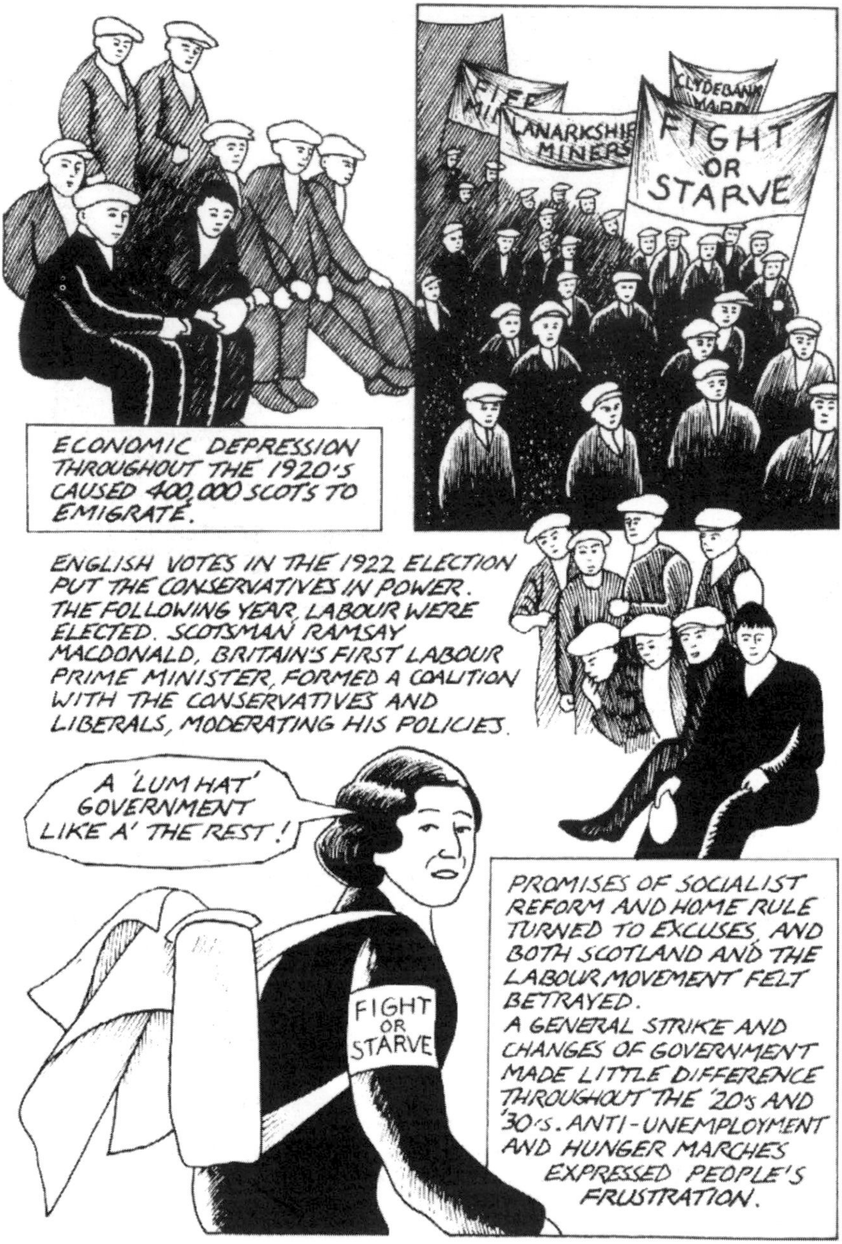
ECONOMIC DEPRESSION THROUGHOUT THE 1920'S CAUSED 400,000 SCOTS TO EMIGRATE.
LANARKSHIR MINERS
FIGHT OR STARVE
ENGLISH VOTES IN THE 1922 ELECTION PUT THE CONSERVATIVES IN POWER. THE FOLLOWING YEAR, LABOUR WERE ELECTED. SCOTSMAN RAMSAY MACDONALD, BRITAIN'S FIRST LABOUR PRIME MINISTER, FORMED A COALITION WITH THE CONSERVATIVES AND LIBERALS, MODERATING HIS POLICIES.
A 'LUM HAT' GOVERNMENT LIKE A' THE REST!
FIGHT OR STARVE
PROMISES OF SOCIALIST REFORM AND HOME RULE TURNED TO EXCUSES, AND BOTH SCOTLAND AND THE LABOUR MOVEMENT FELT BETRAYED.
A GENERAL STRIKE AND CHANGES OF GOVERNMENT MADE LITTLE DIFFERENCE THROUGHOUT THE '20'S AND '30'S. ANTI-UNEMPLOYMENT AND HUNGER MARCHES EXPRESSED PEOPLE'S FRUSTRATION.

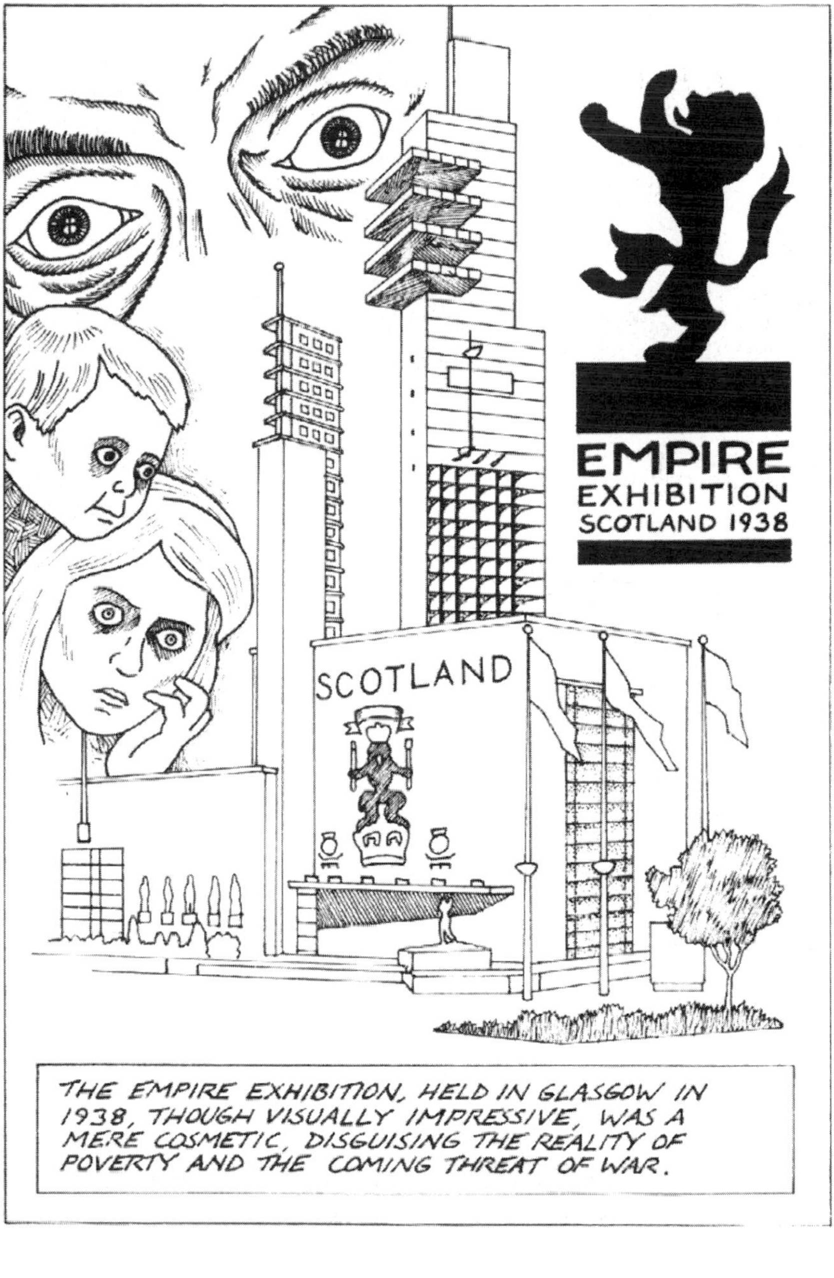
EMPIRE
EXHIBITION
SCOTLAND 1938
SCOTLAND
THE EMPIRE EXHIBITION, HELD IN GLASGOW IN 1938, THOUGH VISUALLY IMPRESSIVE, WAS A MERE COSMETIC, DISGUISING THE REALITY OF POVERTY AND THE COMING THREAT OF WAR.

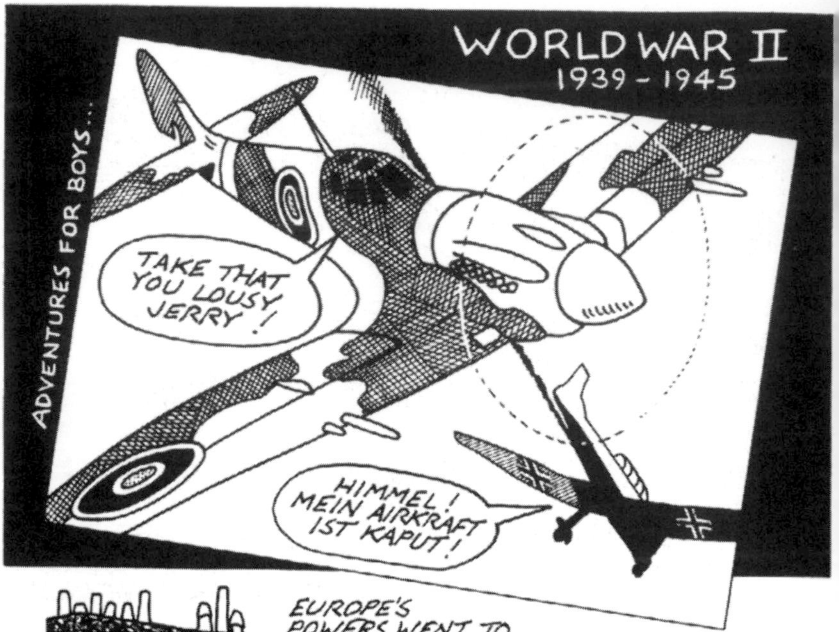
WORLD WAR II
1939 - 1945
ADVENTURES FOR BOYS...
TAKE THAT YOU LOUSY JERRY!
HIMMEL! MEIN AIRKRAFT IST KAPUT!

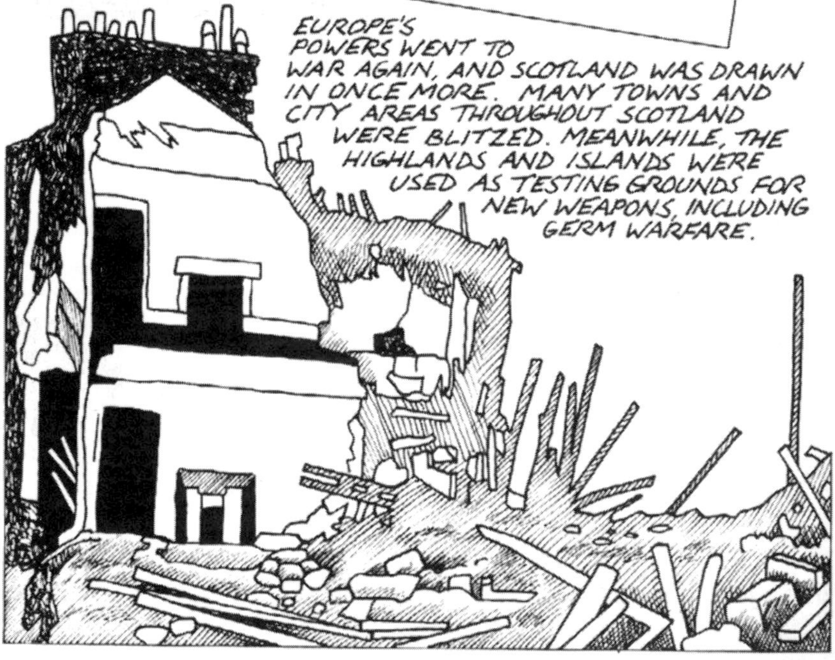
EUROPE'S POWERS WENT TO WAR AGAIN, AND SCOTLAND WAS DRAWN IN ONCE MORE. MANY TOWNS AND CITY AREAS THROUGHOUT SCOTLAND WERE BLITZED. MEANWHILE, THE HIGHLANDS AND ISLANDS WERE USED AS TESTING GROUNDS FOR NEW WEAPONS, INCLUDING GERM WARFARE.

57,720 SCOTS DIED IN THE SECOND WORLD WAR. AFTER THE WAR, A NEW AGE OF PROSPERITY PROMISED BY THE GOVERNMENT FAILED TO REACH EXPECTATIONS.

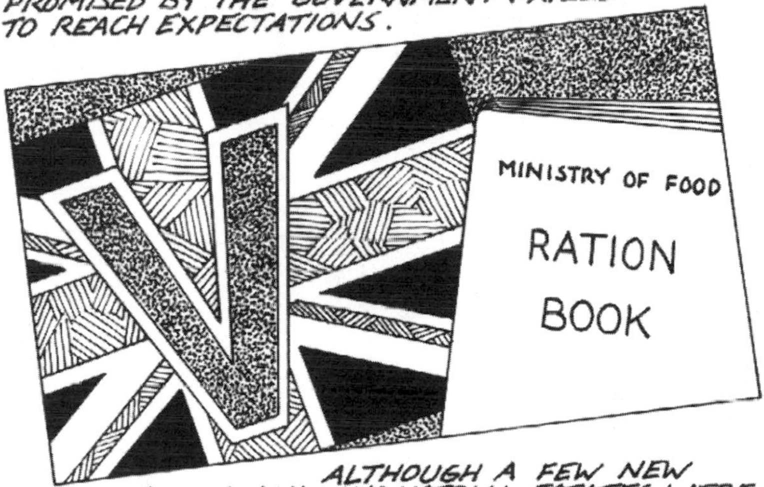
MINISTRY OF FOOD
RATION BOOK

ALTHOUGH A FEW NEW TOWNS AND INDUSTRIAL ESTATES WERE CREATED, SCOTLAND DID NOT PROSPER NEARLY AS MUCH AS ENGLAND.

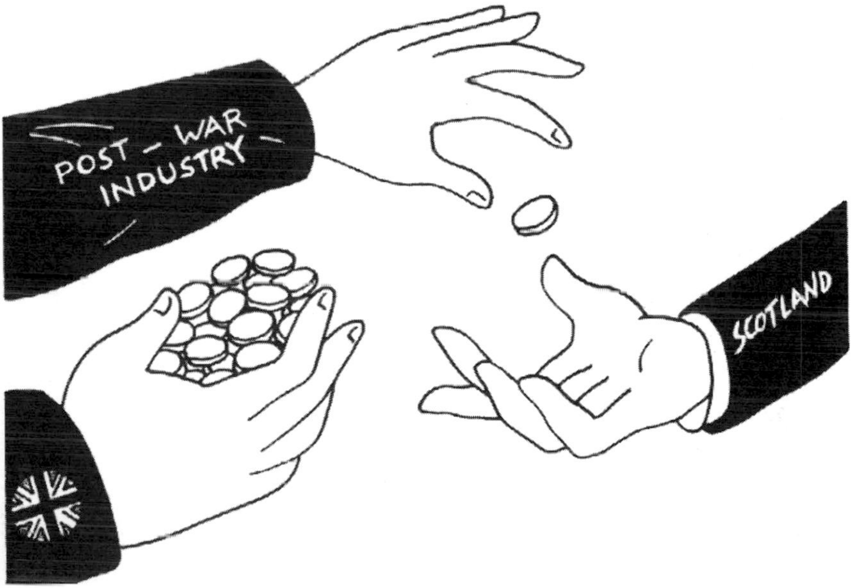
POST-WAR INDUSTRY
SCOTLAND

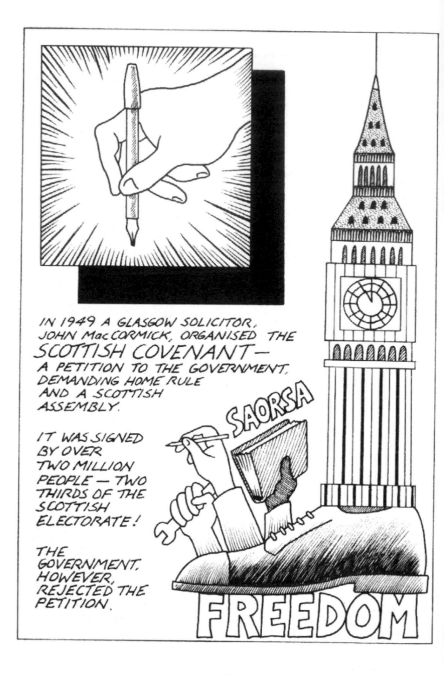

IN 1949 A GLASGOW SOLICITOR,
JOHN MacCORMICK, ORGANISED THE
SCOTTISH COVENANT—
A PETITION TO THE GOVERNMENT,
DEMANDING HOME RULE
AND A SCOTTISH
ASSEMBLY.

IT WAS SIGNED
BY OVER
TWO MILLION
PEOPLE — TWO
THIRDS OF THE
SCOTTISH
ELECTORATE!

THE
GOVERNMENT,
HOWEVER,
REJECTED THE
PETITION.

SAORSA

FREEDOM

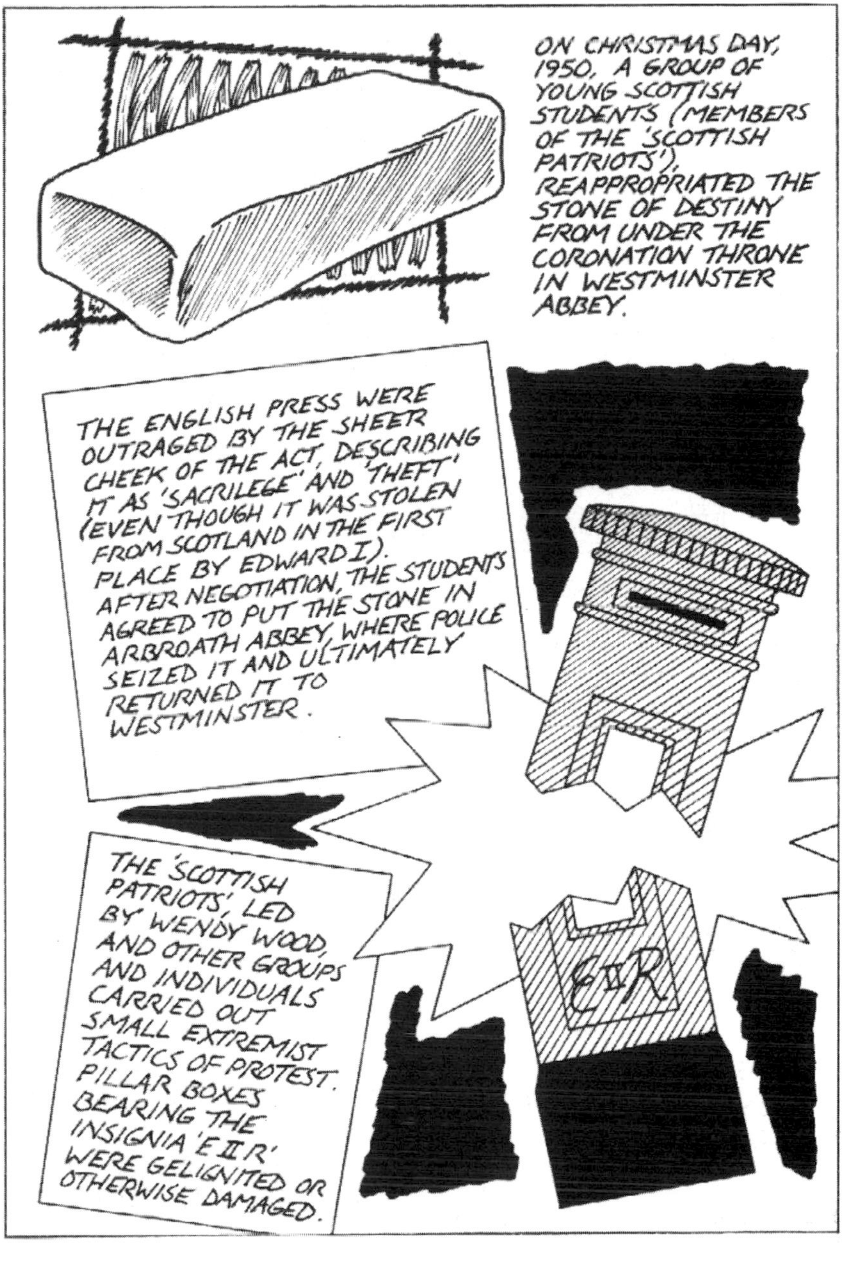
ON CHRISTMAS DAY, 1950, A GROUP OF YOUNG SCOTTISH STUDENTS (MEMBERS OF THE 'SCOTTISH PATRIOTS'), REAPPROPRIATED THE STONE OF DESTINY FROM UNDER THE CORONATION THRONE IN WESTMINSTER ABBEY.
THE ENGLISH PRESS WERE OUTRAGED BY THE SHEER CHEEK OF THE ACT, DESCRIBING IT AS 'SACRILEGE' AND 'THEFT' (EVEN THOUGH IT WAS STOLEN FROM SCOTLAND IN THE FIRST PLACE BY EDWARD I). AFTER NEGOTIATION, THE STUDENTS AGREED TO PUT THE STONE IN ARBROATH ABBEY, WHERE POLICE SEIZED IT AND ULTIMATELY RETURNED IT TO WESTMINSTER.
THE 'SCOTTISH PATRIOTS', LED BY WENDY WOOD, AND OTHER GROUPS AND INDIVIDUALS CARRIED OUT SMALL EXTREMIST TACTICS OF PROTEST. PILLAR BOXES BEARING THE INSIGNIA 'E II R' WERE GELIGNITED OR OTHERWISE DAMAGED.
E II R

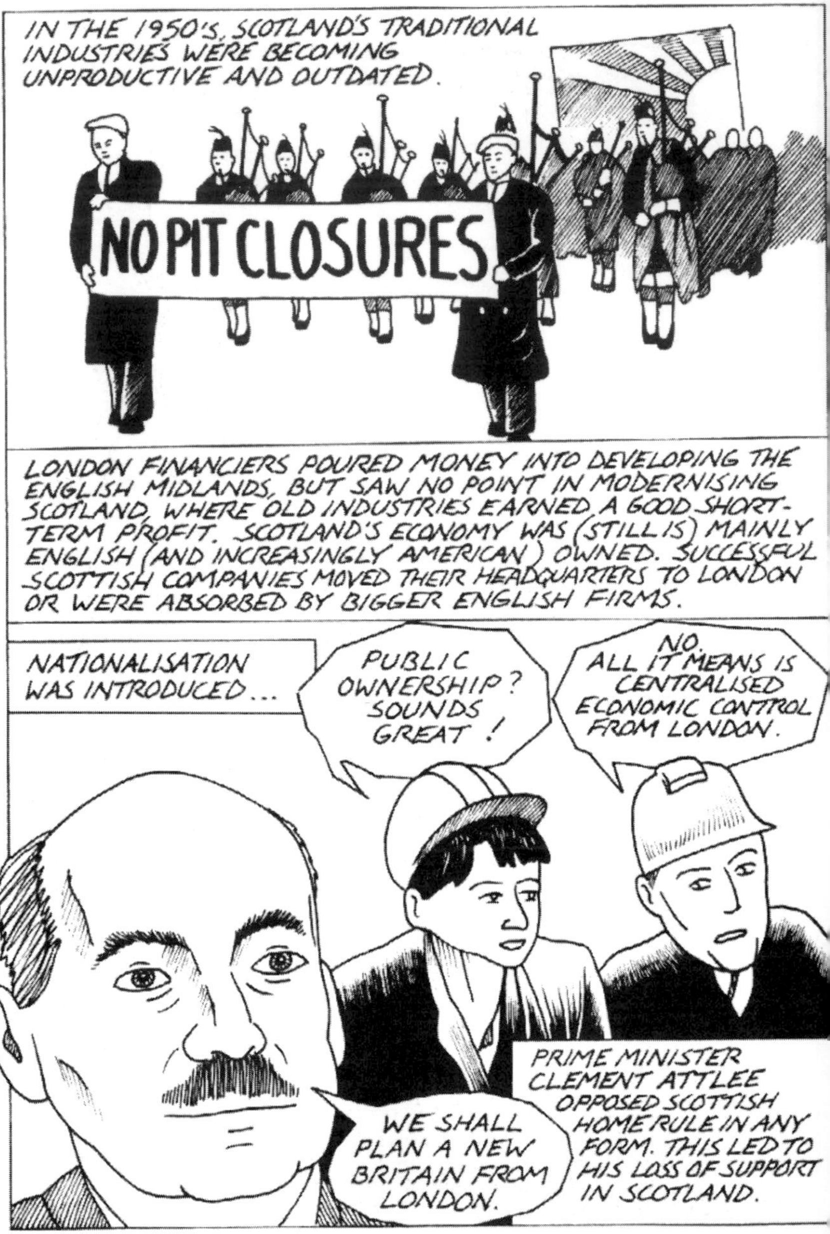
IN THE 1950'S, SCOTLAND'S TRADITIONAL INDUSTRIES WERE BECOMING UNPRODUCTIVE AND OUTDATED.
NO PIT CLOSURES
LONDON FINANCIERS POURED MONEY INTO DEVELOPING THE ENGLISH MIDLANDS, BUT SAW NO POINT IN MODERNISING SCOTLAND, WHERE OLD INDUSTRIES EARNED A GOOD SHORT-TERM PROFIT. SCOTLAND'S ECONOMY WAS (STILL IS) MAINLY ENGLISH (AND INCREASINGLY AMERICAN) OWNED. SUCCESSFUL SCOTTISH COMPANIES MOVED THEIR HEADQUARTERS TO LONDON OR WERE ABSORBED BY BIGGER ENGLISH FIRMS.
NATIONALISATION WAS INTRODUCED...
PUBLIC OWNERSHIP? SOUNDS GREAT!
NO. ALL IT MEANS IS CENTRALISED ECONOMIC CONTROL FROM LONDON.
WE SHALL PLAN A NEW BRITAIN FROM LONDON.
PRIME MINISTER CLEMENT ATTLEE OPPOSED SCOTTISH HOME RULE IN ANY FORM. THIS LED TO HIS LOSS OF SUPPORT IN SCOTLAND.

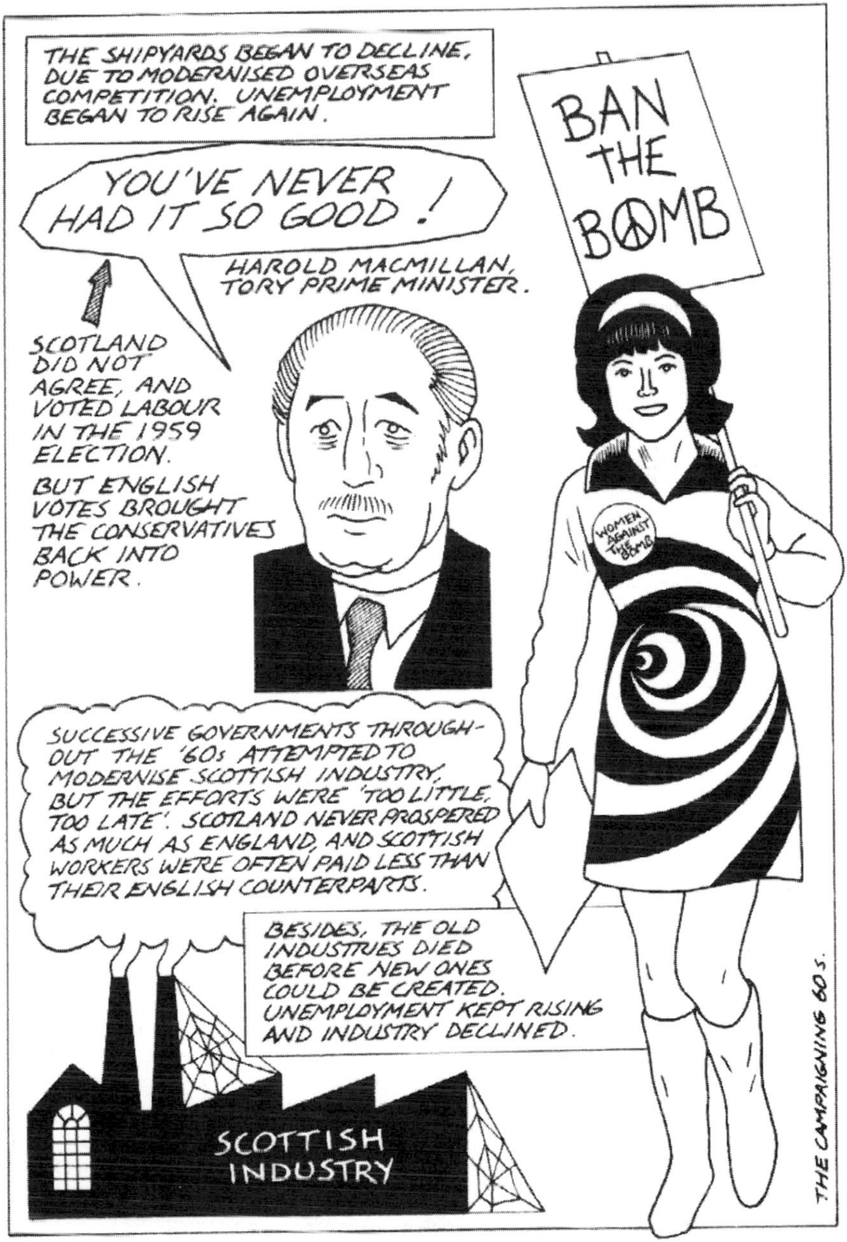
THE SHIPYARDS BEGAN TO DECLINE, DUE TO MODERNISED OVERSEAS COMPETITION. UNEMPLOYMENT BEGAN TO RISE AGAIN.
YOU'VE NEVER HAD IT SO GOOD!
HAROLD MACMILLAN, TORY PRIME MINISTER.
SCOTLAND DID NOT AGREE, AND VOTED LABOUR IN THE 1959 ELECTION.
BUT ENGLISH VOTES BROUGHT THE CONSERVATIVES BACK INTO POWER.
BAN THE BOMB
WOMEN AGAINST THE BOMB
SUCCESSIVE GOVERNMENTS THROUGHOUT THE '60s ATTEMPTED TO MODERNISE SCOTTISH INDUSTRY, BUT THE EFFORTS WERE 'TOO LITTLE, TOO LATE'. SCOTLAND NEVER PROSPERED AS MUCH AS ENGLAND, AND SCOTTISH WORKERS WERE OFTEN PAID LESS THAN THEIR ENGLISH COUNTERPARTS.
BESIDES, THE OLD INDUSTRIES DIED BEFORE NEW ONES COULD BE CREATED. UNEMPLOYMENT KEPT RISING AND INDUSTRY DECLINED.
SCOTTISH INDUSTRY
THE CAMPAIGNING 60s.

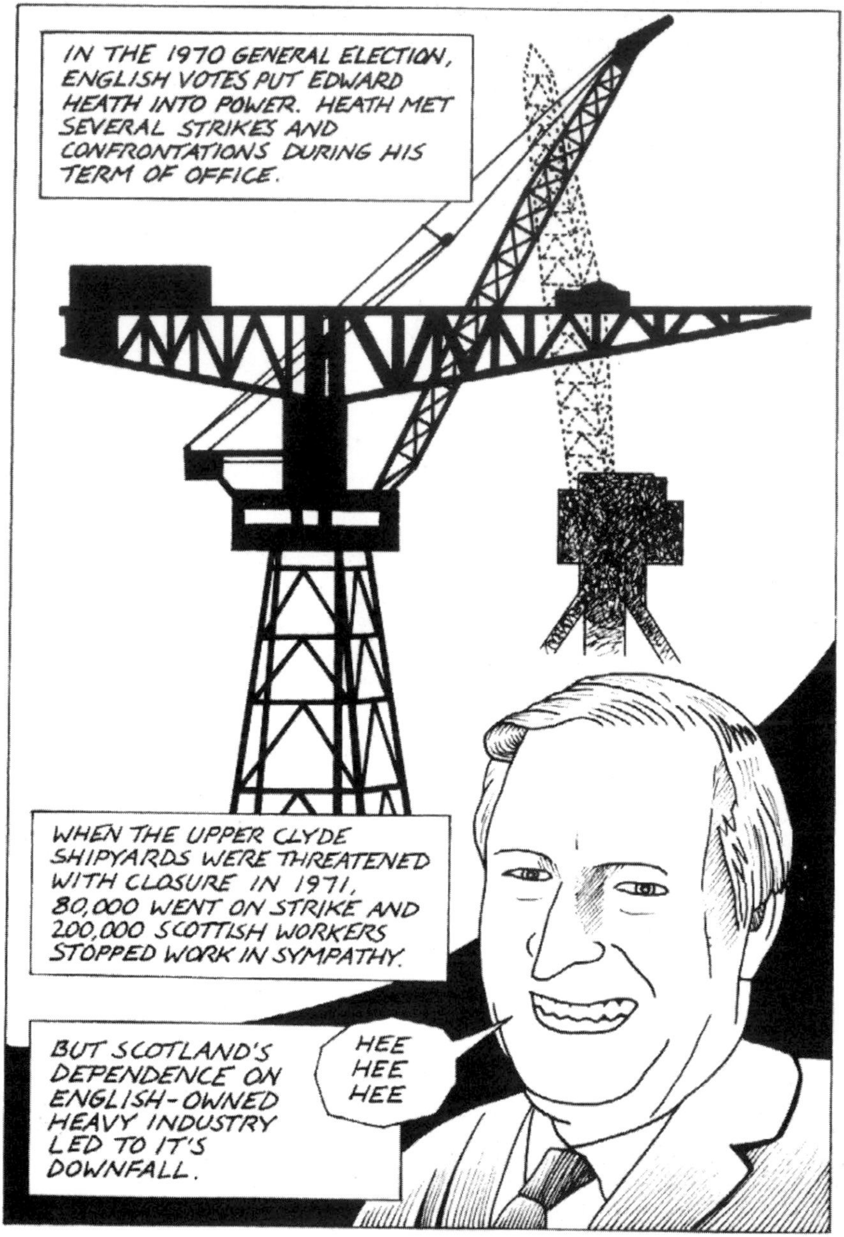
IN THE 1970 GENERAL ELECTION, ENGLISH VOTES PUT EDWARD HEATH INTO POWER. HEATH MET SEVERAL STRIKES AND CONFRONTATIONS DURING HIS TERM OF OFFICE.
WHEN THE UPPER CLYDE SHIPYARDS WERE THREATENED WITH CLOSURE IN 1971, 80,000 WENT ON STRIKE AND 200,000 SCOTTISH WORKERS STOPPED WORK IN SYMPATHY.
BUT SCOTLAND'S DEPENDENCE ON ENGLISH-OWNED HEAVY INDUSTRY LED TO IT'S DOWNFALL.
HEE HEE HEE

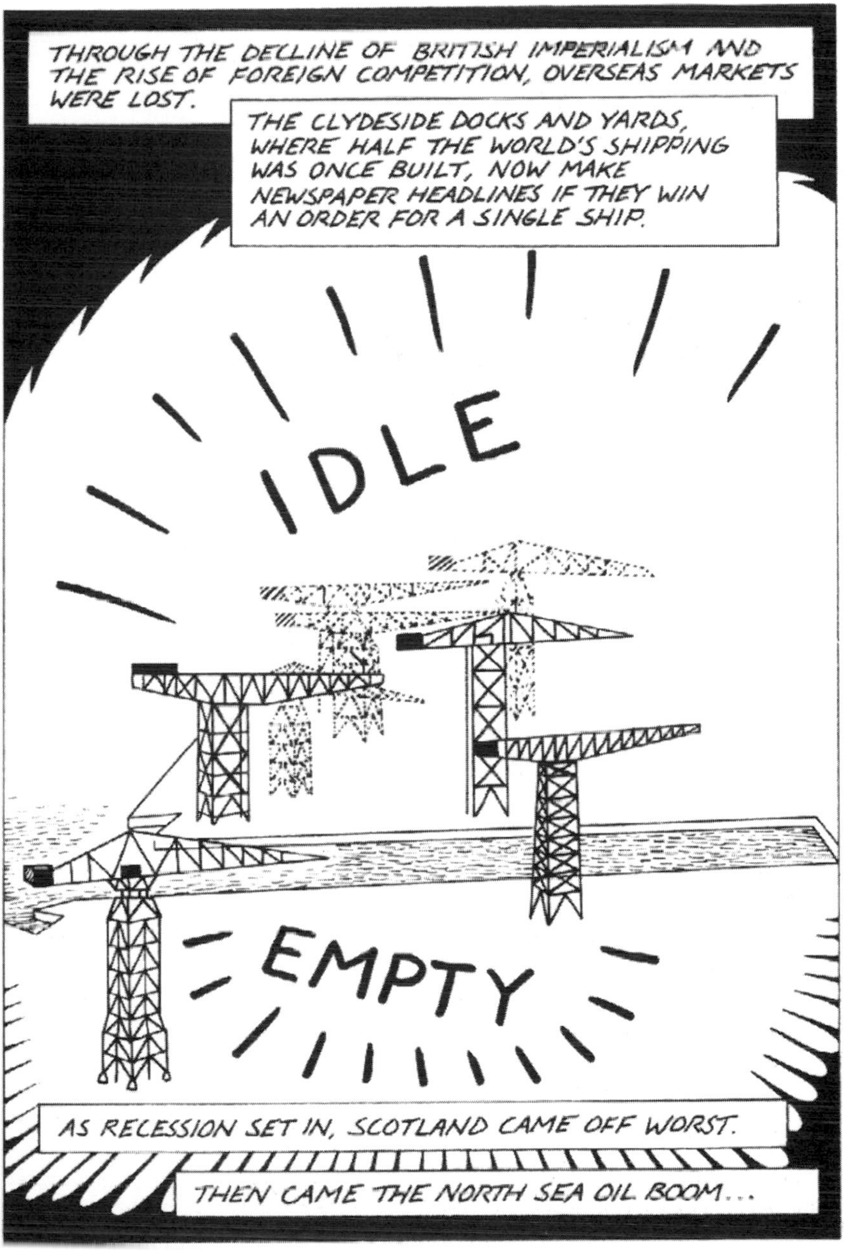
THROUGH THE DECLINE OF BRITISH IMPERIALISM AND THE RISE OF FOREIGN COMPETITION, OVERSEAS MARKETS WERE LOST.
THE CLYDESIDE DOCKS AND YARDS, WHERE HALF THE WORLD'S SHIPPING WAS ONCE BUILT, NOW MAKE NEWSPAPER HEADLINES IF THEY WIN AN ORDER FOR A SINGLE SHIP.
IDLE
EMPTY
AS RECESSION SET IN, SCOTLAND CAME OFF WORST.
THEN CAME THE NORTH SEA OIL BOOM...

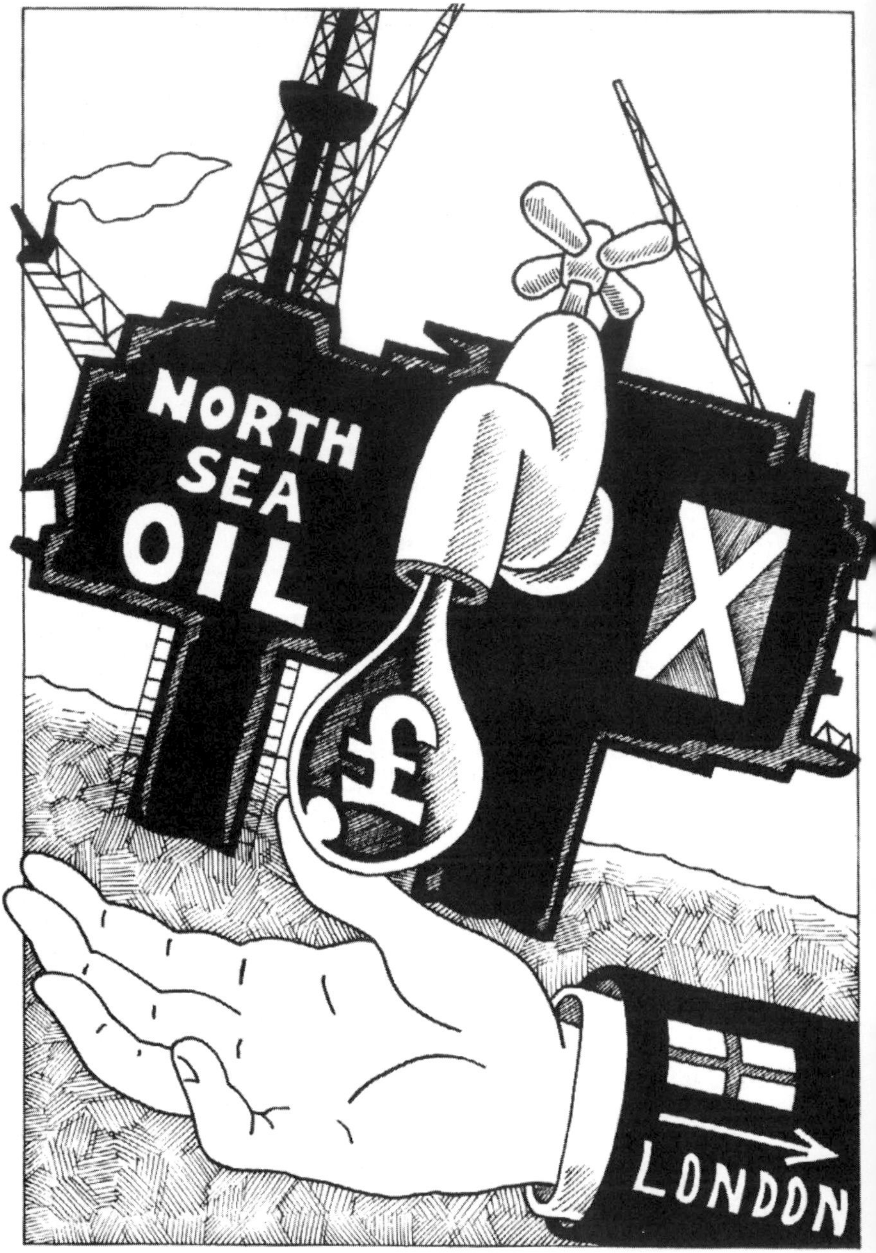
NORTH
SEA
OIL
£
LONDON

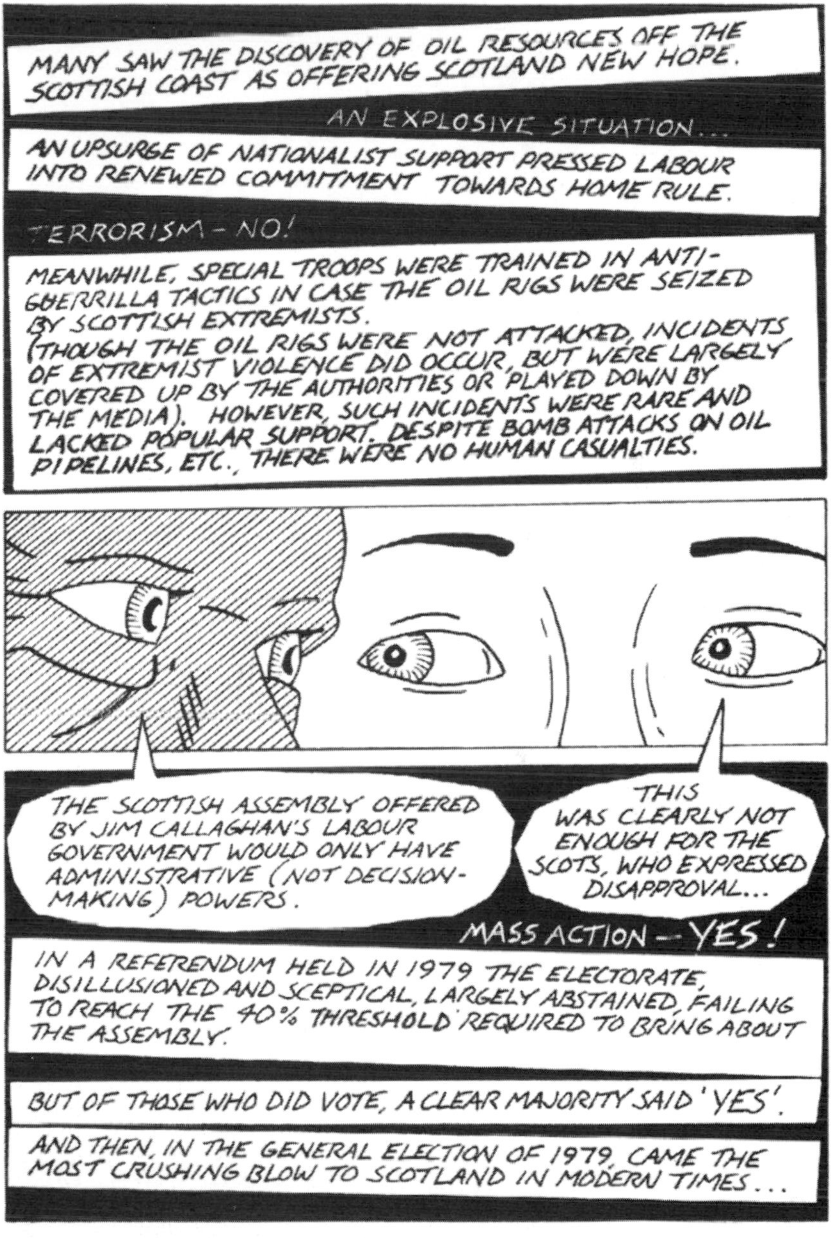
MANY SAW THE DISCOVERY OF OIL RESOURCES OFF THE SCOTTISH COAST AS OFFERING SCOTLAND NEW HOPE.
AN EXPLOSIVE SITUATION...
AN UPSURGE OF NATIONALIST SUPPORT PRESSED LABOUR INTO RENEWED COMMITMENT TOWARDS HOME RULE.
TERRORISM – NO!
MEANWHILE, SPECIAL TROOPS WERE TRAINED IN ANTI-GUERRILLA TACTICS IN CASE THE OIL RIGS WERE SEIZED BY SCOTTISH EXTREMISTS. (THOUGH THE OIL RIGS WERE NOT ATTACKED, INCIDENTS OF EXTREMIST VIOLENCE DID OCCUR, BUT WERE LARGELY COVERED UP BY THE AUTHORITIES OR PLAYED DOWN BY THE MEDIA). HOWEVER, SUCH INCIDENTS WERE RARE AND LACKED POPULAR SUPPORT. DESPITE BOMB ATTACKS ON OIL PIPELINES, ETC., THERE WERE NO HUMAN CASUALTIES.
THE SCOTTISH ASSEMBLY OFFERED BY JIM CALLAGHAN'S LABOUR GOVERNMENT WOULD ONLY HAVE ADMINISTRATIVE (NOT DECISION-MAKING) POWERS.
THIS WAS CLEARLY NOT ENOUGH FOR THE SCOTS, WHO EXPRESSED DISAPPROVAL...
MASS ACTION – YES!
IN A REFERENDUM HELD IN 1979 THE ELECTORATE, DISILLUSIONED AND SCEPTICAL, LARGELY ABSTAINED, FAILING TO REACH THE 40% THRESHOLD REQUIRED TO BRING ABOUT THE ASSEMBLY.
BUT OF THOSE WHO DID VOTE, A CLEAR MAJORITY SAID 'YES'.
AND THEN, IN THE GENERAL ELECTION OF 1979, CAME THE MOST CRUSHING BLOW TO SCOTLAND IN MODERN TIMES...

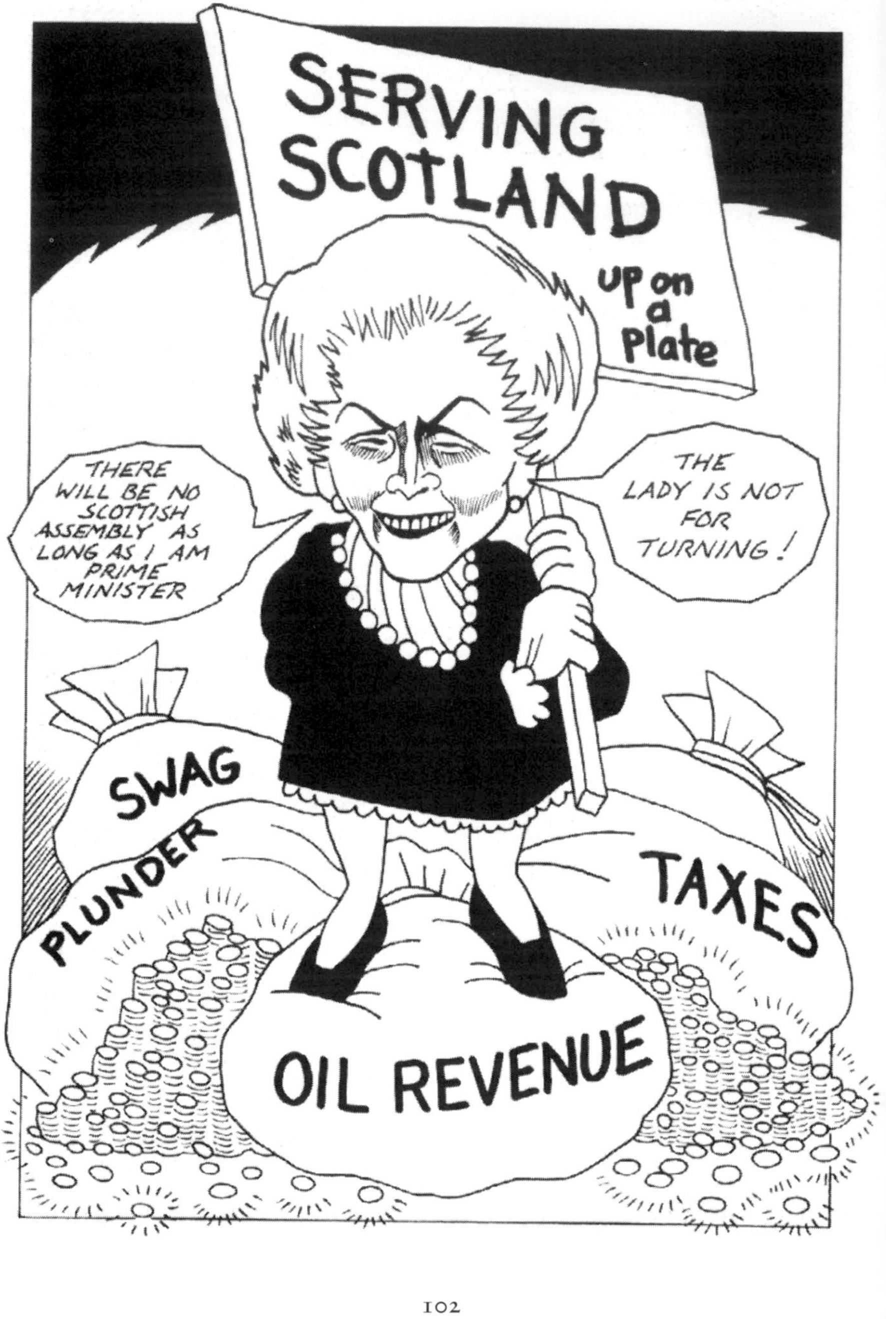
SERVING SCOTLAND
up on a Plate
THERE WILL BE NO SCOTTISH ASSEMBLY AS LONG AS I AM PRIME MINISTER
THE LADY IS NOT FOR TURNING!
SWAG
PLUNDER
TAXES
OIL REVENUE

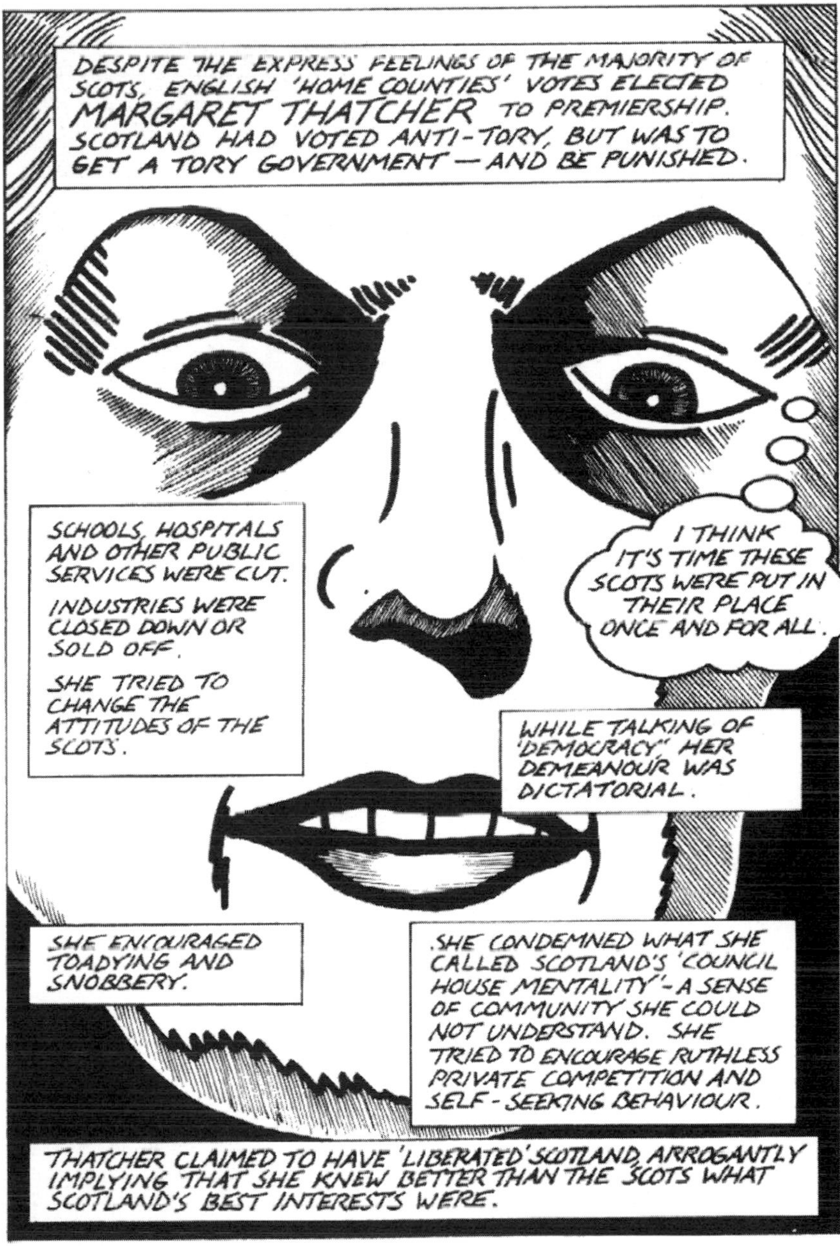
DESPITE THE EXPRESS FEELINGS OF THE MAJORITY OF SCOTS, ENGLISH 'HOME COUNTIES' VOTES ELECTED MARGARET THATCHER TO PREMIERSHIP. SCOTLAND HAD VOTED ANTI-TORY, BUT WAS TO GET A TORY GOVERNMENT — AND BE PUNISHED.
SCHOOLS, HOSPITALS AND OTHER PUBLIC SERVICES WERE CUT.
INDUSTRIES WERE CLOSED DOWN OR SOLD OFF.
SHE TRIED TO CHANGE THE ATTITUDES OF THE SCOTS.
I THINK IT'S TIME THESE SCOTS WERE PUT IN THEIR PLACE ONCE AND FOR ALL.
WHILE TALKING OF 'DEMOCRACY,' HER DEMEANOUR WAS DICTATORIAL.
SHE ENCOURAGED TOADYING AND SNOBBERY.
SHE CONDEMNED WHAT SHE CALLED SCOTLAND'S 'COUNCIL HOUSE MENTALITY' – A SENSE OF COMMUNITY SHE COULD NOT UNDERSTAND. SHE TRIED TO ENCOURAGE RUTHLESS PRIVATE COMPETITION AND SELF-SEEKING BEHAVIOUR.
THATCHER CLAIMED TO HAVE 'LIBERATED' SCOTLAND, ARROGANTLY IMPLYING THAT SHE KNEW BETTER THAN THE SCOTS WHAT SCOTLAND'S BEST INTERESTS WERE.

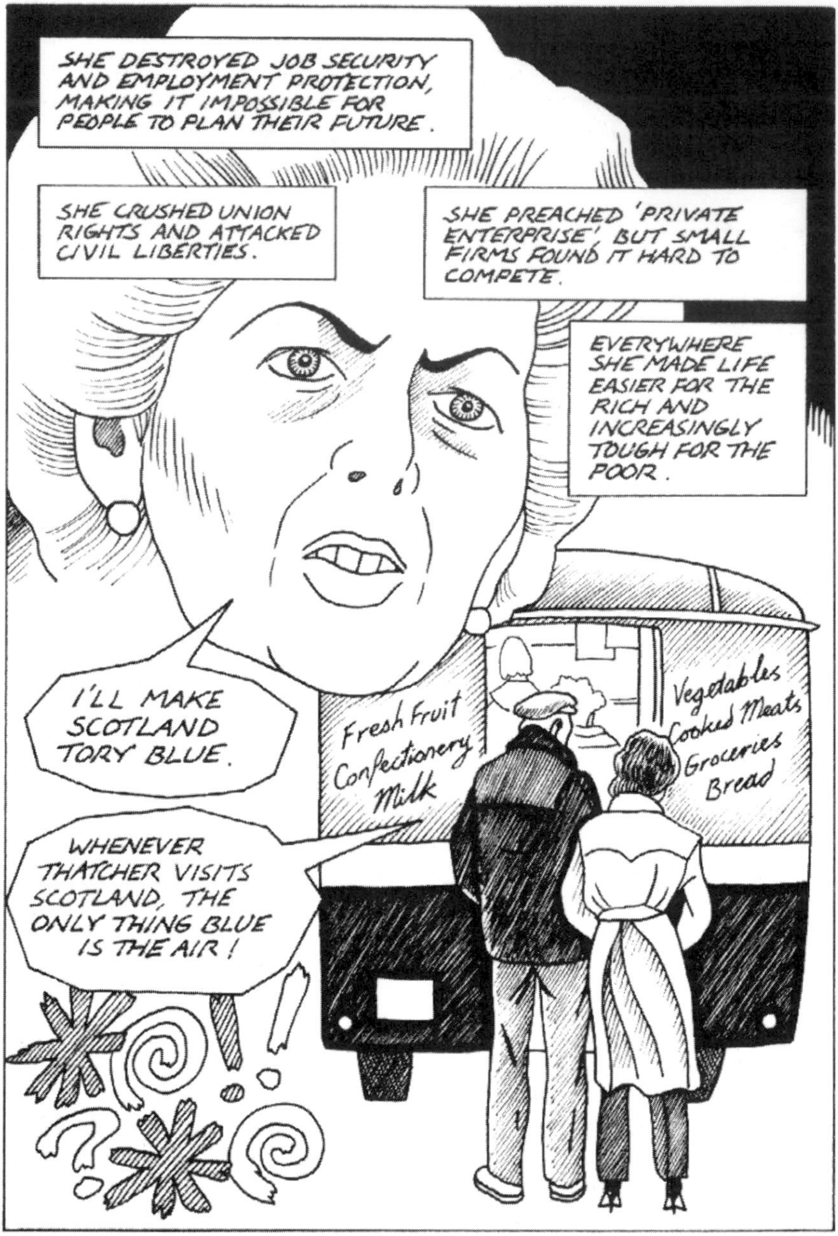
SHE DESTROYED JOB SECURITY AND EMPLOYMENT PROTECTION, MAKING IT IMPOSSIBLE FOR PEOPLE TO PLAN THEIR FUTURE.
SHE CRUSHED UNION RIGHTS AND ATTACKED CIVIL LIBERTIES.
SHE PREACHED 'PRIVATE ENTERPRISE', BUT SMALL FIRMS FOUND IT HARD TO COMPETE.
EVERYWHERE SHE MADE LIFE EASIER FOR THE RICH AND INCREASINGLY TOUGH FOR THE POOR.
I'LL MAKE SCOTLAND TORY BLUE.
Fresh Fruit Confectionery Milk
Vegetables Cooked Meats Groceries Bread
WHENEVER THATCHER VISITS SCOTLAND, THE ONLY THING BLUE IS THE AIR!

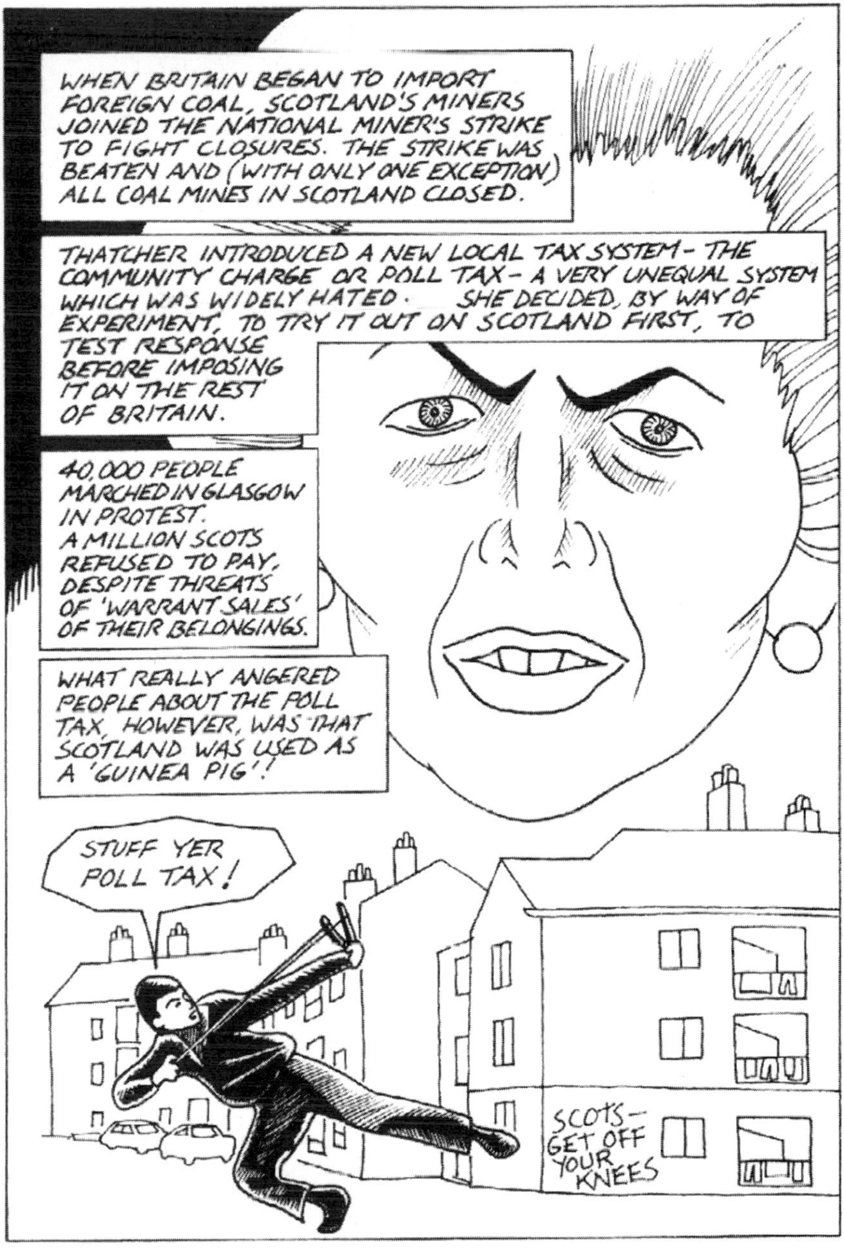
WHEN BRITAIN BEGAN TO IMPORT FOREIGN COAL, SCOTLAND'S MINERS JOINED THE NATIONAL MINER'S STRIKE TO FIGHT CLOSURES. THE STRIKE WAS BEATEN AND (WITH ONLY ONE EXCEPTION) ALL COAL MINES IN SCOTLAND CLOSED.
THATCHER INTRODUCED A NEW LOCAL TAX SYSTEM - THE COMMUNITY CHARGE OR POLL TAX - A VERY UNEQUAL SYSTEM WHICH WAS WIDELY HATED. SHE DECIDED, BY WAY OF EXPERIMENT, TO TRY IT OUT ON SCOTLAND FIRST, TO TEST RESPONSE BEFORE IMPOSING IT ON THE REST OF BRITAIN.
40,000 PEOPLE MARCHED IN GLASGOW IN PROTEST. A MILLION SCOTS REFUSED TO PAY, DESPITE THREATS OF 'WARRANT SALES' OF THEIR BELONGINGS.
WHAT REALLY ANGERED PEOPLE ABOUT THE POLL TAX, HOWEVER, WAS THAT SCOTLAND WAS USED AS A 'GUINEA PIG'!
STUFF YER POLL TAX!
SCOTS - GET OFF YOUR KNEES

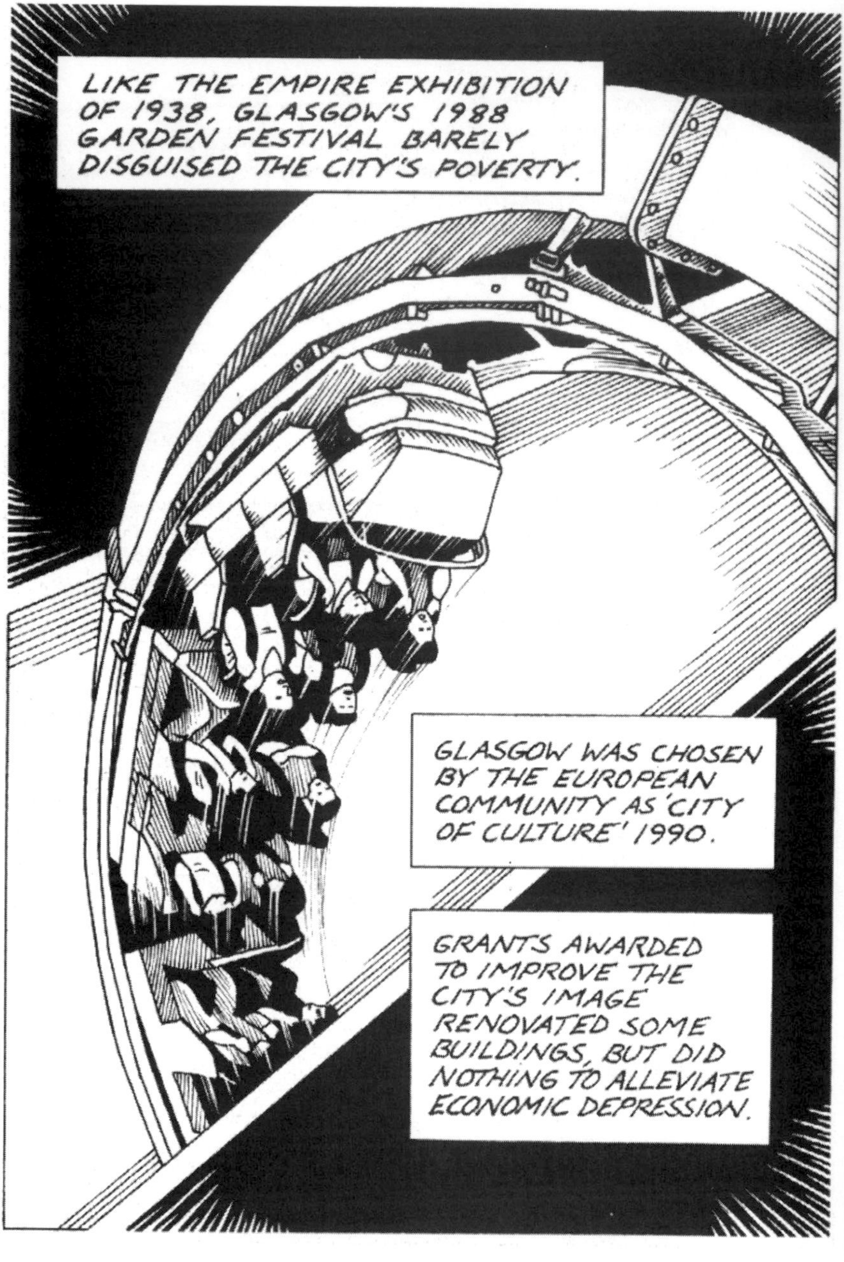
LIKE THE EMPIRE EXHIBITION OF 1938, GLASGOW'S 1988 GARDEN FESTIVAL BARELY DISGUISED THE CITY'S POVERTY.
GLASGOW WAS CHOSEN BY THE EUROPEAN COMMUNITY AS 'CITY OF CULTURE' 1990.
GRANTS AWARDED TO IMPROVE THE CITY'S IMAGE RENOVATED SOME BUILDINGS, BUT DID NOTHING TO ALLEVIATE ECONOMIC DEPRESSION.

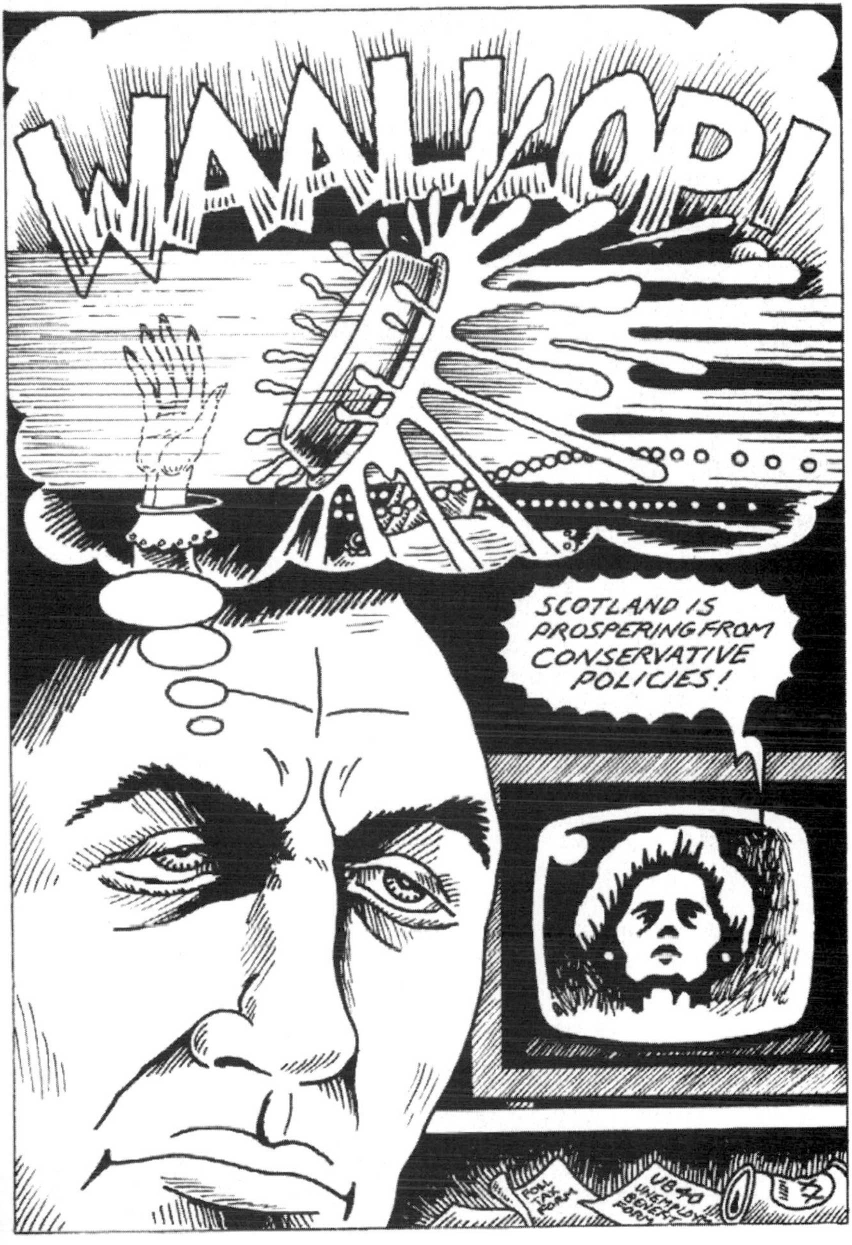
WAALLOP!
SCOTLAND IS PROSPERING FROM CONSERVATIVE POLICIES!
POLL TAX FORM
UB40

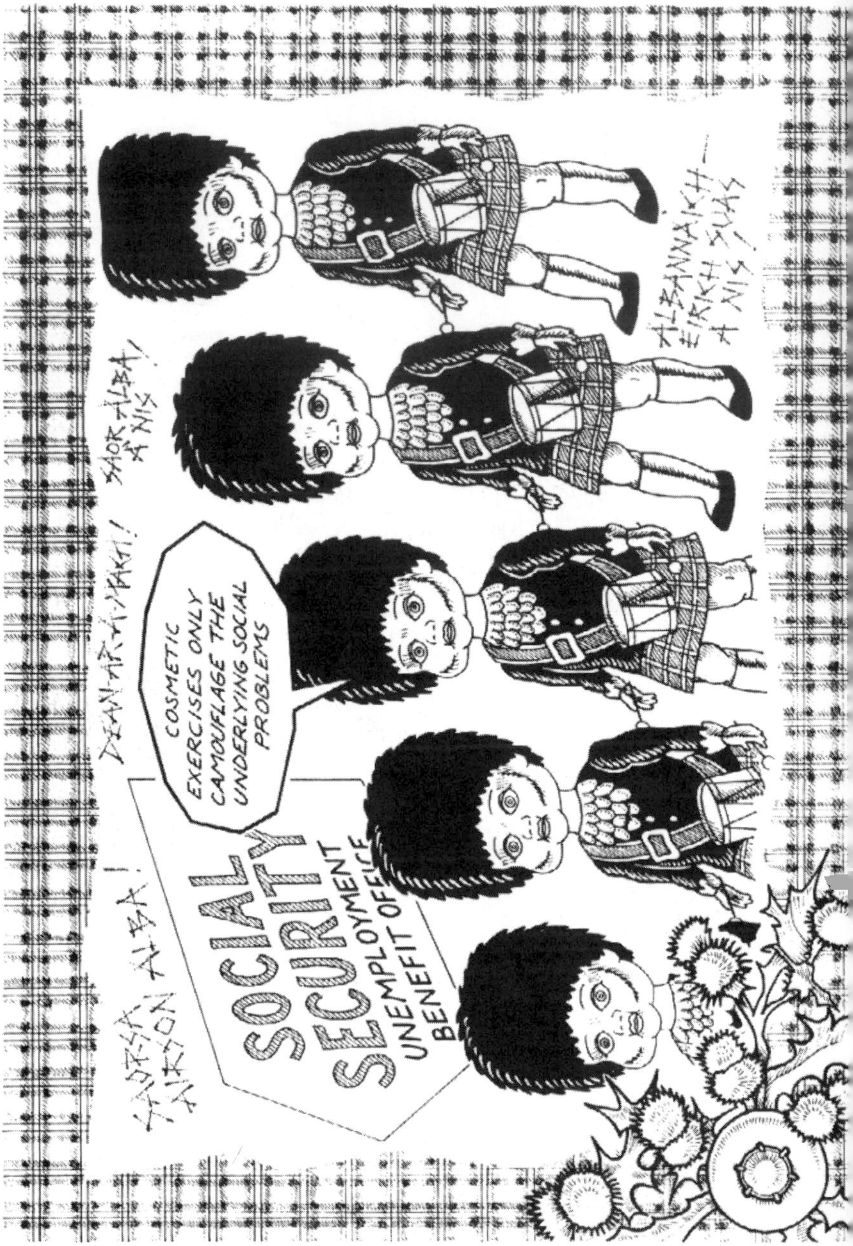
SOCIAL SECURITY
UNEMPLOYMENT BENEFIT OFFICE
COSMETIC EXERCISES ONLY CAMOUFLAGE THE UNDERLYING SOCIAL PROBLEMS
SAOR ALBA A NIS!
ALBANNAICH EIRICH SUAS A NIS!

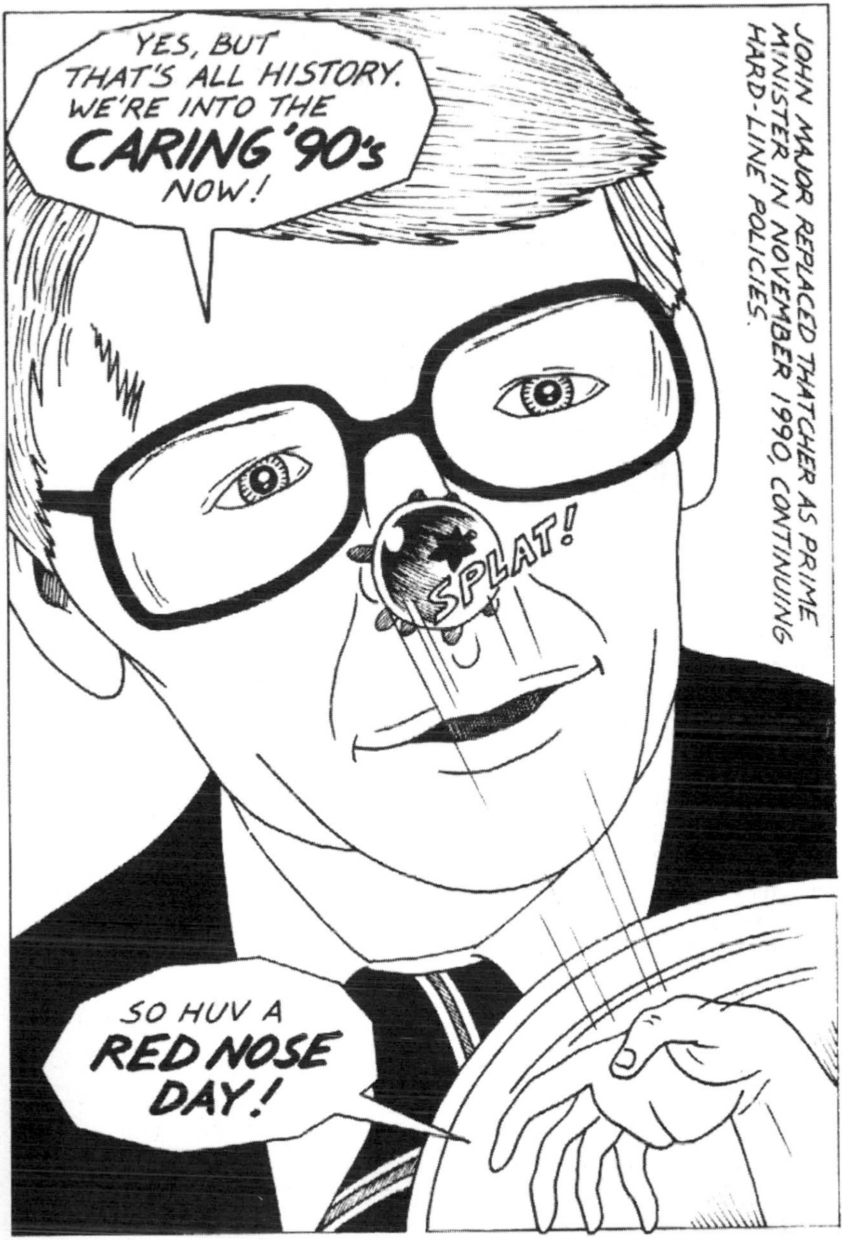
YES, BUT THAT'S ALL HISTORY. WE'RE INTO THE CARING '90's NOW!
JOHN MAJOR REPLACED THATCHER AS PRIME MINISTER IN NOVEMBER 1990, CONTINUING HARD-LINE POLICIES.
SPLAT!
SO HUV A RED NOSE DAY!

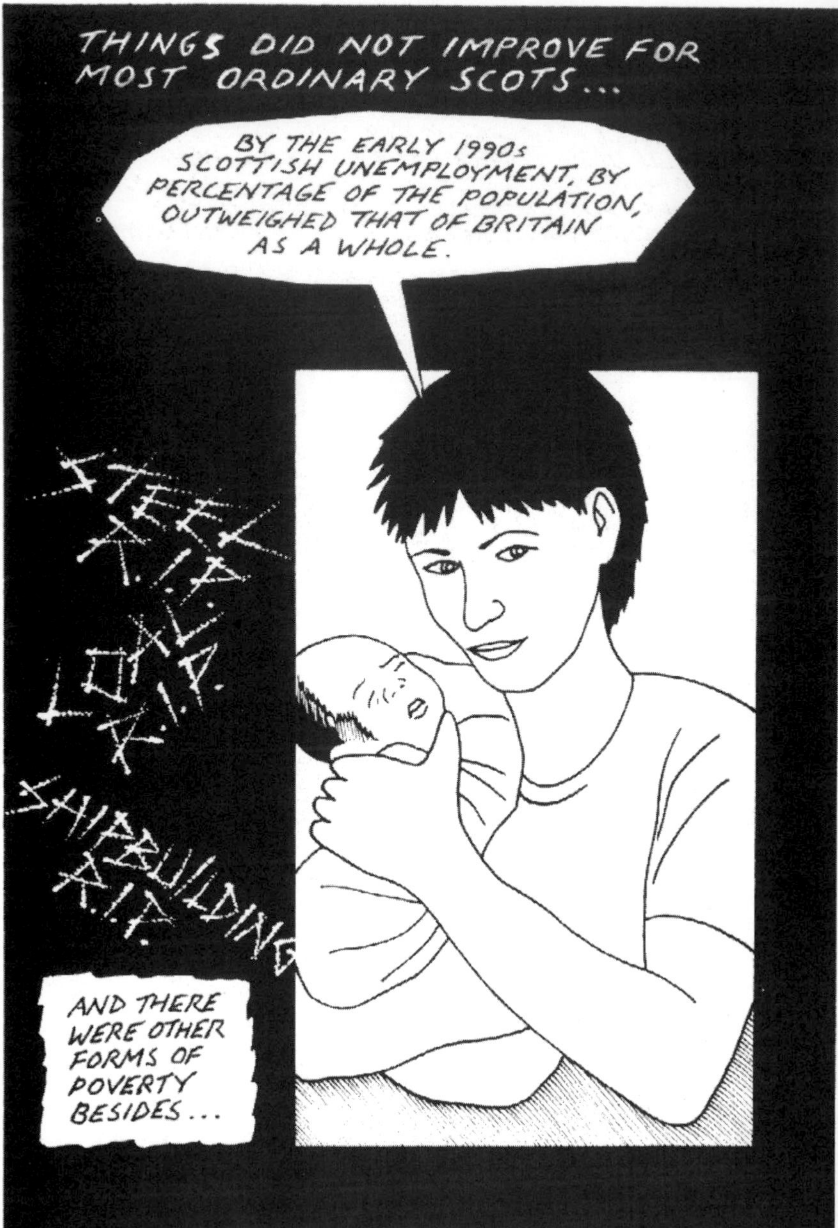
THINGS DID NOT IMPROVE FOR MOST ORDINARY SCOTS...
BY THE EARLY 1990s SCOTTISH UNEMPLOYMENT, BY PERCENTAGE OF THE POPULATION, OUTWEIGHED THAT OF BRITAIN AS A WHOLE.
STEEL R.I.P.
COAL R.I.P.
SHIPBUILDING R.I.P.
AND THERE WERE OTHER FORMS OF POVERTY BESIDES...

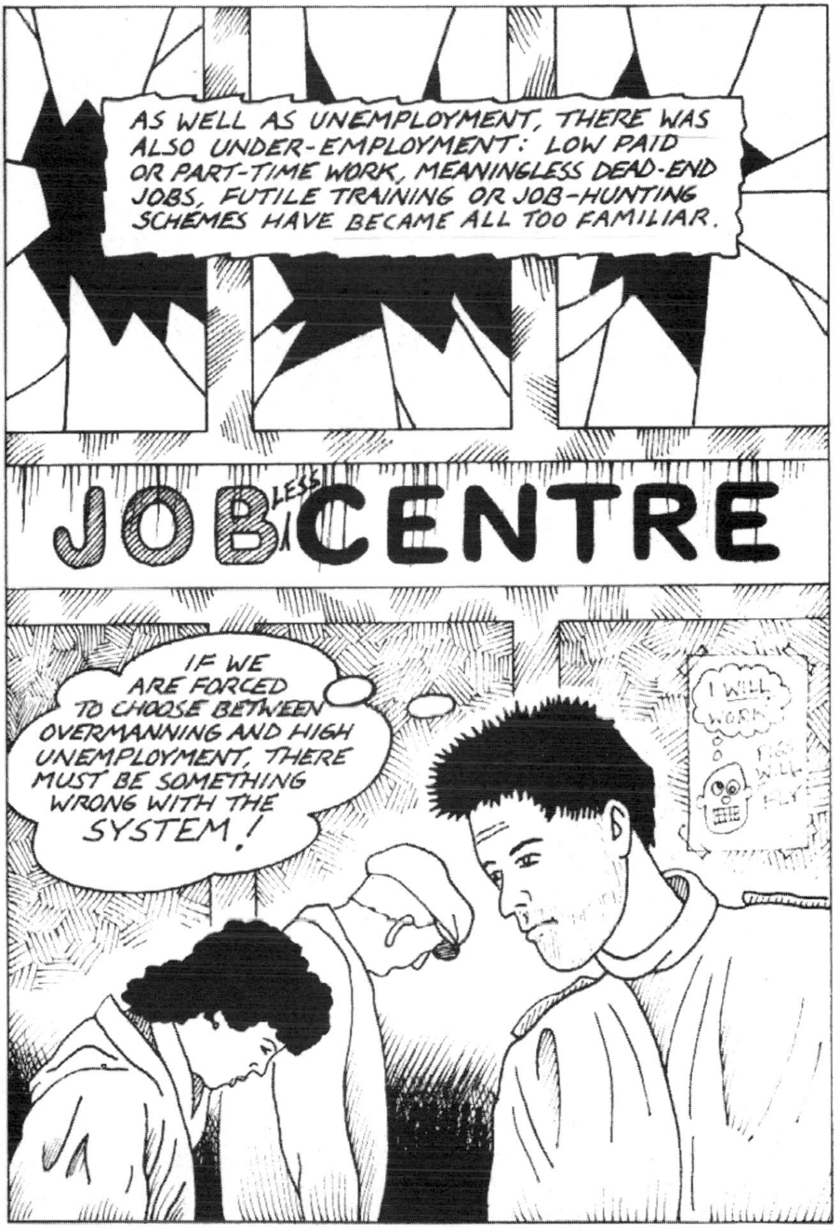
AS WELL AS UNEMPLOYMENT, THERE WAS ALSO UNDER-EMPLOYMENT: LOW PAID OR PART-TIME WORK, MEANINGLESS DEAD-END JOBS, FUTILE TRAINING OR JOB-HUNTING SCHEMES HAVE BECAME ALL TOO FAMILIAR.
JOB LESS CENTRE
IF WE ARE FORCED TO CHOOSE BETWEEN OVERMANNING AND HIGH UNEMPLOYMENT, THERE MUST BE SOMETHING WRONG WITH THE SYSTEM!
I WILL WORK

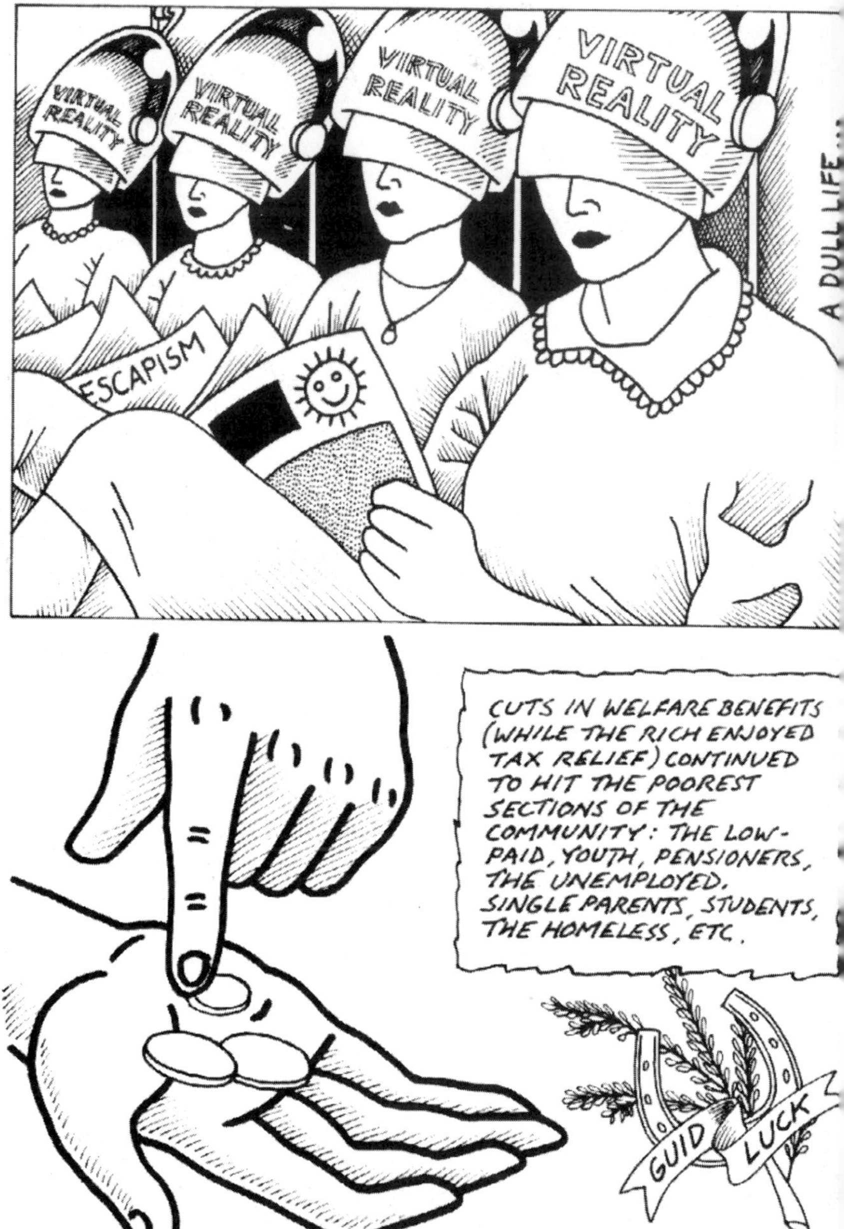
VIRTUAL REALITY
VIRTUAL REALITY
VIRTUAL REALITY
VIRTUAL REALITY
ESCAPISM
A DULL LIFE
CUTS IN WELFARE BENEFITS (WHILE THE RICH ENJOYED TAX RELIEF) CONTINUED TO HIT THE POOREST SECTIONS OF THE COMMUNITY: THE LOW-PAID, YOUTH, PENSIONERS, THE UNEMPLOYED. SINGLE PARENTS, STUDENTS, THE HOMELESS, ETC.
GUID LUCK

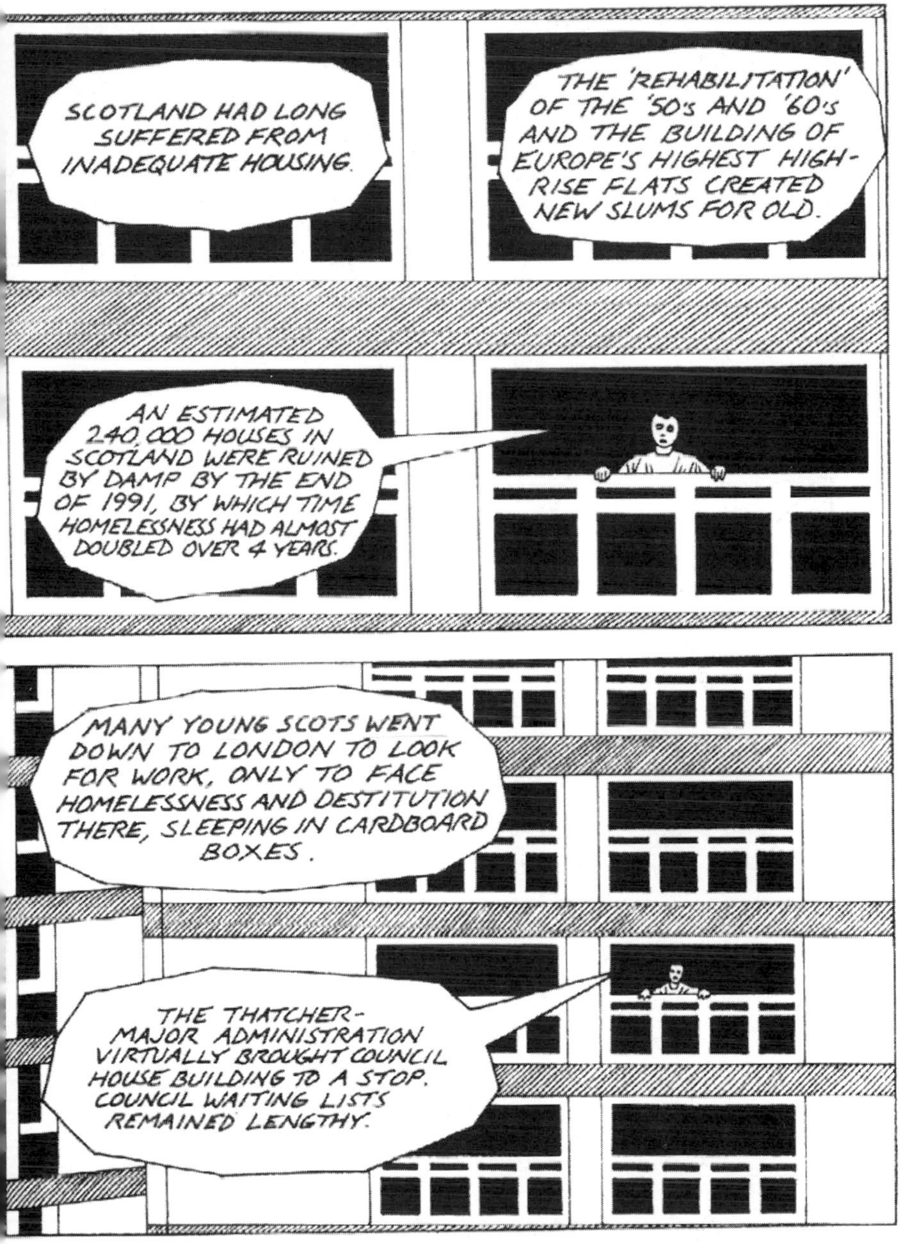
SCOTLAND HAD LONG SUFFERED FROM INADEQUATE HOUSING.
THE 'REHABILITATION' OF THE '50's AND '60's AND THE BUILDING OF EUROPE'S HIGHEST HIGH-RISE FLATS CREATED NEW SLUMS FOR OLD.
AN ESTIMATED 240,000 HOUSES IN SCOTLAND WERE RUINED BY DAMP BY THE END OF 1991, BY WHICH TIME HOMELESSNESS HAD ALMOST DOUBLED OVER 4 YEARS.
MANY YOUNG SCOTS WENT DOWN TO LONDON TO LOOK FOR WORK, ONLY TO FACE HOMELESSNESS AND DESTITUTION THERE, SLEEPING IN CARDBOARD BOXES.
THE THATCHER-MAJOR ADMINISTRATION VIRTUALLY BROUGHT COUNCIL HOUSE BUILDING TO A STOP. COUNCIL WAITING LISTS REMAINED LENGTHY.

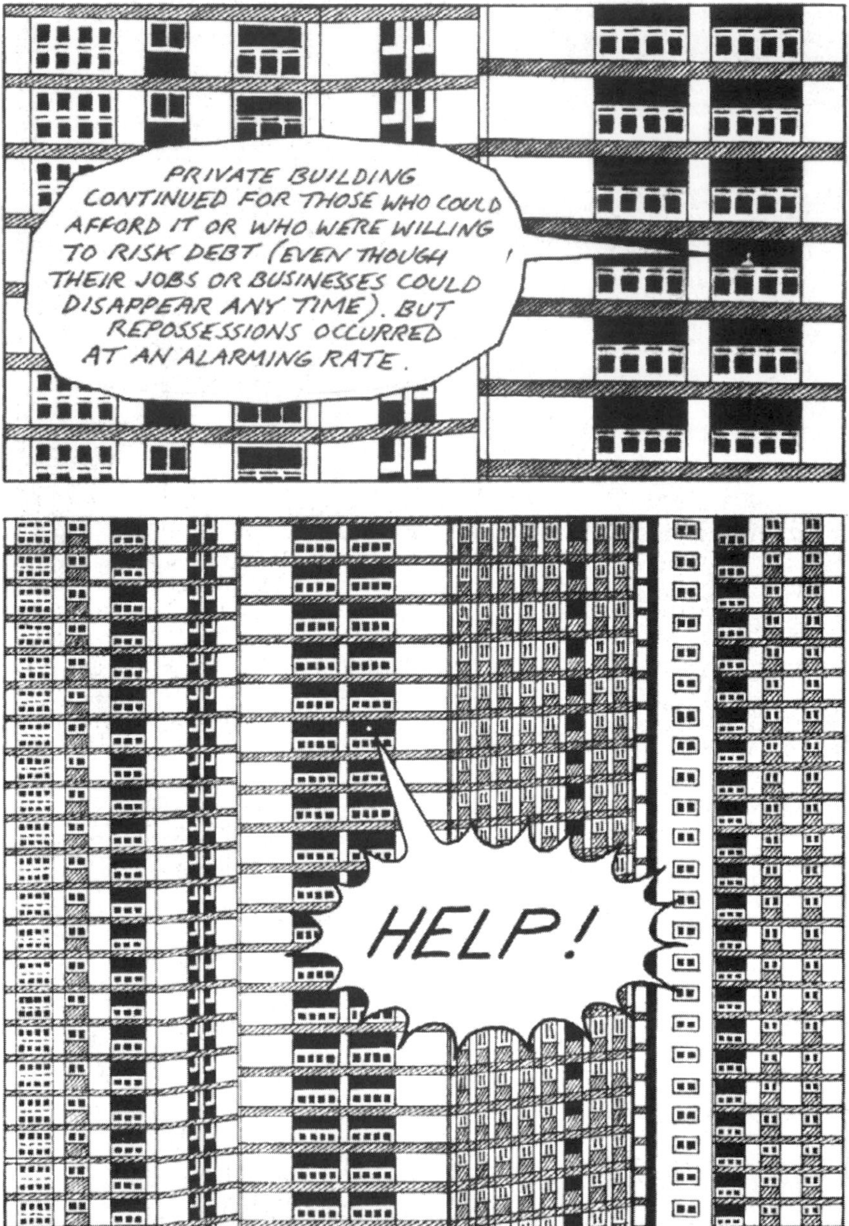
PRIVATE BUILDING CONTINUED FOR THOSE WHO COULD AFFORD IT OR WHO WERE WILLING TO RISK DEBT (EVEN THOUGH THEIR JOBS OR BUSINESSES COULD DISAPPEAR ANY TIME). BUT REPOSSESSIONS OCCURRED AT AN ALARMING RATE.
HELP!

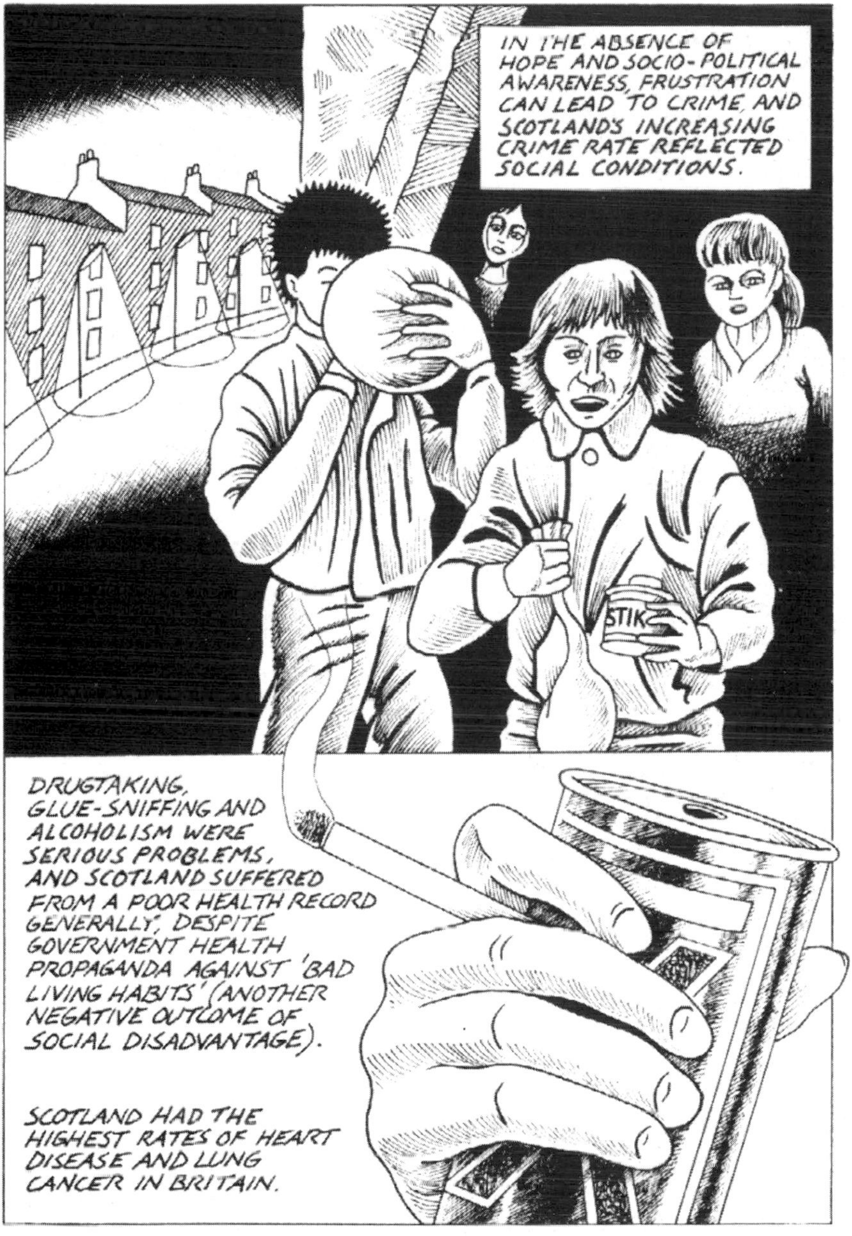
IN THE ABSENCE OF HOPE AND SOCIO-POLITICAL AWARENESS, FRUSTRATION CAN LEAD TO CRIME AND SCOTLAND'S INCREASING CRIME RATE REFLECTED SOCIAL CONDITIONS.
STIK
DRUGTAKING, GLUE-SNIFFING AND ALCOHOLISM WERE SERIOUS PROBLEMS, AND SCOTLAND SUFFERED FROM A POOR HEALTH RECORD GENERALLY, DESPITE GOVERNMENT HEALTH PROPAGANDA AGAINST 'BAD LIVING HABITS' (ANOTHER NEGATIVE OUTCOME OF SOCIAL DISADVANTAGE).
SCOTLAND HAD THE HIGHEST RATES OF HEART DISEASE AND LUNG CANCER IN BRITAIN.

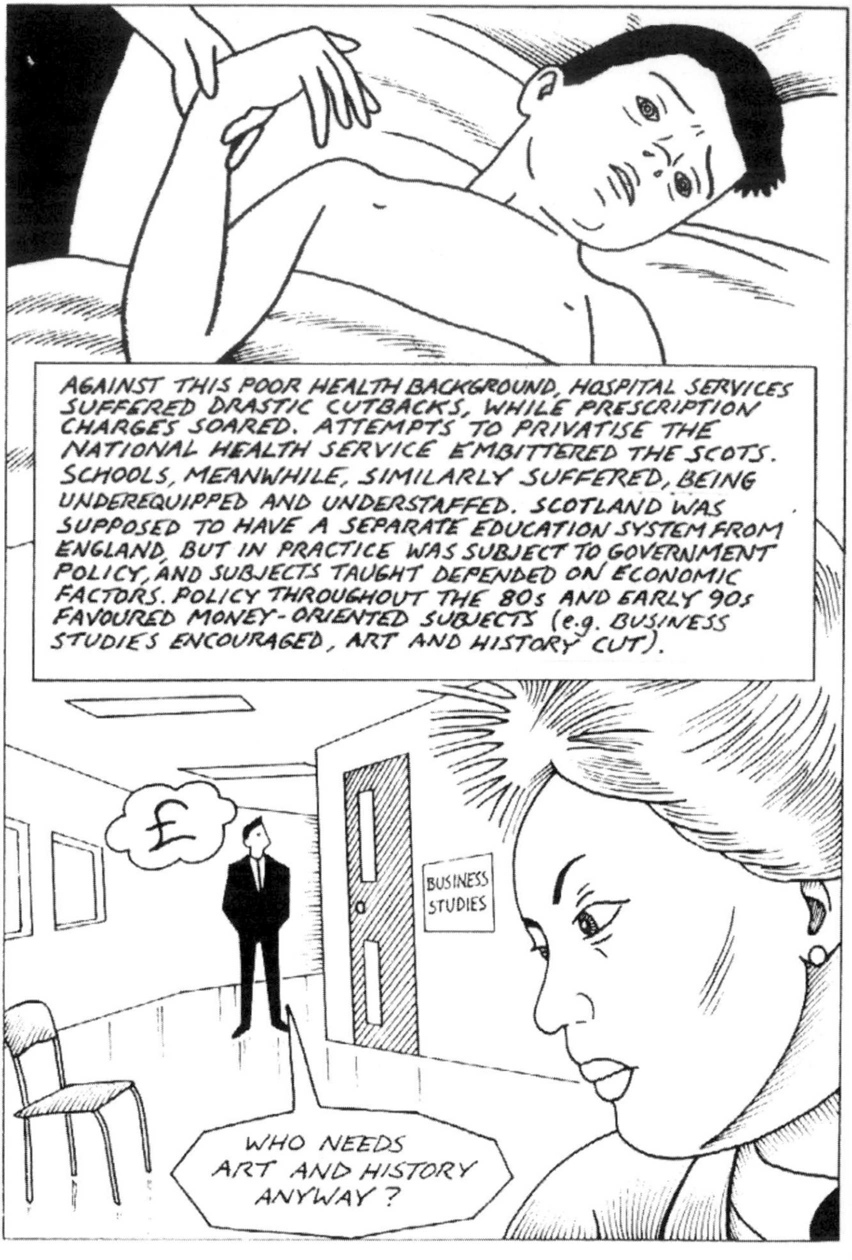
AGAINST THIS POOR HEALTH BACKGROUND, HOSPITAL SERVICES SUFFERED DRASTIC CUTBACKS, WHILE PRESCRIPTION CHARGES SOARED. ATTEMPTS TO PRIVATISE THE NATIONAL HEALTH SERVICE EMBITTERED THE SCOTS. SCHOOLS, MEANWHILE, SIMILARLY SUFFERED, BEING UNDEREQUIPPED AND UNDERSTAFFED. SCOTLAND WAS SUPPOSED TO HAVE A SEPARATE EDUCATION SYSTEM FROM ENGLAND, BUT IN PRACTICE WAS SUBJECT TO GOVERNMENT POLICY, AND SUBJECTS TAUGHT DEPENDED ON ECONOMIC FACTORS. POLICY THROUGHOUT THE 80s AND EARLY 90s FAVOURED MONEY-ORIENTED SUBJECTS (e.g. BUSINESS STUDIES ENCOURAGED, ART AND HISTORY CUT).
£
BUSINESS STUDIES
WHO NEEDS ART AND HISTORY ANYWAY?

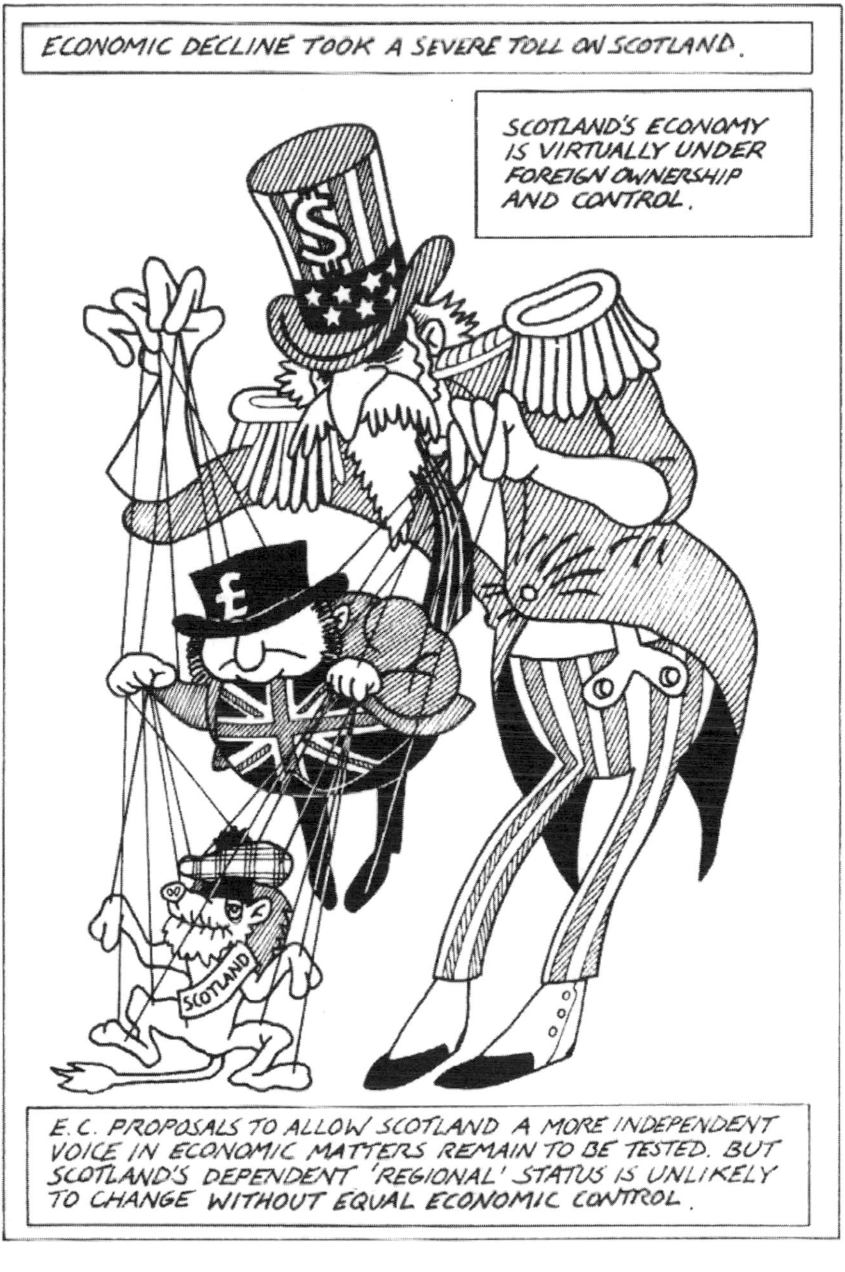
ECONOMIC DECLINE TOOK A SEVERE TOLL ON SCOTLAND.
SCOTLAND'S ECONOMY IS VIRTUALLY UNDER FOREIGN OWNERSHIP AND CONTROL.
$
£
SCOTLAND
E.C. PROPOSALS TO ALLOW SCOTLAND A MORE INDEPENDENT VOICE IN ECONOMIC MATTERS REMAIN TO BE TESTED. BUT SCOTLAND'S DEPENDENT 'REGIONAL' STATUS IS UNLIKELY TO CHANGE WITHOUT EQUAL ECONOMIC CONTROL.

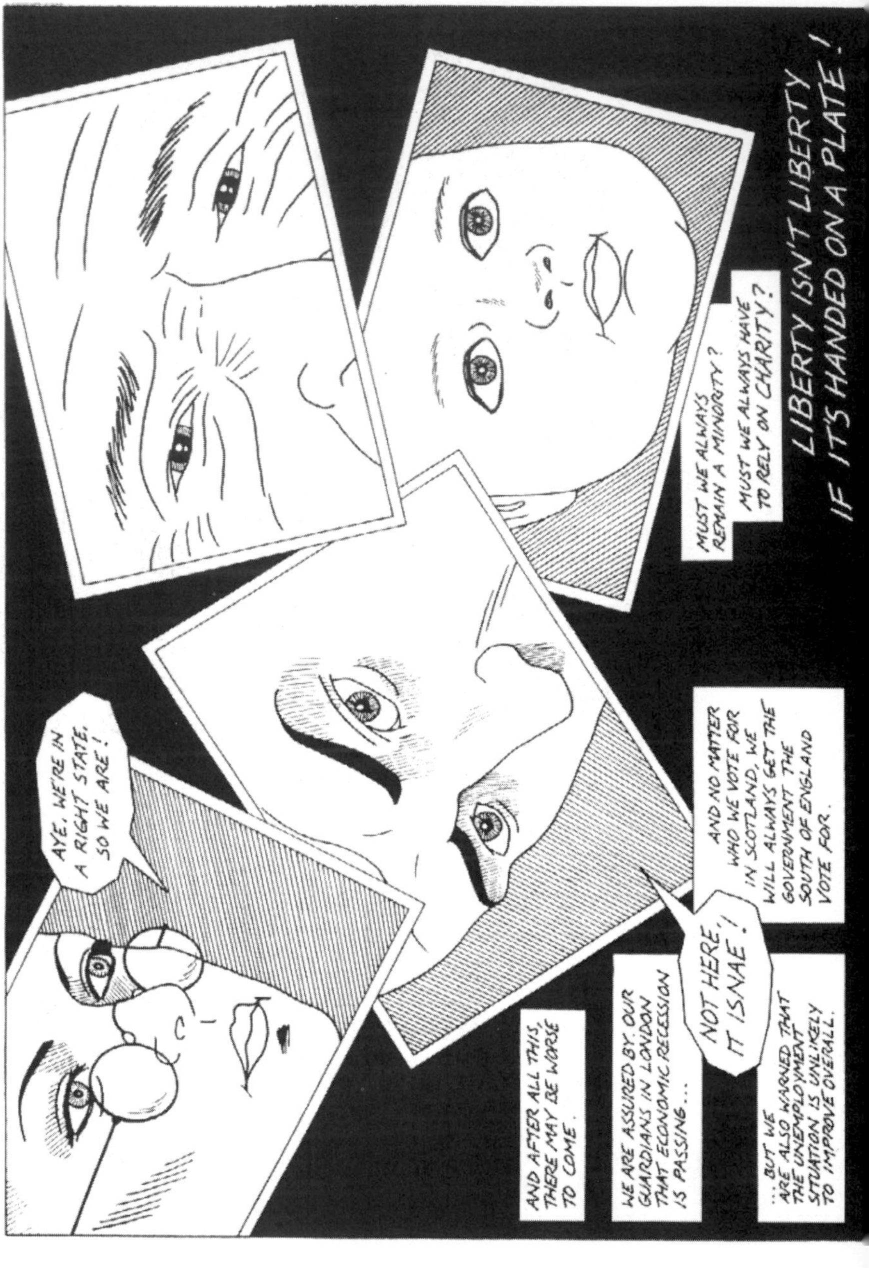
AND AFTER ALL THIS, THERE MAY BE WORSE TO COME.
WE ARE ASSURED BY OUR GUARDIANS IN LONDON THAT ECONOMIC RECESSION IS PASSING...
...BUT WE ARE ALSO WARNED THAT THE UNEMPLOYMENT SITUATION IS UNLIKELY TO IMPROVE OVERALL.
NOT HERE, IT ISNAE!
AYE. WE'RE IN A RIGHT STATE, SO WE ARE!
AND NO MATTER WHO WE VOTE FOR IN SCOTLAND, WE WILL ALWAYS GET THE GOVERNMENT THE SOUTH OF ENGLAND VOTE FOR.
MUST WE ALWAYS REMAIN A MINORITY?
MUST WE ALWAYS HAVE TO RELY ON CHARITY?
LIBERTY ISN'T LIBERTY IF IT'S HANDED ON A PLATE!

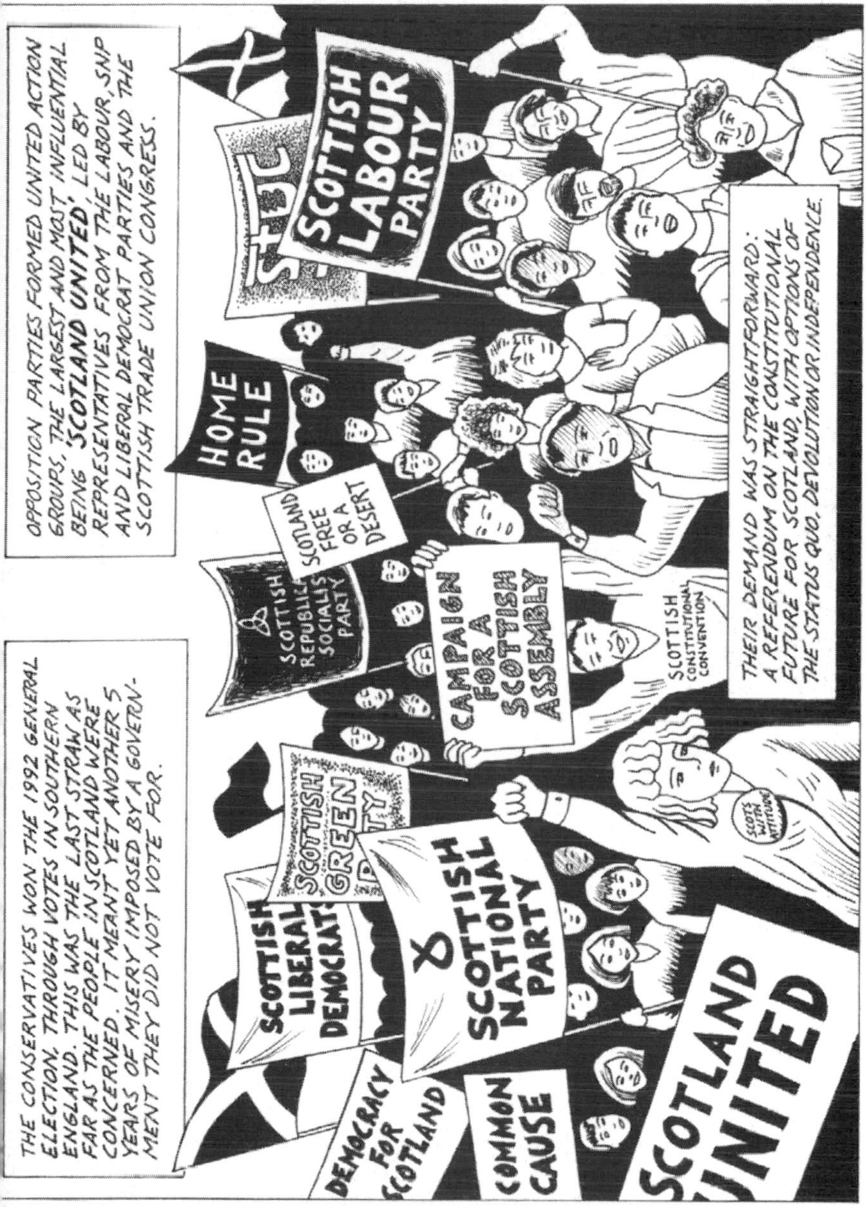
THE CONSERVATIVES WON THE 1992 GENERAL ELECTION, THROUGH VOTES IN SOUTHERN ENGLAND. THIS WAS THE LAST STRAW AS FAR AS THE PEOPLE IN SCOTLAND WERE CONCERNED. IT MEANT YET ANOTHER 5 YEARS OF MISERY IMPOSED BY A GOVERN-MENT THEY DID NOT VOTE FOR.
OPPOSITION PARTIES FORMED UNITED ACTION GROUPS, THE LARGEST AND MOST INFLUENTIAL BEING **'SCOTLAND UNITED'**, LED BY REPRESENTATIVES FROM THE LABOUR, SNP AND LIBERAL DEMOCRAT PARTIES AND THE SCOTTISH TRADE UNION CONGRESS.
SCOTTISH LIBERAL DEMOCRATS
SCOTTISH GREEN
SCOTTISH NATIONAL PARTY
DEMOCRACY FOR SCOTLAND
COMMON CAUSE
SCOTLAND UNITED
SCOTS WITH ATTITUDE
SCOTTISH REPUBLIC SOCIALIS PARTY
CAMPAIGN FOR A SCOTTISH ASSEMBLY
SCOTTISH CONSTITUTIONAL CONVENTION
SCOTLAND FREE OR A DESERT
HOME RULE
STUC
SCOTTISH LABOUR PARTY
THEIR DEMAND WAS STRAIGHTFORWARD: A REFERENDUM ON THE CONSTITUTIONAL FUTURE FOR SCOTLAND, WITH OPTIONS OF THE STATUS QUO, DEVOLUTION OR INDEPENDENCE.

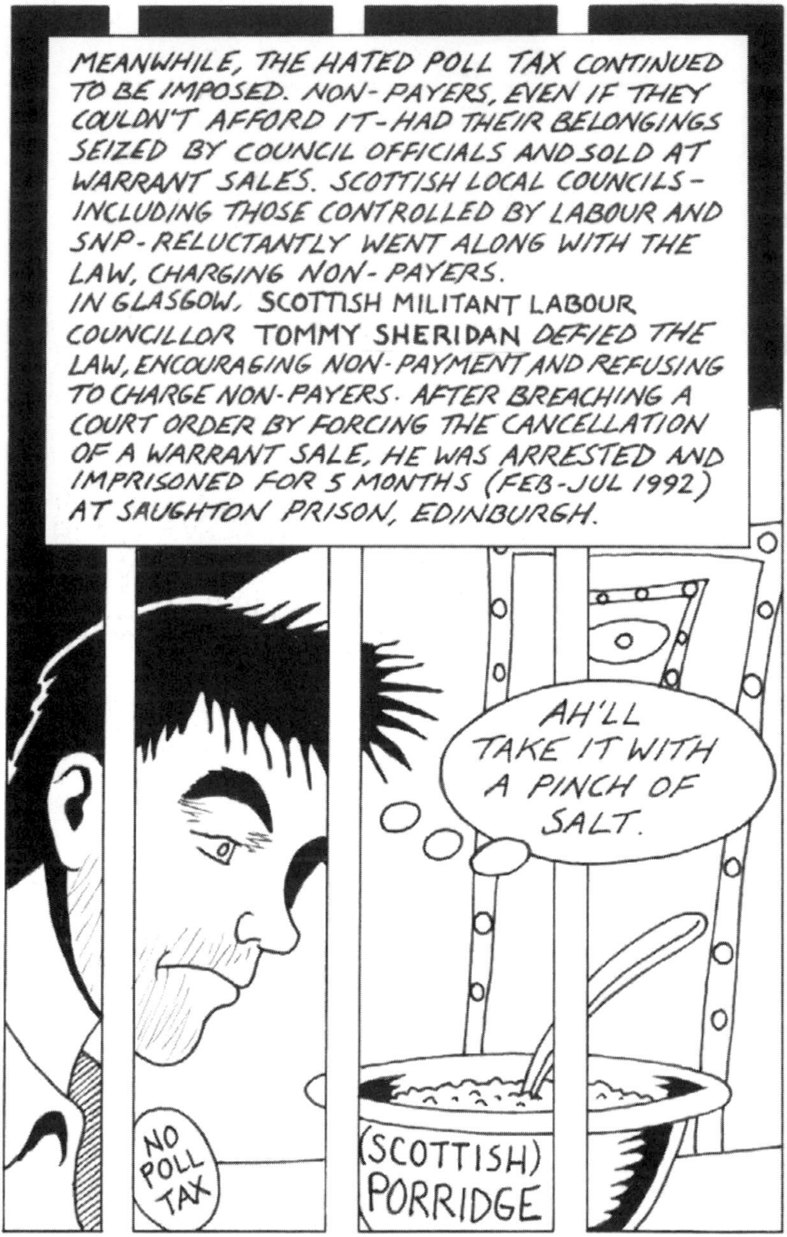
MEANWHILE, THE HATED POLL TAX CONTINUED TO BE IMPOSED. NON-PAYERS, EVEN IF THEY COULDN'T AFFORD IT - HAD THEIR BELONGINGS SEIZED BY COUNCIL OFFICIALS AND SOLD AT WARRANT SALES. SCOTTISH LOCAL COUNCILS - INCLUDING THOSE CONTROLLED BY LABOUR AND SNP - RELUCTANTLY WENT ALONG WITH THE LAW, CHARGING NON-PAYERS.
IN GLASGOW, SCOTTISH MILITANT LABOUR COUNCILLOR TOMMY SHERIDAN DEFIED THE LAW, ENCOURAGING NON-PAYMENT AND REFUSING TO CHARGE NON-PAYERS. AFTER BREACHING A COURT ORDER BY FORCING THE CANCELLATION OF A WARRANT SALE, HE WAS ARRESTED AND IMPRISONED FOR 5 MONTHS (FEB-JUL 1992) AT SAUGHTON PRISON, EDINBURGH.
AH'LL TAKE IT WITH A PINCH OF SALT.
NO POLL TAX
(SCOTTISH) PORRIDGE

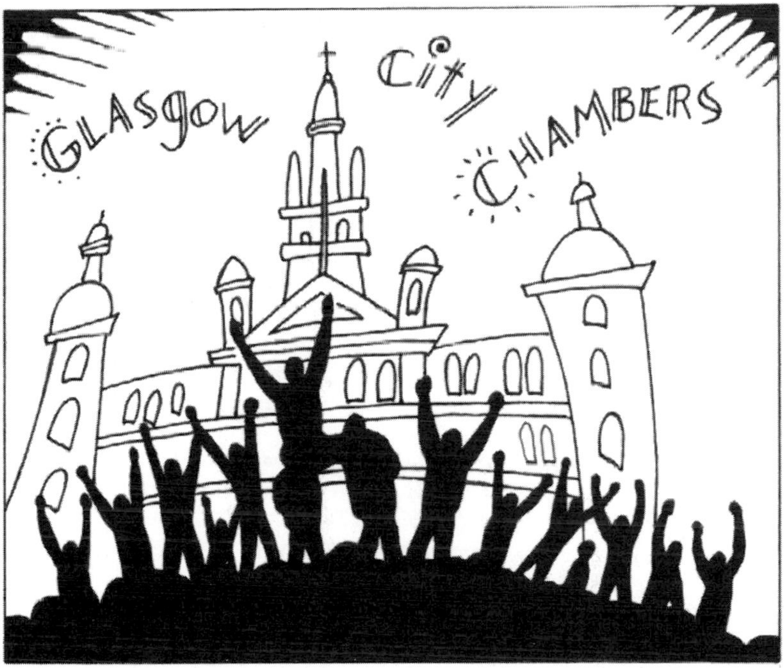
GLASGOW CITY CHAMBERS

SHERIDAN CONDUCTED TWO ELECTION CAMPAIGNS FROM HIS CELL, ALSO GIVING PRESS, RADIO AND TV INTERVIEWS.

ON HIS RELEASE, HE RETURNED TO AN UPROARIOUS WELCOME IN GLASGOW. BUT HIS ACTIVITIES HAD DEPRIVED THE COUNCIL OF PUBLIC FUNDS, AND HIS CONSTITUENTS WERE ULTIMATELY FORCED TO PAY UP.

A NEW LAW WAS PASSED, MAKING IT ILLEGAL FOR ANYONE TO STAND AS A COUNCILLOR WHILE SERVING A PRISON SENTENCE.

LIKE MOST OTHER ISSUES, THE ONLY HOPE SEEMED TO LIE IN THE CREATION OF A SCOTTISH PARLIAMENT. THE CAMPAIGN BY SCOTLAND UNITED AND OTHERS INTENSIFIED.

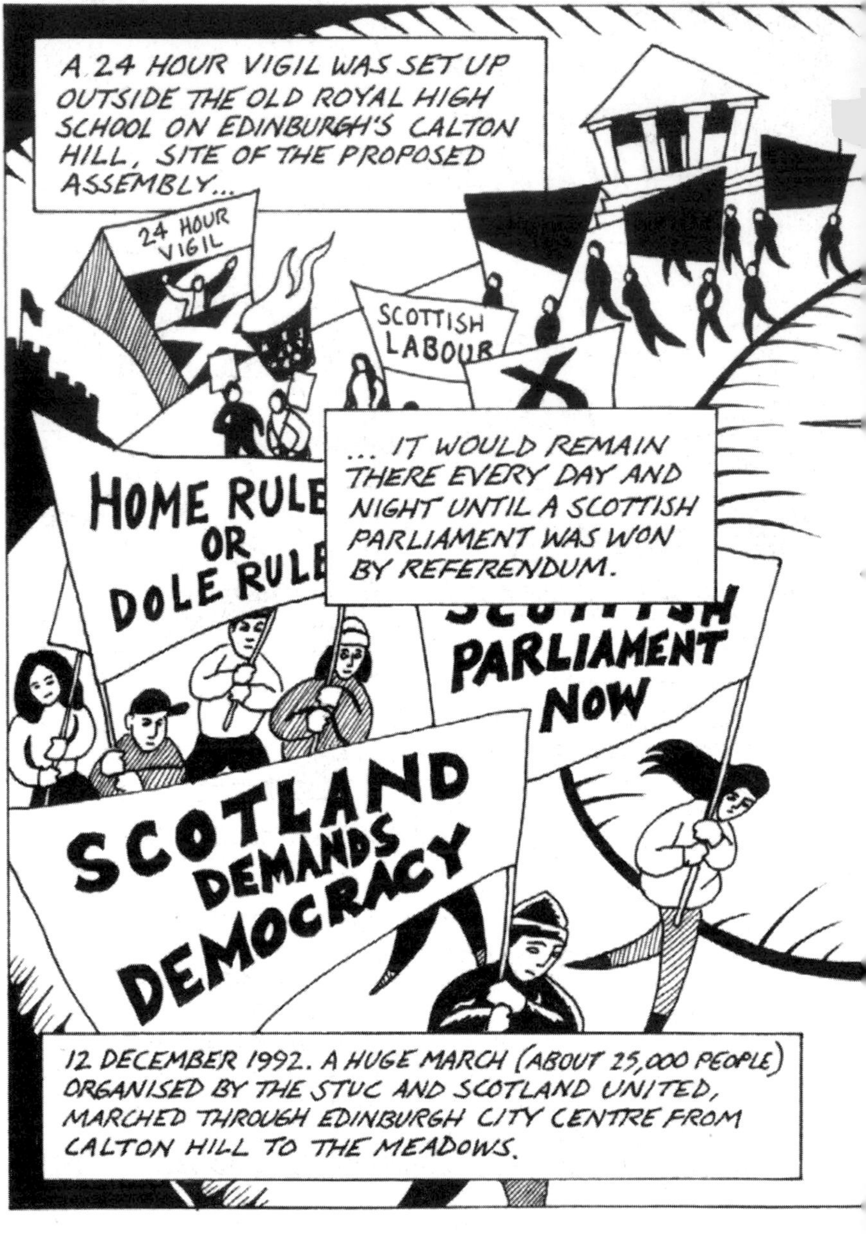
A 24 HOUR VIGIL WAS SET UP OUTSIDE THE OLD ROYAL HIGH SCHOOL ON EDINBURGH'S CALTON HILL, SITE OF THE PROPOSED ASSEMBLY...
24 HOUR VIGIL
SCOTTISH LABOUR
... IT WOULD REMAIN THERE EVERY DAY AND NIGHT UNTIL A SCOTTISH PARLIAMENT WAS WON BY REFERENDUM.
HOME RULE OR DOLE RULE
PARLIAMENT NOW
SCOTLAND DEMANDS DEMOCRACY
12 DECEMBER 1992. A HUGE MARCH (ABOUT 25,000 PEOPLE) ORGANISED BY THE STUC AND SCOTLAND UNITED, MARCHED THROUGH EDINBURGH CITY CENTRE FROM CALTON HILL TO THE MEADOWS.

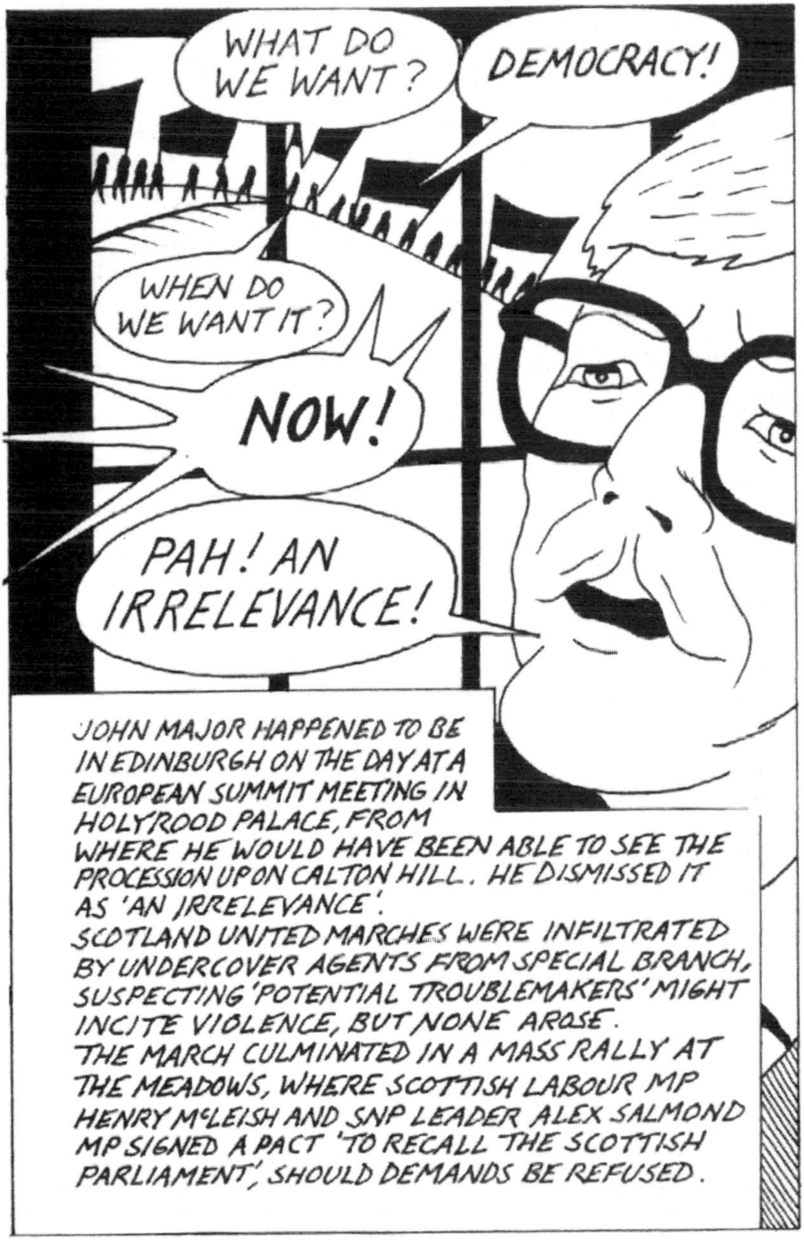
WHAT DO WE WANT?
DEMOCRACY!
WHEN DO WE WANT IT?
NOW!
PAH! AN IRRELEVANCE!
JOHN MAJOR HAPPENED TO BE IN EDINBURGH ON THE DAY AT A EUROPEAN SUMMIT MEETING IN HOLYROOD PALACE, FROM WHERE HE WOULD HAVE BEEN ABLE TO SEE THE PROCESSION UP ON CALTON HILL. HE DISMISSED IT AS 'AN IRRELEVANCE'.
SCOTLAND UNITED MARCHES WERE INFILTRATED BY UNDERCOVER AGENTS FROM SPECIAL BRANCH, SUSPECTING 'POTENTIAL TROUBLEMAKERS' MIGHT INCITE VIOLENCE, BUT NONE AROSE.
THE MARCH CULMINATED IN A MASS RALLY AT THE MEADOWS, WHERE SCOTTISH LABOUR MP HENRY McLEISH AND SNP LEADER ALEX SALMOND MP SIGNED A PACT 'TO RECALL THE SCOTTISH PARLIAMENT', SHOULD DEMANDS BE REFUSED.

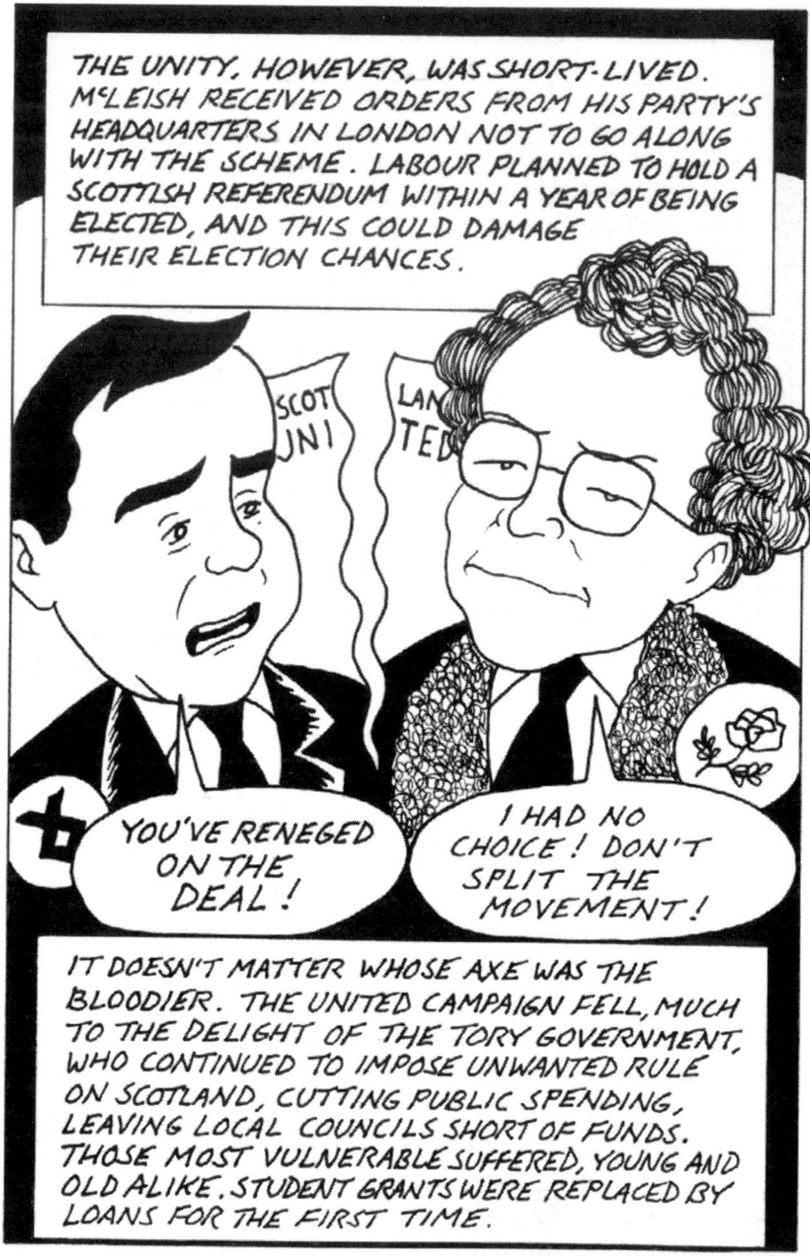
THE UNITY, HOWEVER, WAS SHORT-LIVED. McLEISH RECEIVED ORDERS FROM HIS PARTY'S HEADQUARTERS IN LONDON NOT TO GO ALONG WITH THE SCHEME. LABOUR PLANNED TO HOLD A SCOTTISH REFERENDUM WITHIN A YEAR OF BEING ELECTED, AND THIS COULD DAMAGE THEIR ELECTION CHANCES.
SCOT UNI
LAN TED
YOU'VE RENEGED ON THE DEAL!
I HAD NO CHOICE! DON'T SPLIT THE MOVEMENT!
IT DOESN'T MATTER WHOSE AXE WAS THE BLOODIER. THE UNITED CAMPAIGN FELL, MUCH TO THE DELIGHT OF THE TORY GOVERNMENT, WHO CONTINUED TO IMPOSE UNWANTED RULE ON SCOTLAND, CUTTING PUBLIC SPENDING, LEAVING LOCAL COUNCILS SHORT OF FUNDS. THOSE MOST VULNERABLE SUFFERED, YOUNG AND OLD ALIKE. STUDENT GRANTS WERE REPLACED BY LOANS FOR THE FIRST TIME.

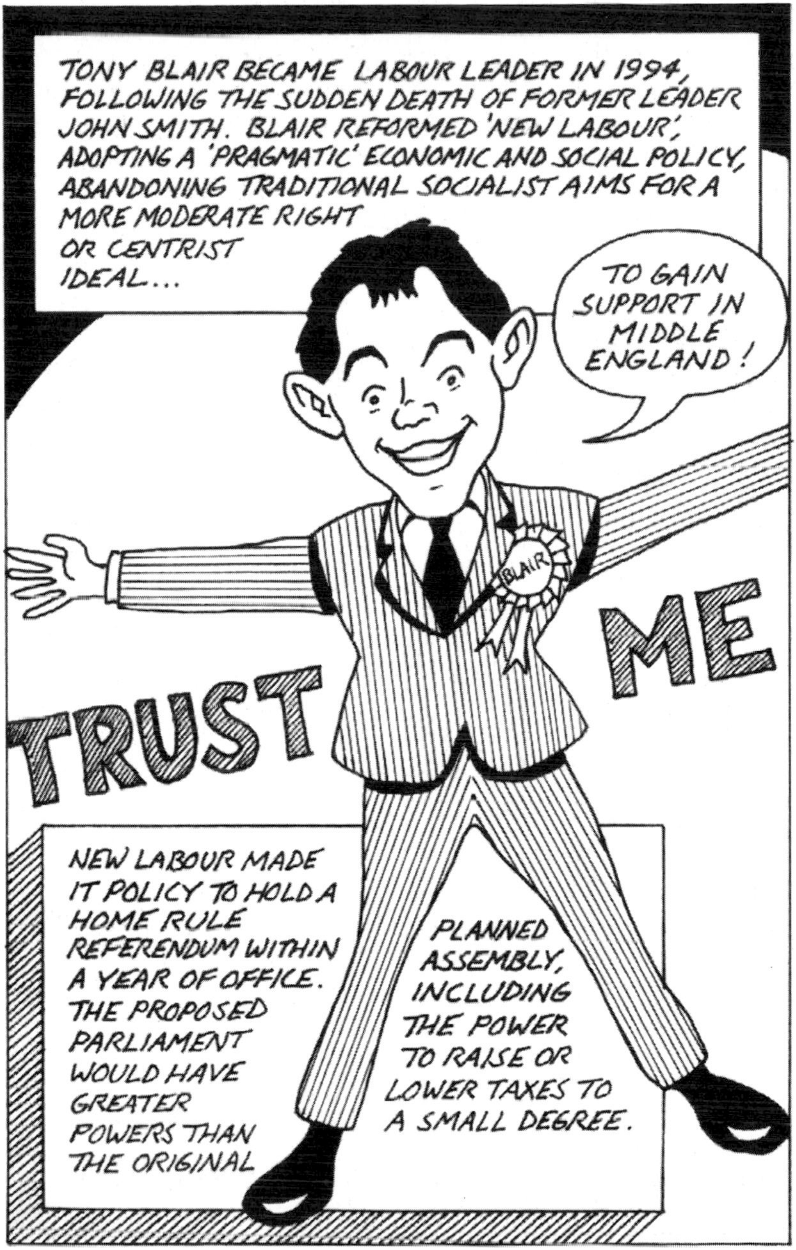
TONY BLAIR BECAME LABOUR LEADER IN 1994, FOLLOWING THE SUDDEN DEATH OF FORMER LEADER JOHN SMITH. BLAIR REFORMED 'NEW LABOUR', ADOPTING A 'PRAGMATIC' ECONOMIC AND SOCIAL POLICY, ABANDONING TRADITIONAL SOCIALIST AIMS FOR A MORE MODERATE RIGHT OR CENTRIST IDEAL...
TO GAIN SUPPORT IN MIDDLE ENGLAND!
BLAIR
TRUST ME
NEW LABOUR MADE IT POLICY TO HOLD A HOME RULE REFERENDUM WITHIN A YEAR OF OFFICE. THE PROPOSED PARLIAMENT WOULD HAVE GREATER POWERS THAN THE ORIGINAL
PLANNED ASSEMBLY, INCLUDING THE POWER TO RAISE OR LOWER TAXES TO A SMALL DEGREE.

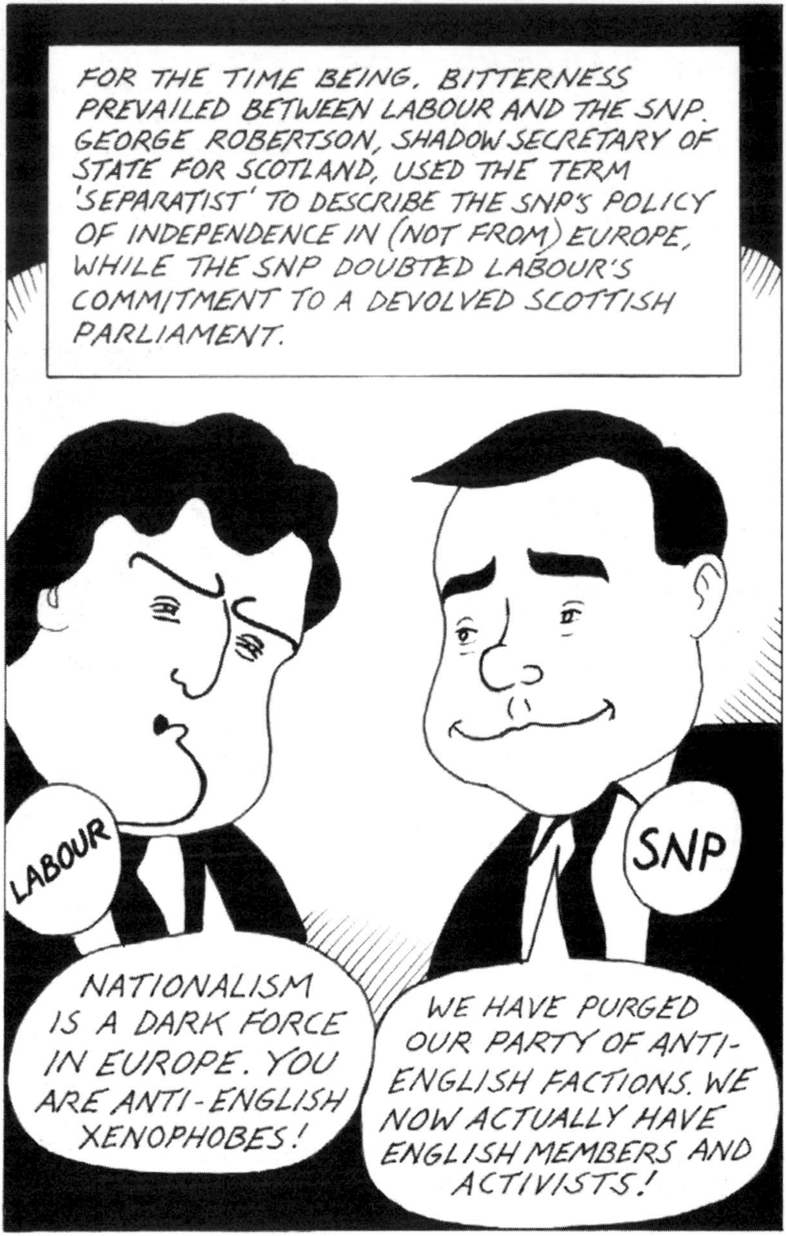
FOR THE TIME BEING, BITTERNESS PREVAILED BETWEEN LABOUR AND THE SNP. GEORGE ROBERTSON, SHADOW SECRETARY OF STATE FOR SCOTLAND, USED THE TERM 'SEPARATIST' TO DESCRIBE THE SNP'S POLICY OF INDEPENDENCE IN (NOT FROM) EUROPE, WHILE THE SNP DOUBTED LABOUR'S COMMITMENT TO A DEVOLVED SCOTTISH PARLIAMENT.
LABOUR
SNP
NATIONALISM IS A DARK FORCE IN EUROPE. YOU ARE ANTI-ENGLISH XENOPHOBES!
WE HAVE PURGED OUR PARTY OF ANTI-ENGLISH FACTIONS. WE NOW ACTUALLY HAVE ENGLISH MEMBERS AND ACTIVISTS!

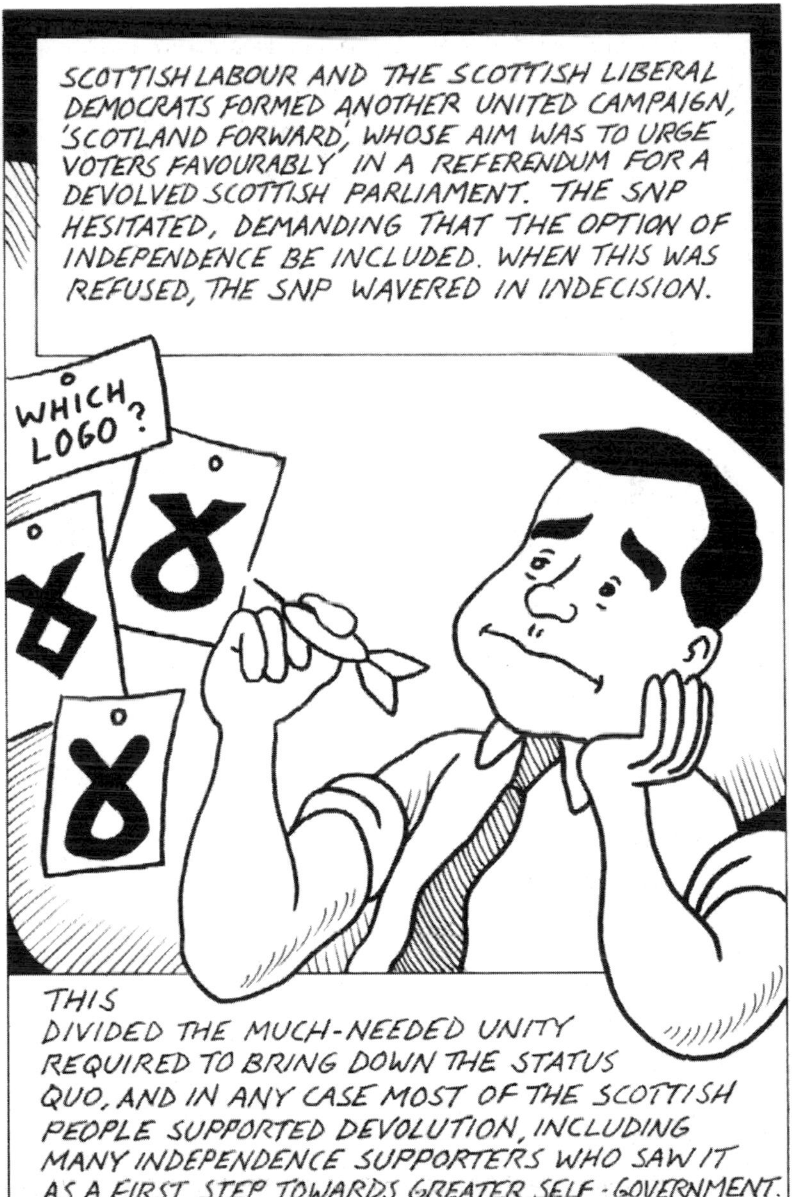
SCOTTISH LABOUR AND THE SCOTTISH LIBERAL DEMOCRATS FORMED ANOTHER UNITED CAMPAIGN, 'SCOTLAND FORWARD,' WHOSE AIM WAS TO URGE VOTERS FAVOURABLY IN A REFERENDUM FOR A DEVOLVED SCOTTISH PARLIAMENT. THE SNP HESITATED, DEMANDING THAT THE OPTION OF INDEPENDENCE BE INCLUDED. WHEN THIS WAS REFUSED, THE SNP WAVERED IN INDECISION.
WHICH LOGO?
THIS DIVIDED THE MUCH-NEEDED UNITY REQUIRED TO BRING DOWN THE STATUS QUO, AND IN ANY CASE MOST OF THE SCOTTISH PEOPLE SUPPORTED DEVOLUTION, INCLUDING MANY INDEPENDENCE SUPPORTERS WHO SAW IT AS A FIRST STEP TOWARDS GREATER SELF-GOVERNMENT.

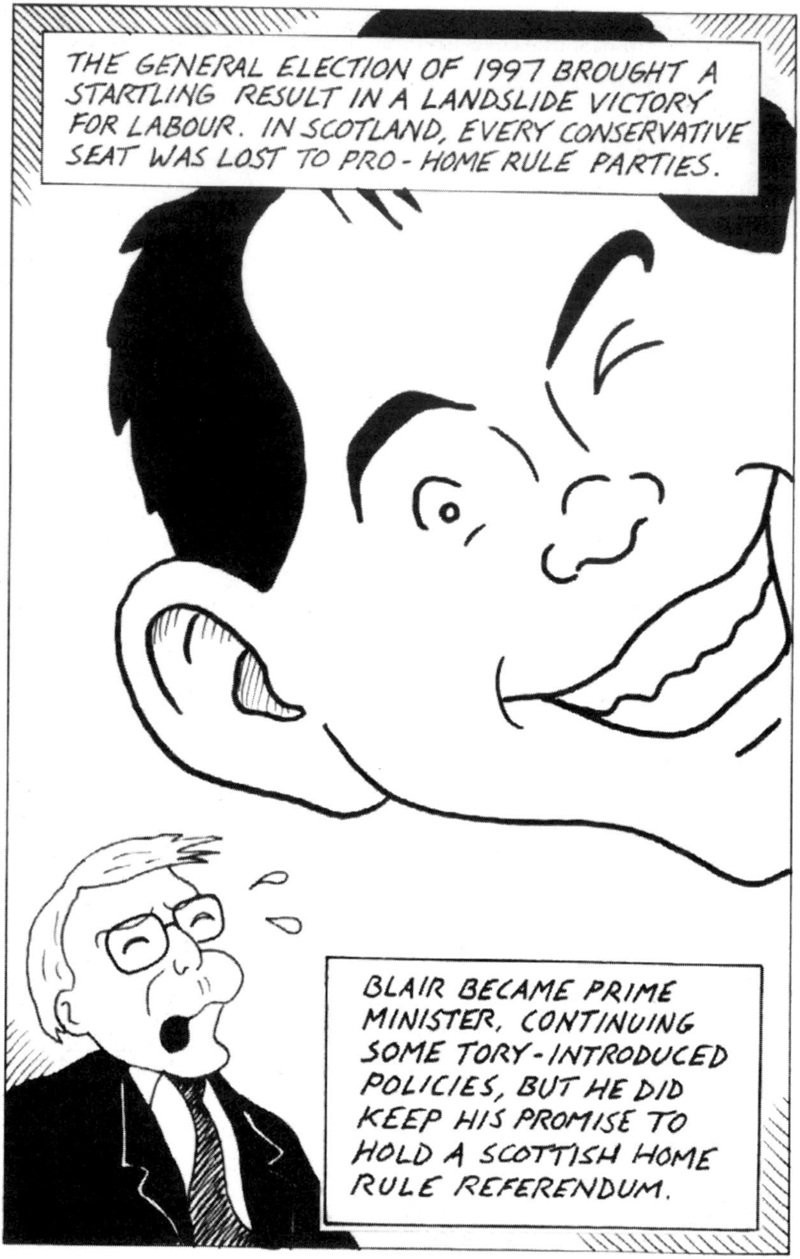
THE GENERAL ELECTION OF 1997 BROUGHT A STARTLING RESULT IN A LANDSLIDE VICTORY FOR LABOUR. IN SCOTLAND, EVERY CONSERVATIVE SEAT WAS LOST TO PRO-HOME RULE PARTIES.
BLAIR BECAME PRIME MINISTER, CONTINUING SOME TORY-INTRODUCED POLICIES, BUT HE DID KEEP HIS PROMISE TO HOLD A SCOTTISH HOME RULE REFERENDUM.

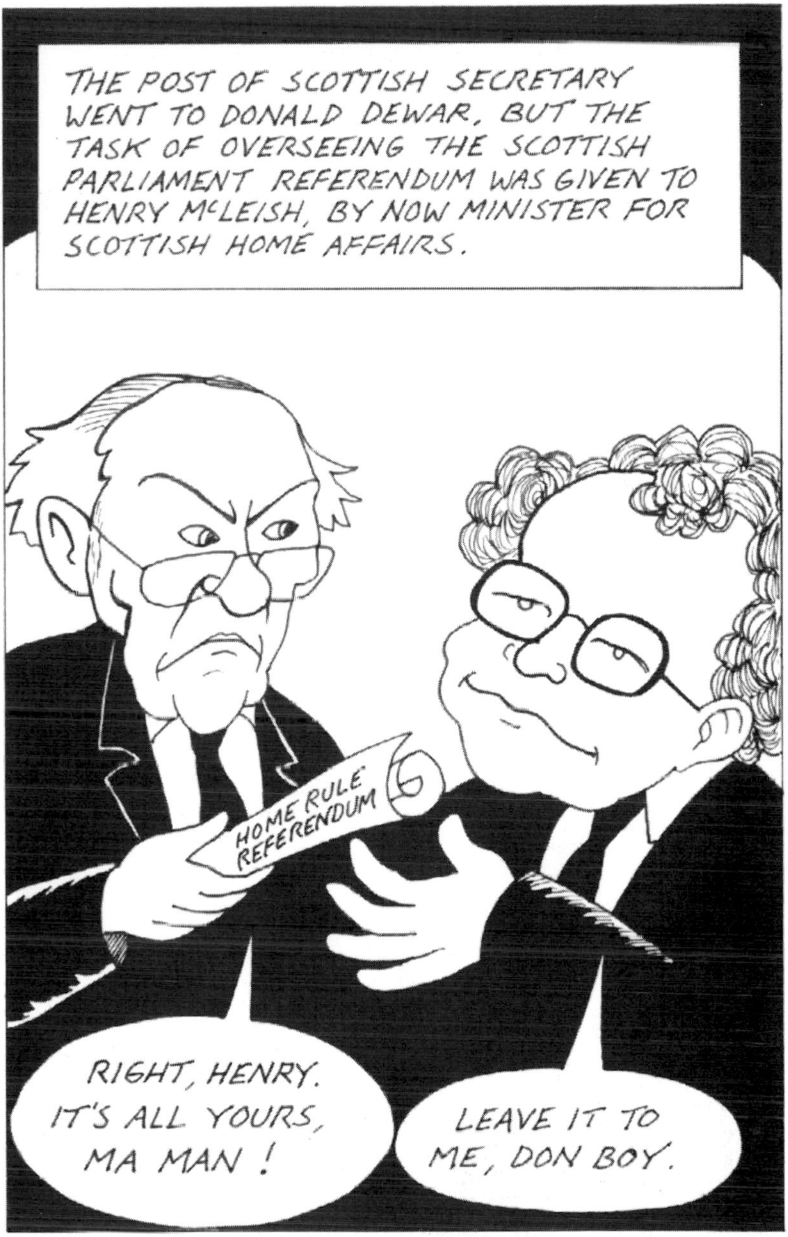
THE POST OF SCOTTISH SECRETARY WENT TO DONALD DEWAR, BUT THE TASK OF OVERSEEING THE SCOTTISH PARLIAMENT REFERENDUM WAS GIVEN TO HENRY McLEISH, BY NOW MINISTER FOR SCOTTISH HOME AFFAIRS.
HOME RULE REFERENDUM
RIGHT, HENRY. IT'S ALL YOURS, MA MAN!
LEAVE IT TO ME, DON BOY.

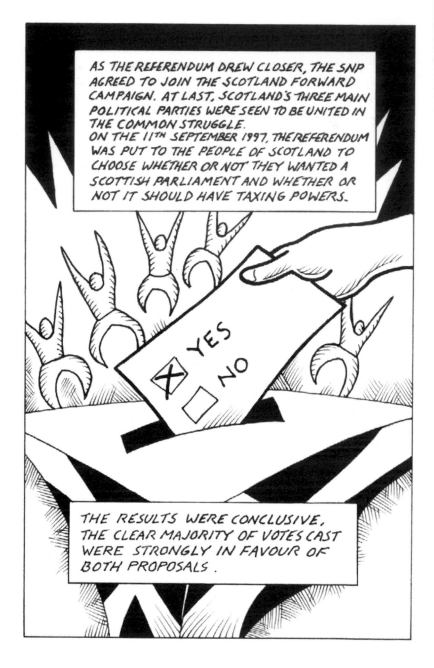

AS THE REFERENDUM DREW CLOSER, THE SNP AGREED TO JOIN THE SCOTLAND FORWARD CAMPAIGN. AT LAST, SCOTLAND'S THREE MAIN POLITICAL PARTIES WERE SEEN TO BE UNITED IN THE COMMON STRUGGLE.
ON THE 11TH SEPTEMBER 1997, THE REFERENDUM WAS PUT TO THE PEOPLE OF SCOTLAND TO CHOOSE WHETHER OR NOT THEY WANTED A SCOTTISH PARLIAMENT AND WHETHER OR NOT IT SHOULD HAVE TAXING POWERS.

YES
NO

THE RESULTS WERE CONCLUSIVE, THE CLEAR MAJORITY OF VOTES CAST WERE STRONGLY IN FAVOUR OF BOTH PROPOSALS.

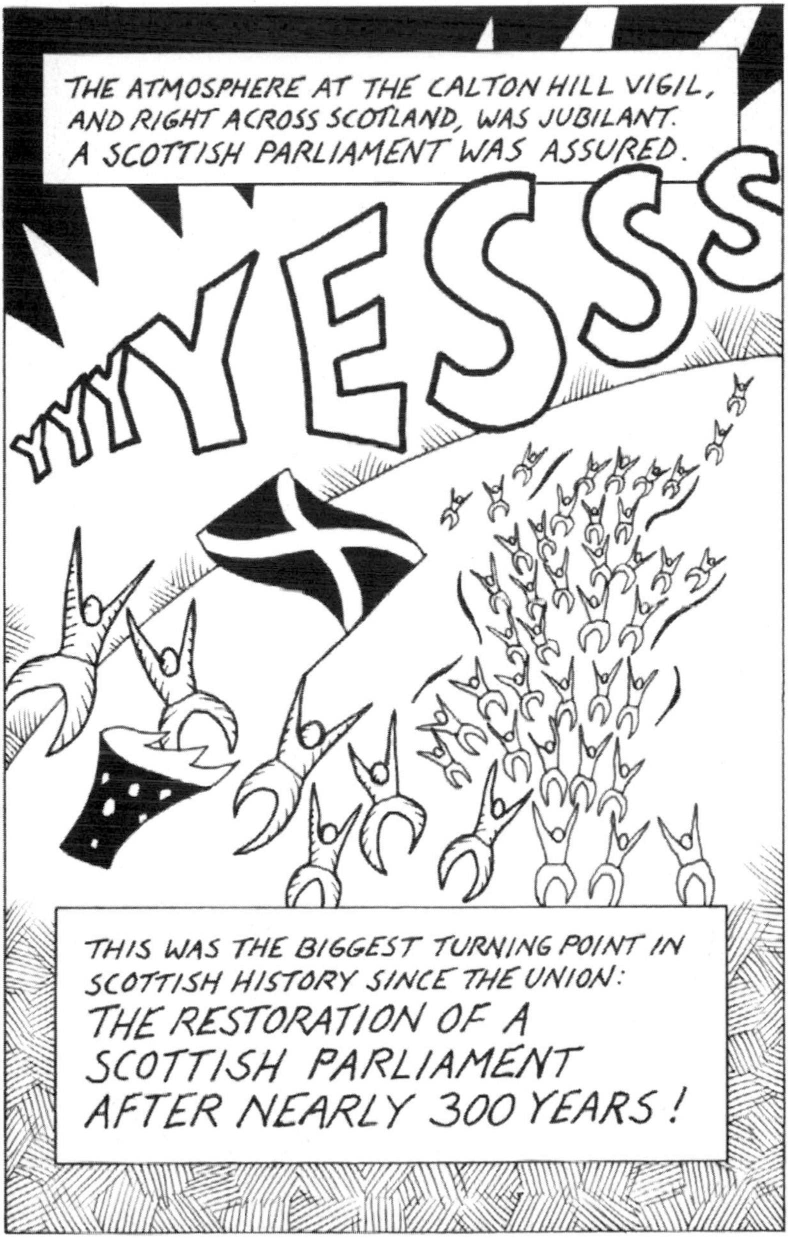
THE ATMOSPHERE AT THE CALTON HILL VIGIL, AND RIGHT ACROSS SCOTLAND, WAS JUBILANT. A SCOTTISH PARLIAMENT WAS ASSURED.
YYYYESSS
THIS WAS THE BIGGEST TURNING POINT IN SCOTTISH HISTORY SINCE THE UNION:
THE RESTORATION OF A SCOTTISH PARLIAMENT AFTER NEARLY 300 YEARS!

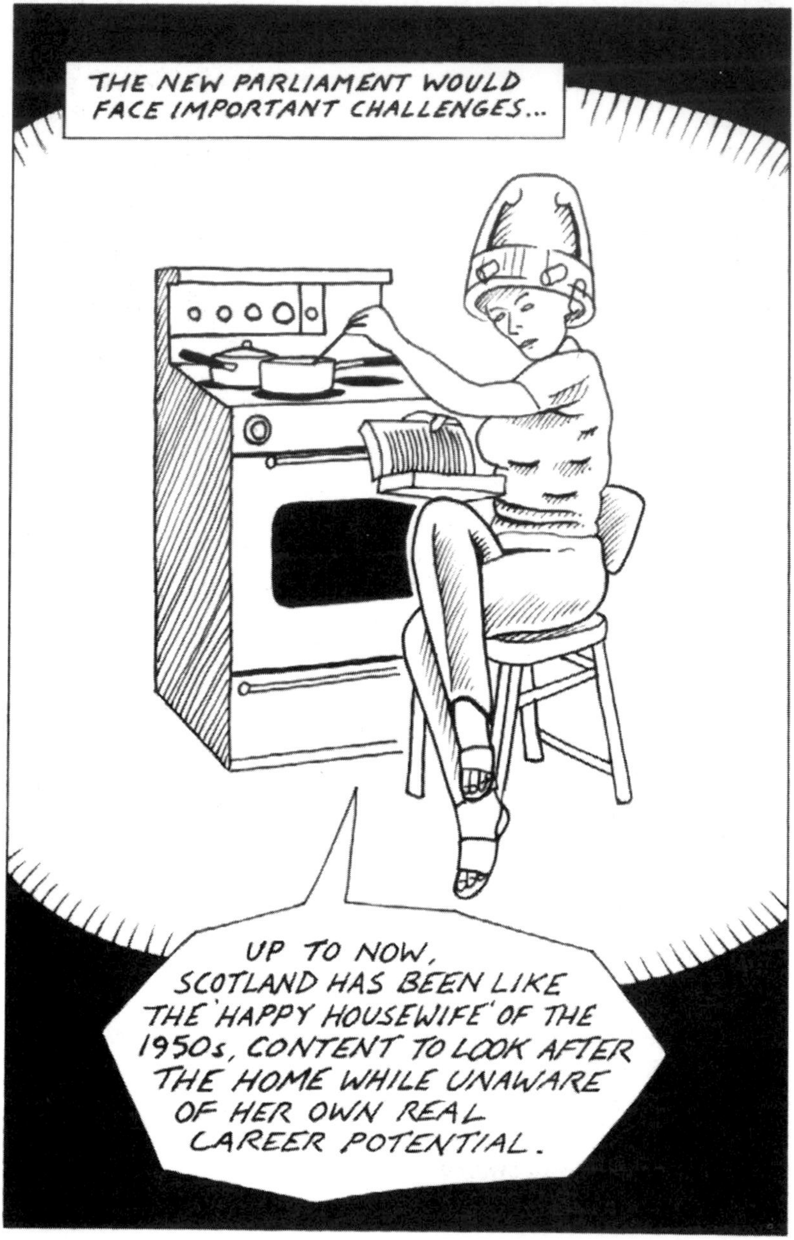
THE NEW PARLIAMENT WOULD FACE IMPORTANT CHALLENGES...
UP TO NOW, SCOTLAND HAS BEEN LIKE THE 'HAPPY HOUSEWIFE' OF THE 1950s, CONTENT TO LOOK AFTER THE HOME WHILE UNAWARE OF HER OWN REAL CAREER POTENTIAL.

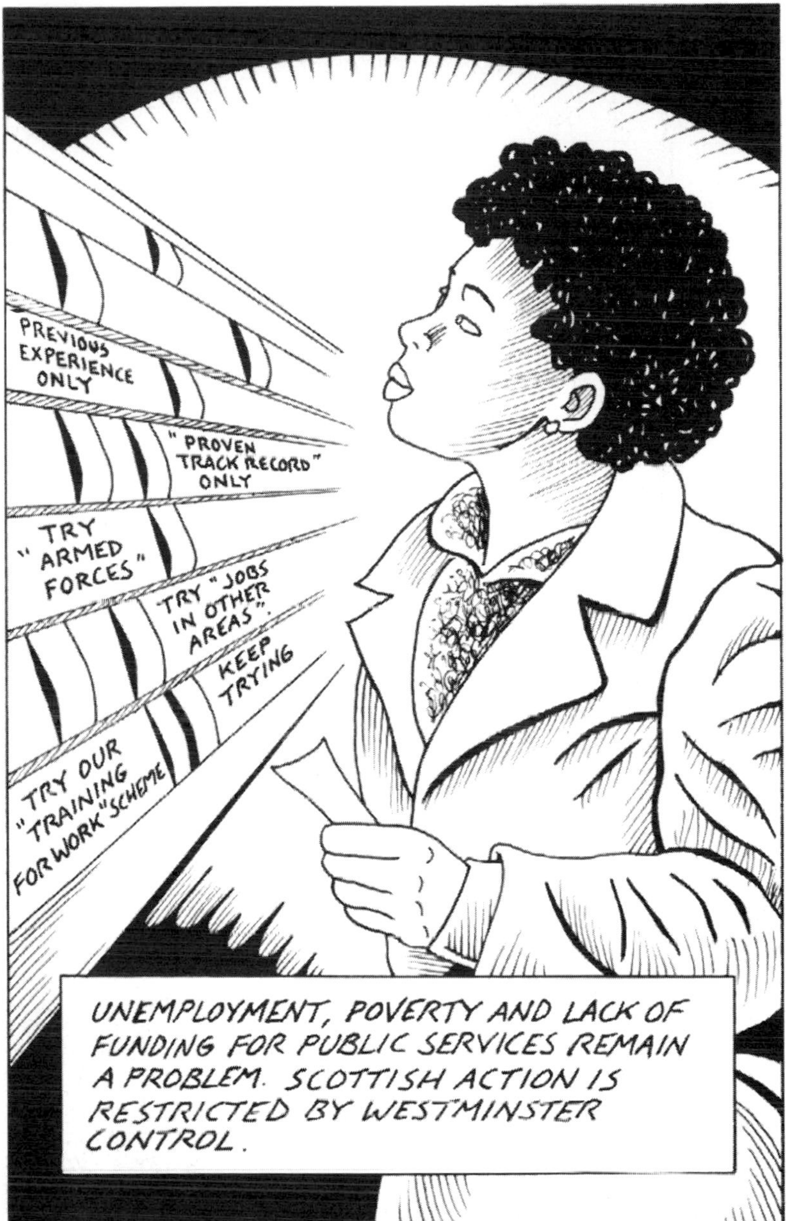
PREVIOUS EXPERIENCE ONLY
"PROVEN TRACK RECORD" ONLY
"TRY ARMED FORCES"
TRY "JOBS IN OTHER AREAS".
KEEP TRYING
TRY OUR "TRAINING FOR WORK" SCHEME
UNEMPLOYMENT, POVERTY AND LACK OF FUNDING FOR PUBLIC SERVICES REMAIN A PROBLEM. SCOTTISH ACTION IS RESTRICTED BY WESTMINSTER CONTROL.

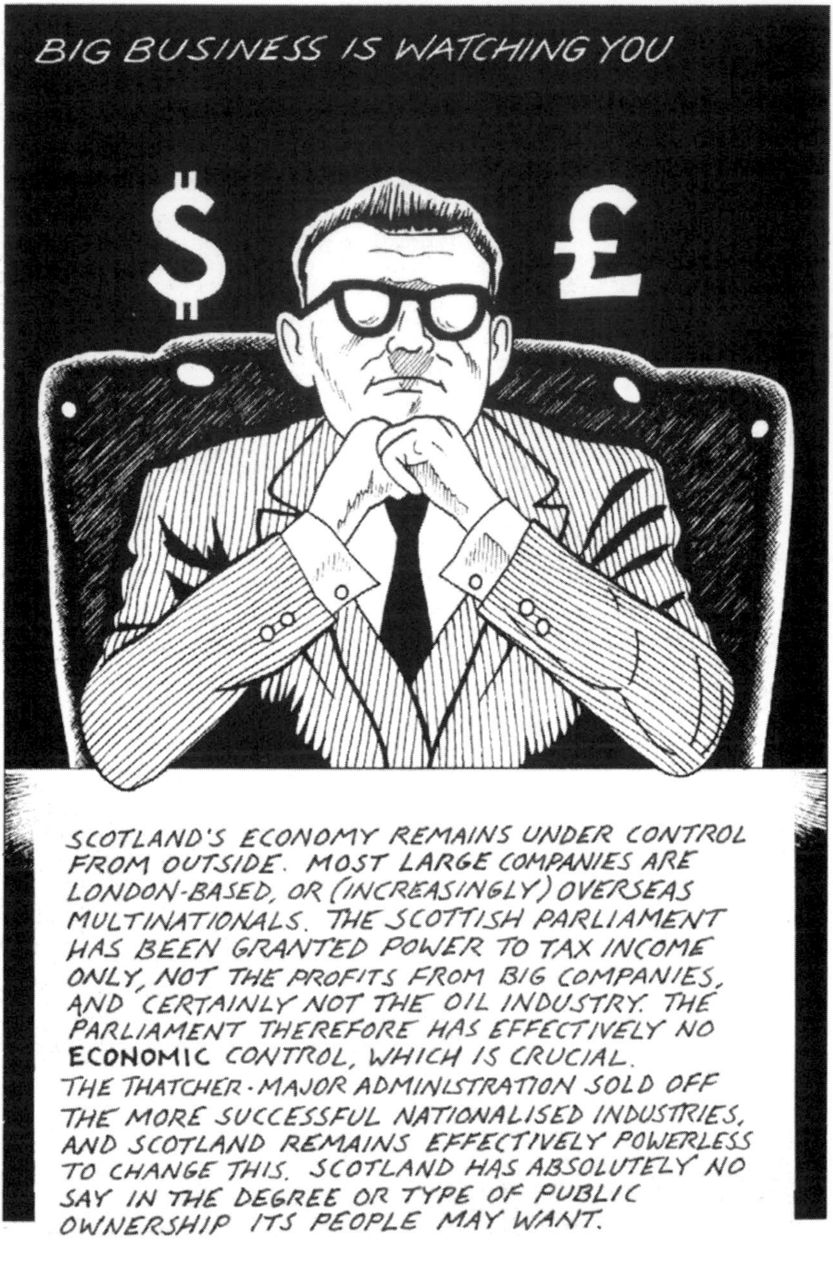
BIG BUSINESS IS WATCHING YOU
$
£
SCOTLAND'S ECONOMY REMAINS UNDER CONTROL FROM OUTSIDE. MOST LARGE COMPANIES ARE LONDON-BASED, OR (INCREASINGLY) OVERSEAS MULTINATIONALS. THE SCOTTISH PARLIAMENT HAS BEEN GRANTED POWER TO TAX INCOME ONLY, NOT THE PROFITS FROM BIG COMPANIES, AND CERTAINLY NOT THE OIL INDUSTRY. THE PARLIAMENT THEREFORE HAS EFFECTIVELY NO ECONOMIC CONTROL, WHICH IS CRUCIAL.
THE THATCHER-MAJOR ADMINISTRATION SOLD OFF THE MORE SUCCESSFUL NATIONALISED INDUSTRIES, AND SCOTLAND REMAINS EFFECTIVELY POWERLESS TO CHANGE THIS. SCOTLAND HAS ABSOLUTELY NO SAY IN THE DEGREE OR TYPE OF PUBLIC OWNERSHIP ITS PEOPLE MAY WANT.

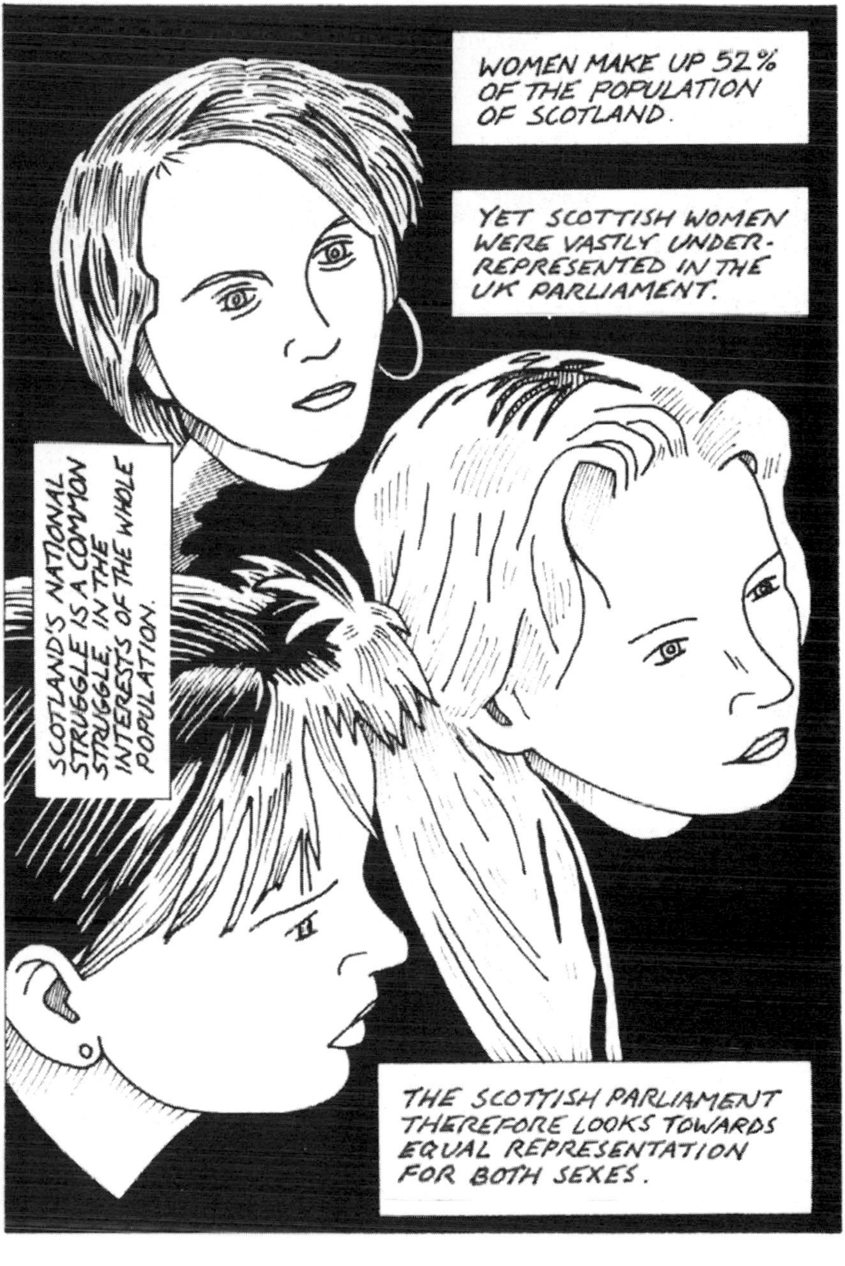
WOMEN MAKE UP 52% OF THE POPULATION OF SCOTLAND.
YET SCOTTISH WOMEN WERE VASTLY UNDER-REPRESENTED IN THE UK PARLIAMENT.
SCOTLAND'S NATIONAL STRUGGLE IS A COMMON STRUGGLE, IN THE INTERESTS OF THE WHOLE POPULATION.
THE SCOTTISH PARLIAMENT THEREFORE LOOKS TOWARDS EQUAL REPRESENTATION FOR BOTH SEXES.

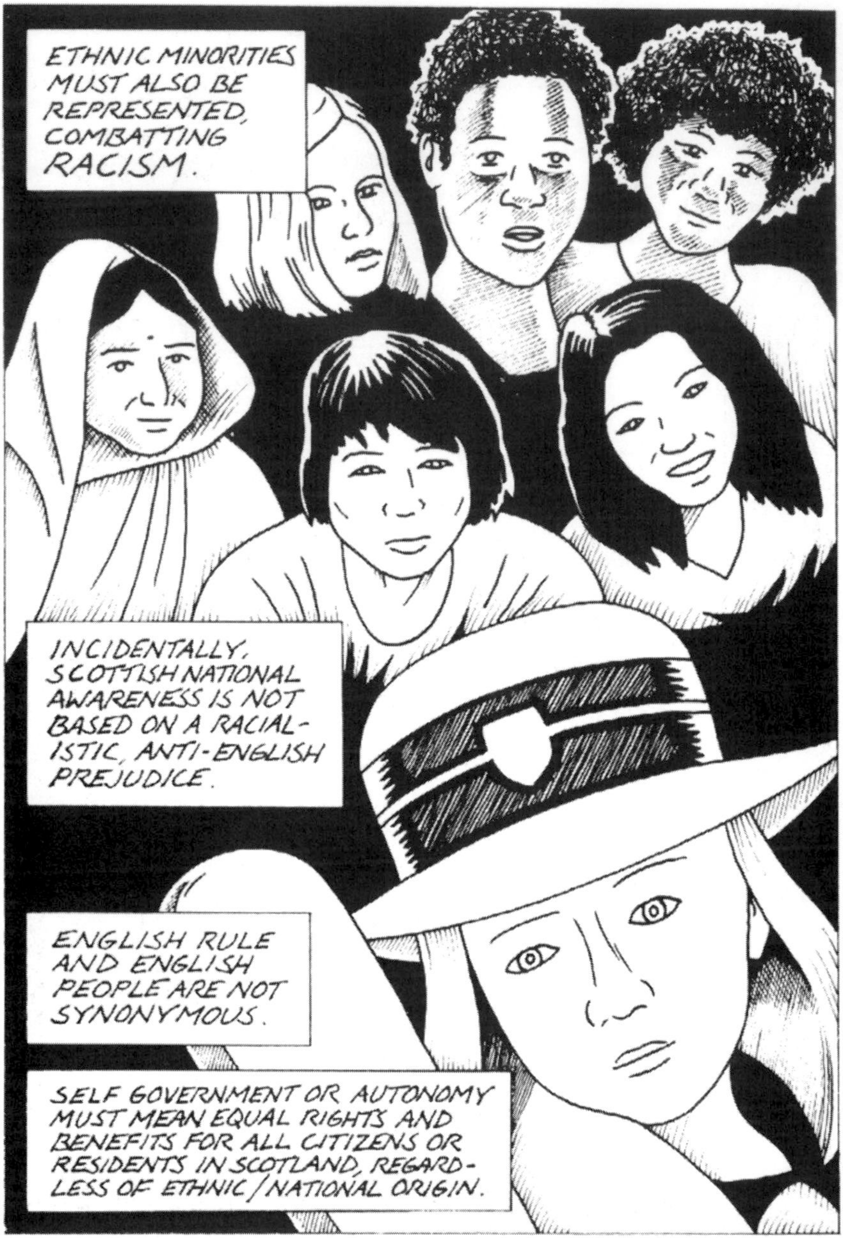
ETHNIC MINORITIES MUST ALSO BE REPRESENTED, COMBATTING RACISM.
INCIDENTALLY, SCOTTISH NATIONAL AWARENESS IS NOT BASED ON A RACIAL-ISTIC, ANTI-ENGLISH PREJUDICE.
ENGLISH RULE AND ENGLISH PEOPLE ARE NOT SYNONYMOUS.
SELF GOVERNMENT OR AUTONOMY MUST MEAN EQUAL RIGHTS AND BENEFITS FOR ALL CITIZENS OR RESIDENTS IN SCOTLAND, REGARD-LESS OF ETHNIC/NATIONAL ORIGIN.

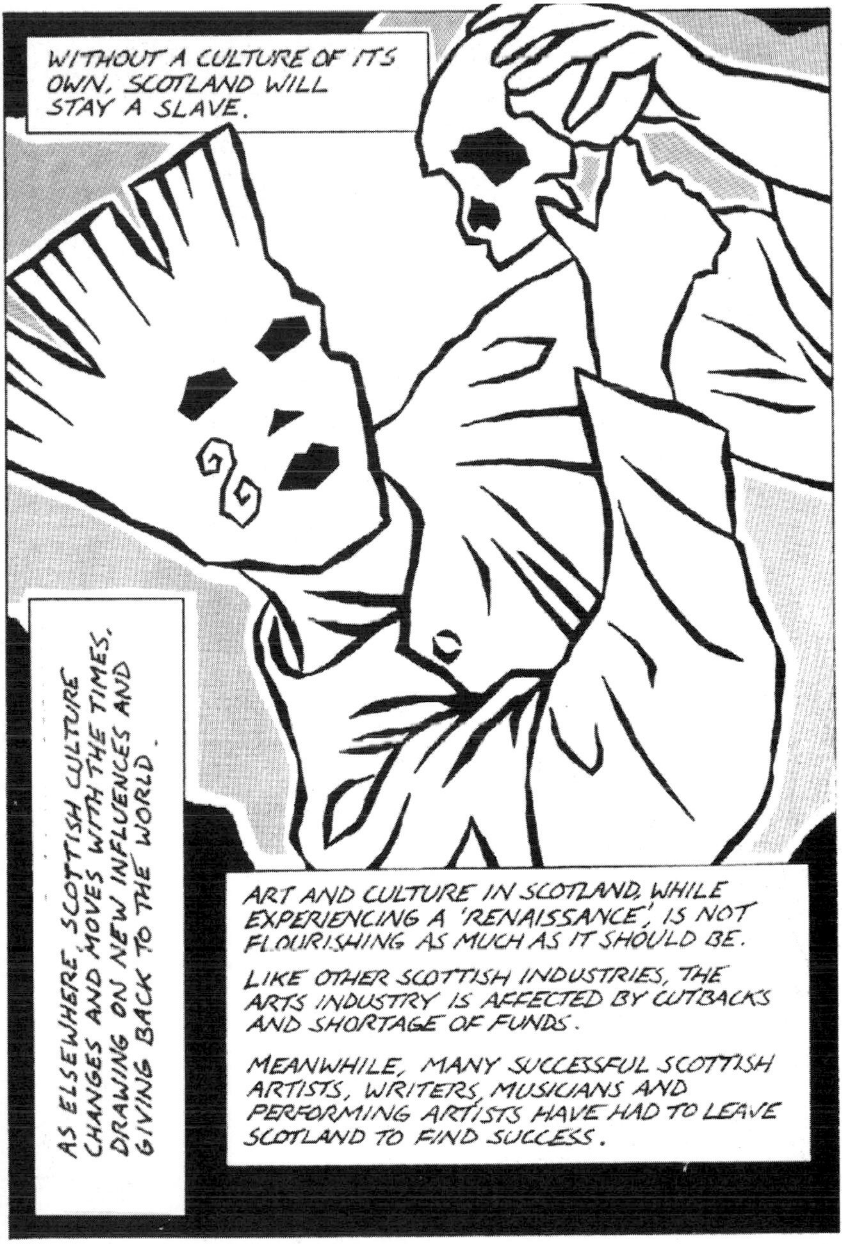
WITHOUT A CULTURE OF ITS OWN, SCOTLAND WILL STAY A SLAVE.
AS ELSEWHERE, SCOTTISH CULTURE CHANGES AND MOVES WITH THE TIMES, DRAWING ON NEW INFLUENCES AND GIVING BACK TO THE WORLD.
ART AND CULTURE IN SCOTLAND, WHILE EXPERIENCING A 'RENAISSANCE', IS NOT FLOURISHING AS MUCH AS IT SHOULD BE.
LIKE OTHER SCOTTISH INDUSTRIES, THE ARTS INDUSTRY IS AFFECTED BY CUTBACKS AND SHORTAGE OF FUNDS.
MEANWHILE, MANY SUCCESSFUL SCOTTISH ARTISTS, WRITERS, MUSICIANS AND PERFORMING ARTISTS HAVE HAD TO LEAVE SCOTLAND TO FIND SUCCESS.

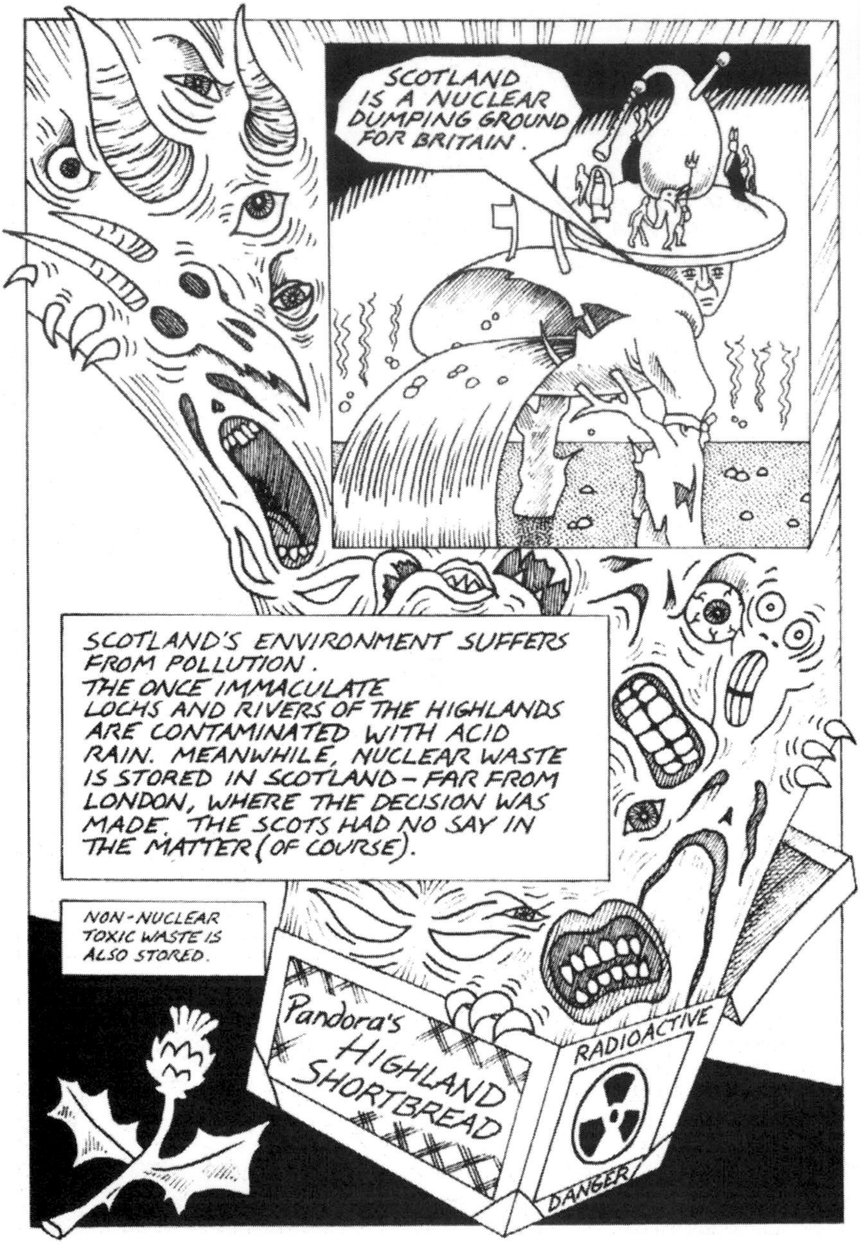
SCOTLAND IS A NUCLEAR DUMPING GROUND FOR BRITAIN.
SCOTLAND'S ENVIRONMENT SUFFERS FROM POLLUTION. THE ONCE IMMACULATE LOCHS AND RIVERS OF THE HIGHLANDS ARE CONTAMINATED WITH ACID RAIN. MEANWHILE, NUCLEAR WASTE IS STORED IN SCOTLAND – FAR FROM LONDON, WHERE THE DECISION WAS MADE. THE SCOTS HAD NO SAY IN THE MATTER (OF COURSE).
NON-NUCLEAR TOXIC WASTE IS ALSO STORED.
Pandora's HIGHLAND SHORTBREAD
RADIOACTIVE
DANGER

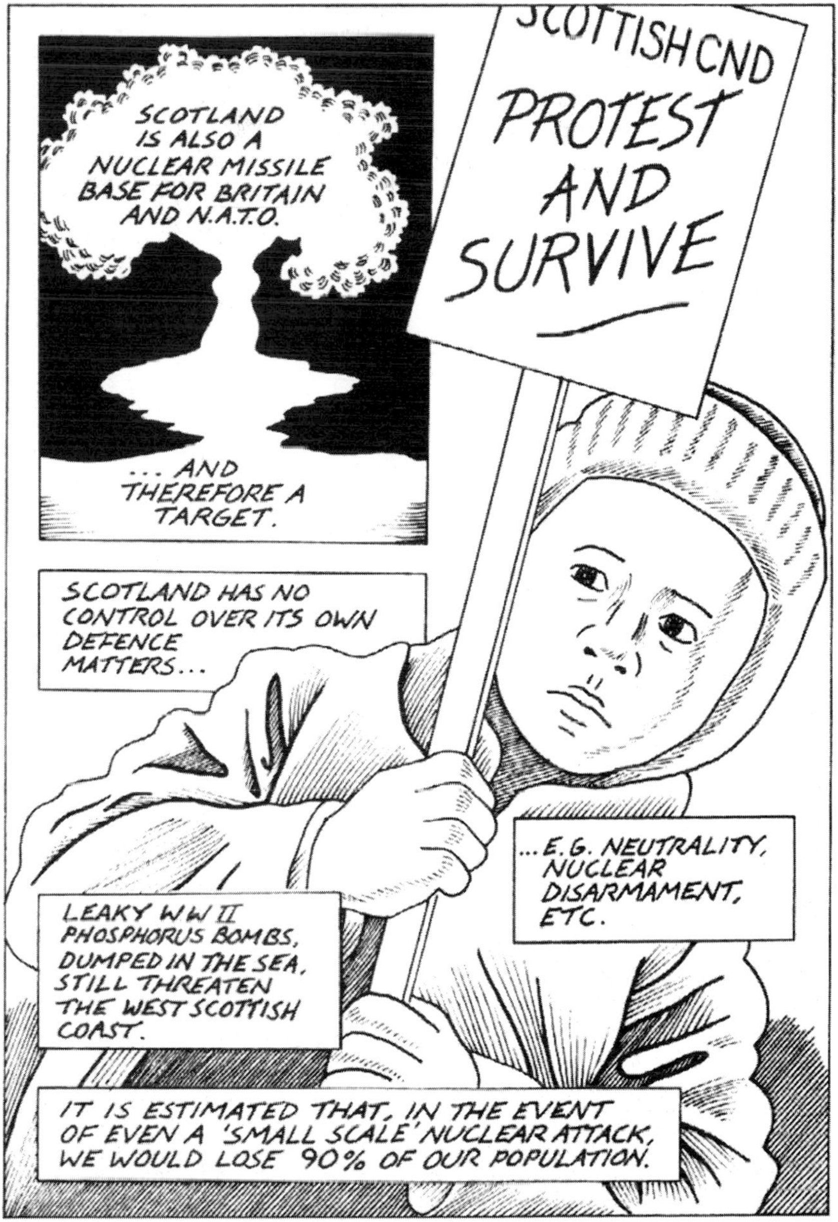
SCOTLAND IS ALSO A NUCLEAR MISSILE BASE FOR BRITAIN AND N.A.T.O.
... AND THEREFORE A TARGET.
SCOTTISH CND
PROTEST AND SURVIVE
SCOTLAND HAS NO CONTROL OVER ITS OWN DEFENCE MATTERS...
...E.G. NEUTRALITY, NUCLEAR DISARMAMENT, ETC.
LEAKY WW II PHOSPHORUS BOMBS, DUMPED IN THE SEA, STILL THREATEN THE WEST SCOTTISH COAST.
IT IS ESTIMATED THAT, IN THE EVENT OF EVEN A 'SMALL SCALE' NUCLEAR ATTACK, WE WOULD LOSE 90% OF OUR POPULATION.

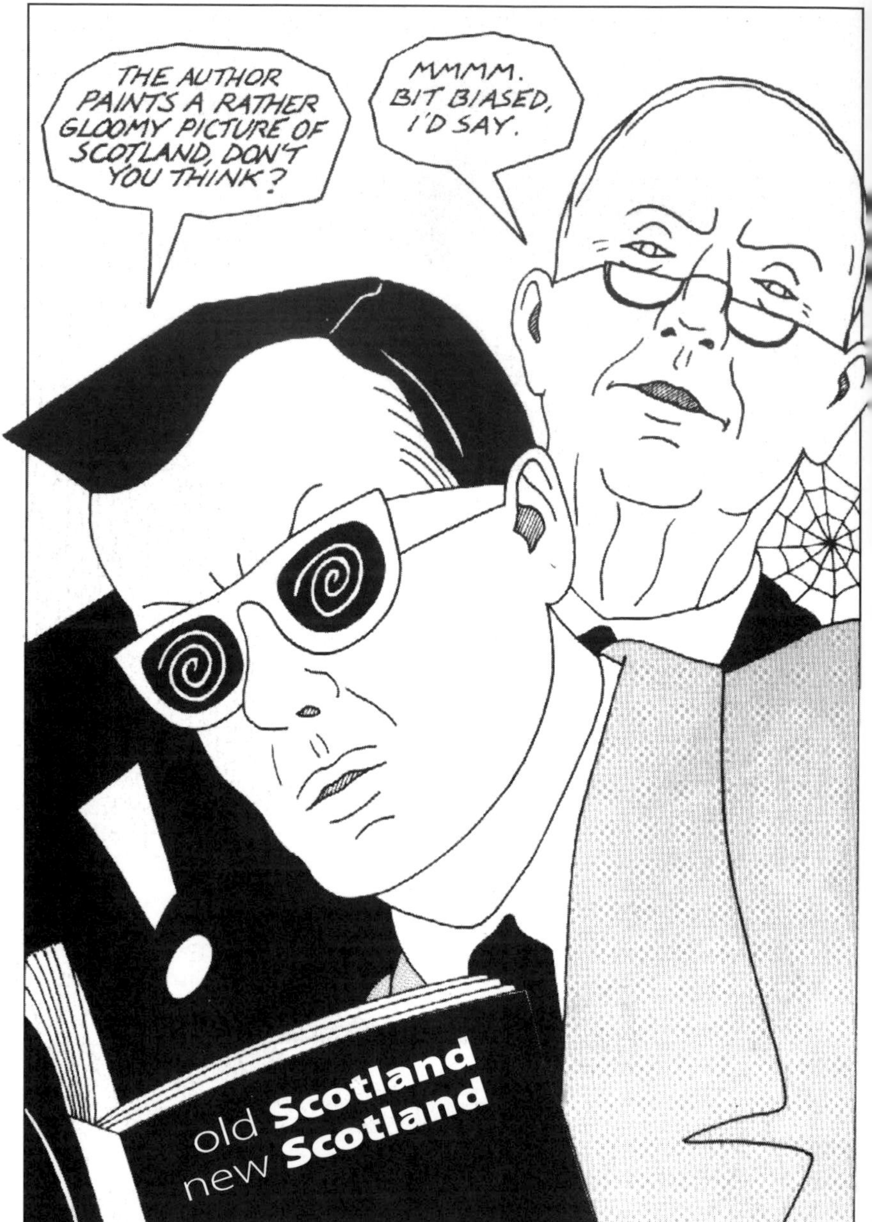
THE AUTHOR PAINTS A RATHER GLOOMY PICTURE OF SCOTLAND, DON'T YOU THINK?
MMMM. BIT BIASED, I'D SAY.
old Scotland new Scotland

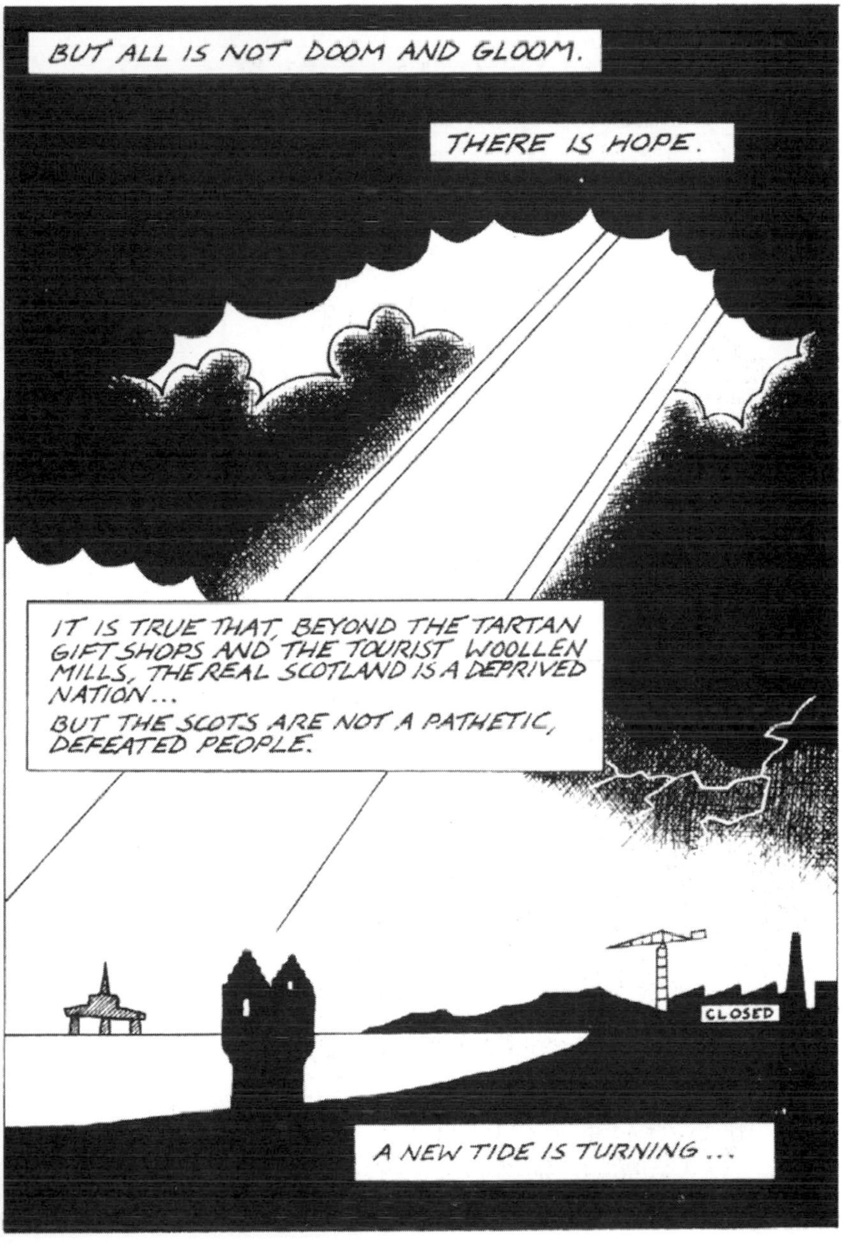
BUT ALL IS NOT DOOM AND GLOOM.
THERE IS HOPE.
IT IS TRUE THAT, BEYOND THE TARTAN GIFT SHOPS AND THE TOURIST WOOLLEN MILLS, THE REAL SCOTLAND IS A DEPRIVED NATION...
BUT THE SCOTS ARE NOT A PATHETIC, DEFEATED PEOPLE.
CLOSED
A NEW TIDE IS TURNING ...

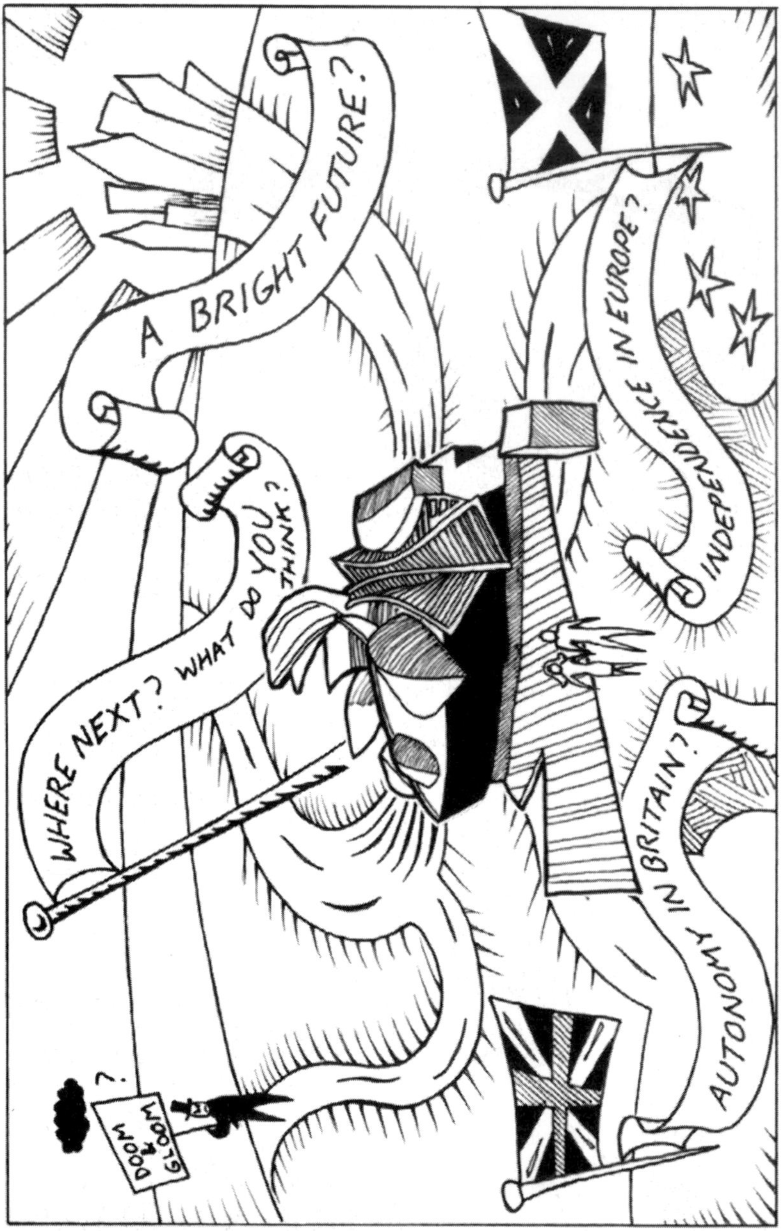
A BRIGHT FUTURE?
WHERE NEXT? WHAT DO YOU THINK?
INDEPENDENCE IN EUROPE?
AUTONOMY IN BRITAIN?
DOOM & GLOOM
?

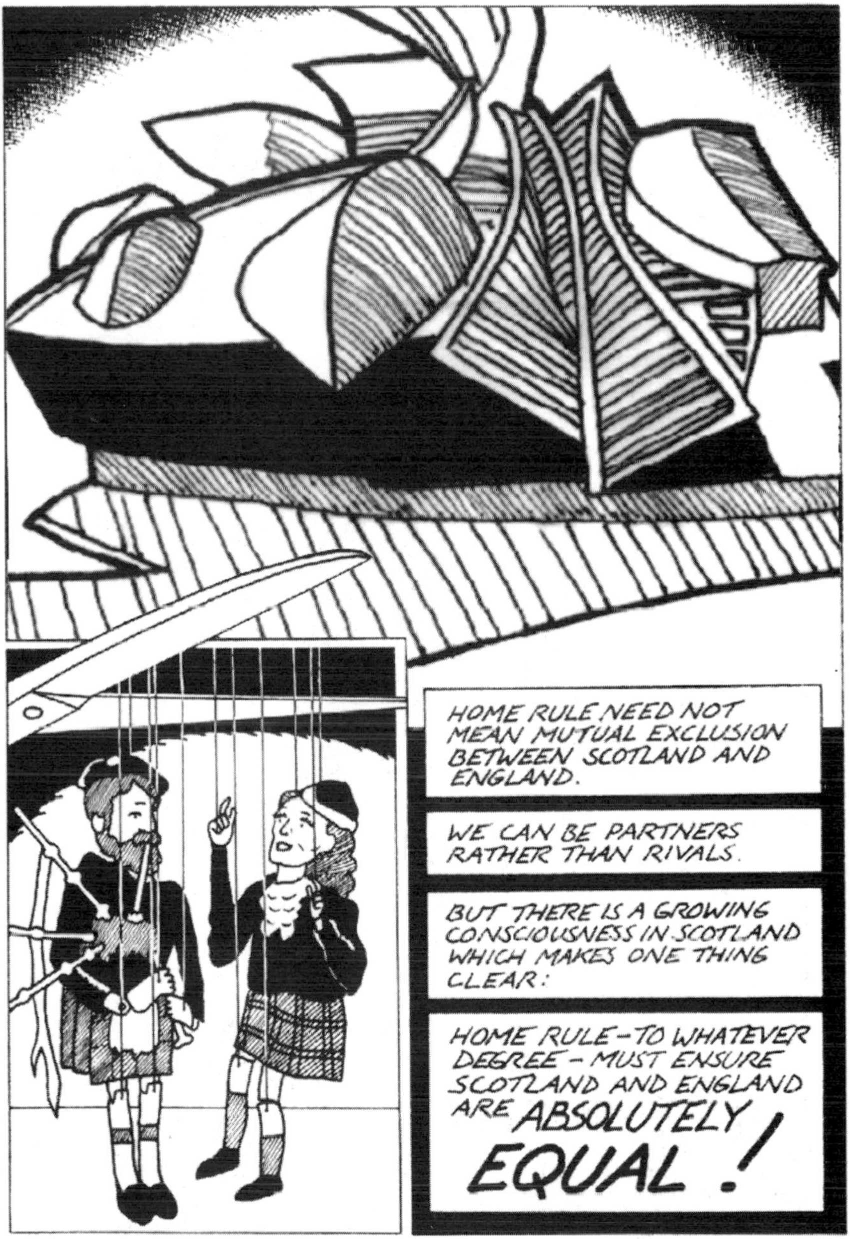
HOME RULE NEED NOT MEAN MUTUAL EXCLUSION BETWEEN SCOTLAND AND ENGLAND.
WE CAN BE PARTNERS RATHER THAN RIVALS.
BUT THERE IS A GROWING CONSCIOUSNESS IN SCOTLAND WHICH MAKES ONE THING CLEAR:
HOME RULE—TO WHATEVER DEGREE—MUST ENSURE SCOTLAND AND ENGLAND ARE ABSOLUTELY EQUAL!

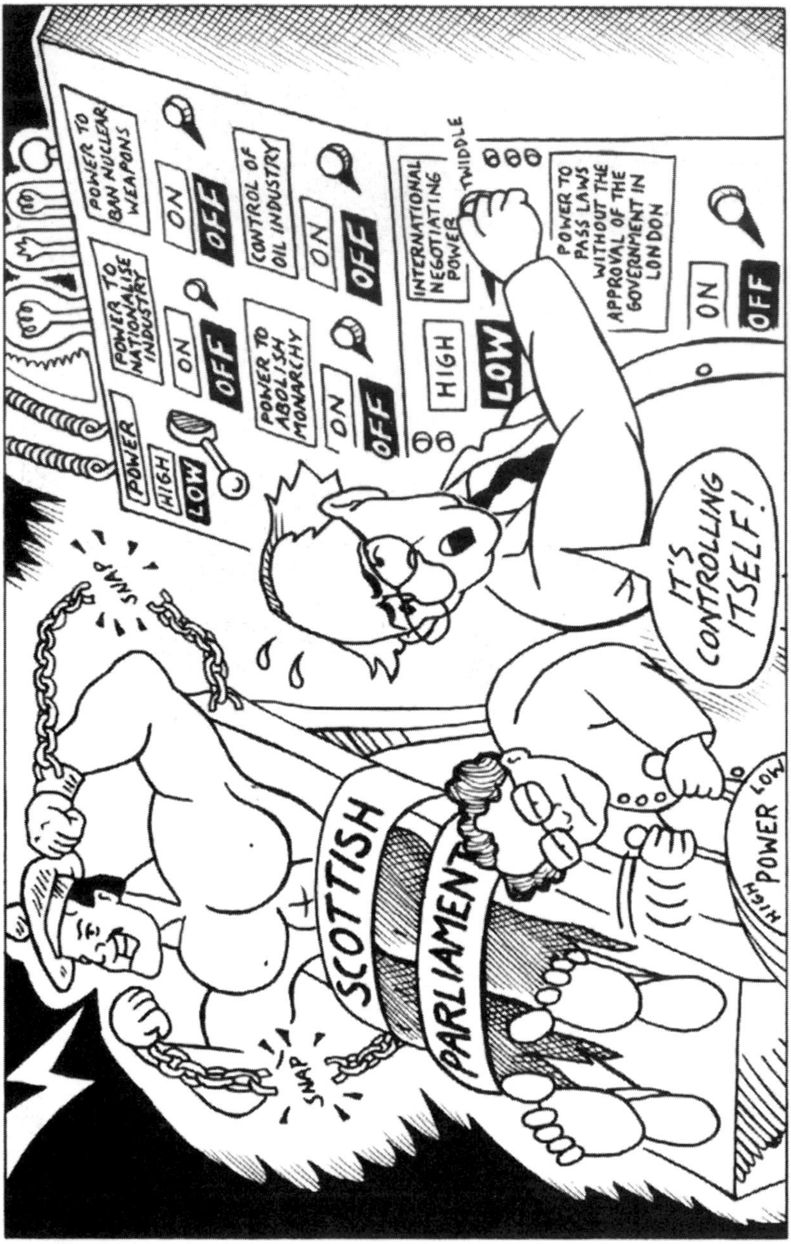
POWER TO BAN NUCLEAR WEAPONS
ON
OFF
POWER TO NATIONALISE INDUSTRY
ON
OFF
CONTROL OF OIL INDUSTRY
ON
OFF
POWER
HIGH
LOW
POWER TO ABOLISH MONARCHY
ON
OFF
INTERNATIONAL NEGOTIATING POWER
HIGH
LOW
TWIDDLE
POWER TO PASS LAWS WITHOUT THE APPROVAL OF THE GOVERNMENT IN LONDON
ON
OFF
SNAP
SNAP
SCOTTISH
PARLIAMENT
IT'S CONTROLLING ITSELF!
HIGH POWER LOW

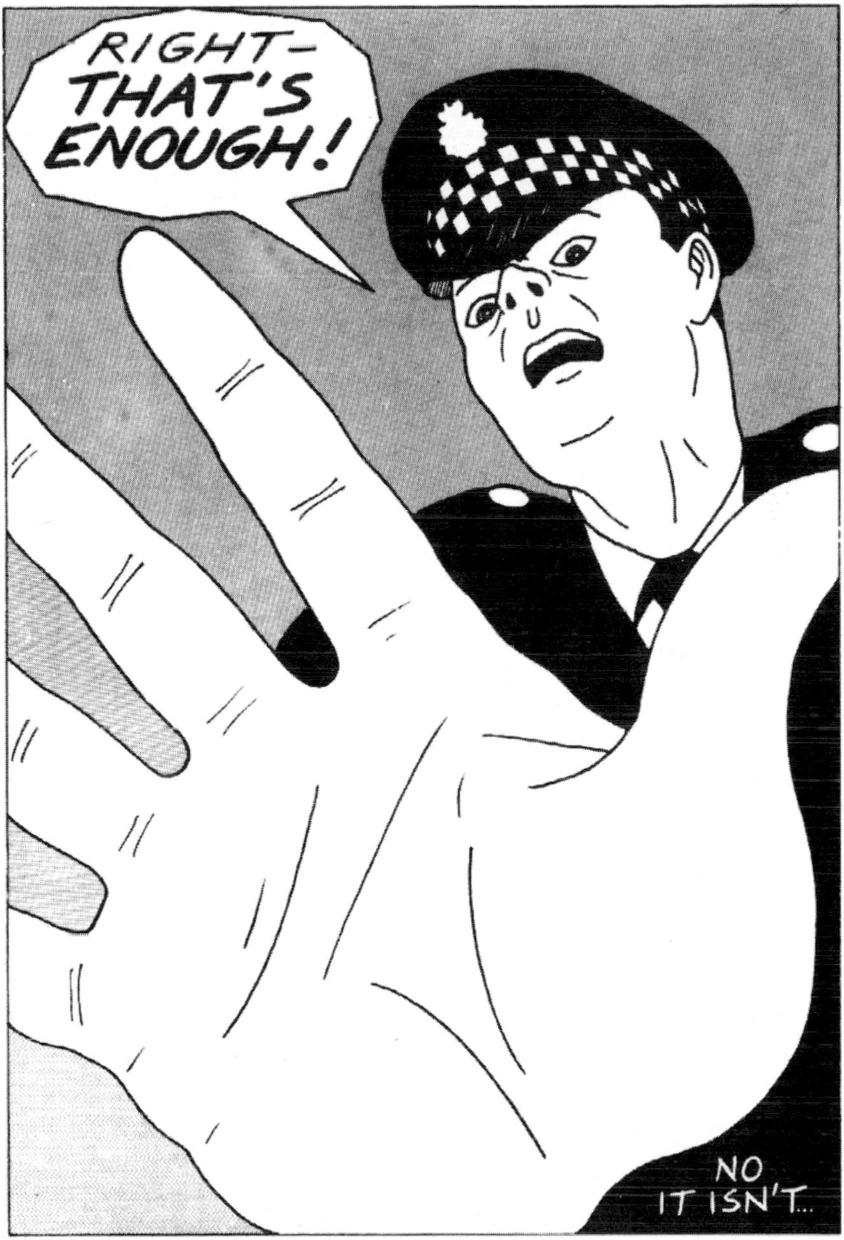
RIGHT–
THAT'S
ENOUGH!
NO
IT ISN'T...

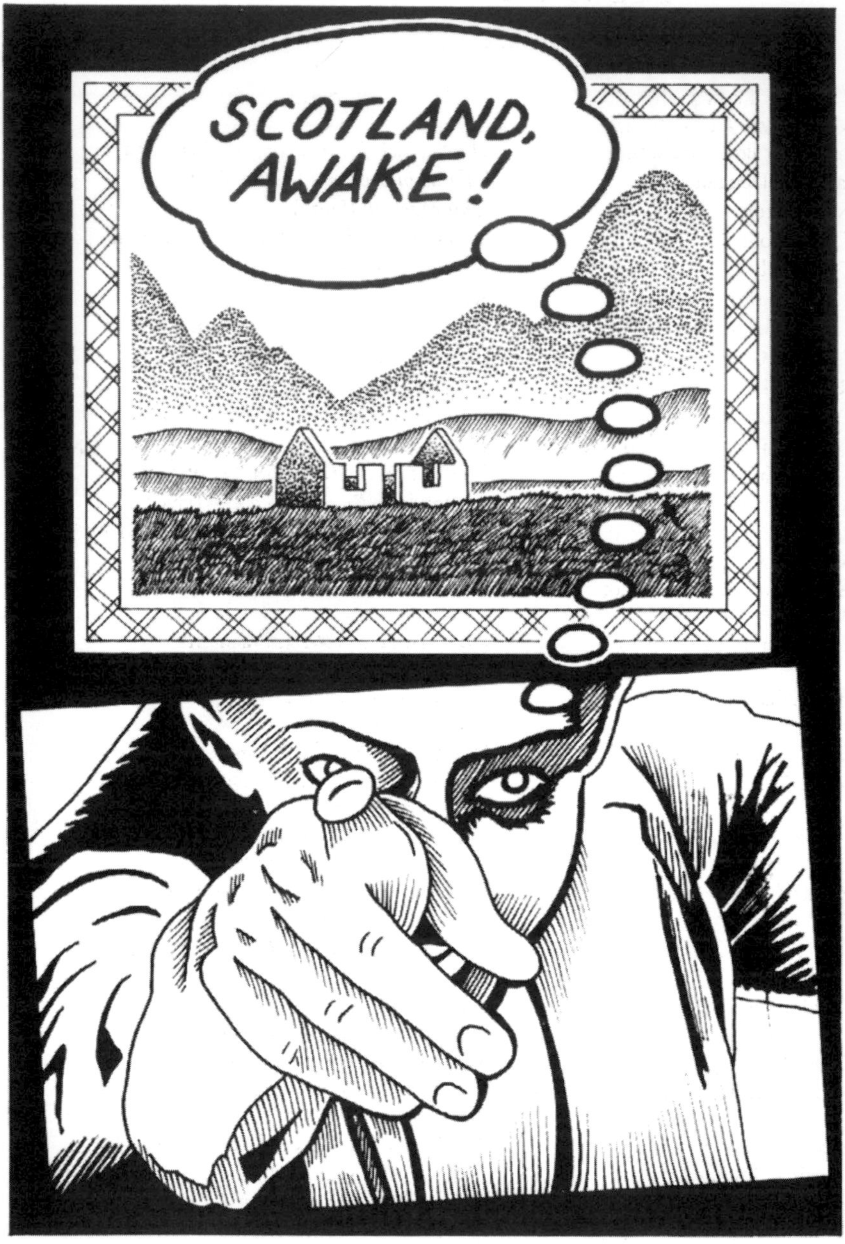
SCOTLAND, AWAKE!

Suggested Further Reading

Kenneth Cargill (Ed.)	*Scotland 2000* (BBC)
Seamus MacA'Ghobhainn and Peter Beresford Ellis	*The Scottish Insurrection of 1820* (Pluto)
Iain MacDougall	*Labour in Scotland* (Mainstream)
Nan Milton	*John Maclean* (Pluto)
T. C. Smout	*A Century of the Scottish People* (Fontana)
Tom Steel	*Scotland's Story* (Fontana)
The Scottish Office	*Scotland's Parliament* (Booklet)
Paul H. Scott	*Towards Independence* (Polygon)
Alasdair Gray	*Why Scots Should Rule Scotland*
Richard J. Finlay	*Independent and Free* (John Donald)
Dudley Edwards	*A Claim of Right for Scotland* (Polygon)
Donnachie & Whatley (Ed.)	*The Manufacture of Scottish History* (Polygon)
Christopher Harvie	*Scotland and Nationalism* (Routledge)
McCrone, Morris & Kelly	*Scotland the Brand – The Making of Scottish Heritage* (Edinburgh University Press)
Kenyon Wright	*The People Say Yes* (Argyll)
Alan Clements Kenny Farquarson & Kirsty Wark	*Restless Nation,* (Mainstream)
Bernie, Brand & Mitchell	*How Scotland Votes* (Manchester University Press)
Angus Calder	*Revolving Culture Notes from the Scottish Republic* (I.B. Tauris)
James Mitchell	*Strategies for Self-Government* (Polygon)
Keith Aitken	*The Bairns o' Adam The Story of the STUC* (Polygon).
Lindsay Paterson	*The Autonomy of Modern Scotland* (Edinburgh University Press)
Michael Lynch	*Scotland: A New History* (Pimlico)
John Prebble	*The Lion in the North* (Penguin)
Alexander Grant	*Independence and Nationhood* (Edinburgh University Press)
Gordon Donaldson	*Scotland's History, Approaches and Reflections* (Scottish Academic Press)
James Halliday	*Scotland – A Concise History* (Gordon Wright)
Fitzroy MacLean	*Scotland – A Concise History* (Thames & Hudson)
Peter & Fiona Somerset Fry	*The History of Scotland* (Routledge)
Rosalind Mitchison	*Why Scottish History Matters* (Saltire Society)
John & Julia Keay (Ed.)	*Collins Encyclopaedia of Scotland* (HarperCollins)

Notes from the North
incorporating a Brief History of the Scots and the English
Emma Wood
ISBN 0 946487 46 4 PBK £8.99

Notes on being English
Notes on being in Scotland
Learning from a shared past
Is it time to recognise that the border between Scotland and England is the dividing line between very different cultures?

As the Scottish nation begins to set its own agenda, will it decide to consign its sense of grievance against England to the dustbin of history?

Will a fresh approach heal these ancient 'sibling rivalries'?

How does a study of Scottish history help to clarify the roots of Scottish-English antagonism?

Does an English 'white settler' have a right to contribute to the debate?

Will the empowering of the citizens of Scotland take us all, Scots and English, towards mutual tolerance and understanding?

Sickened by the English jingoism that surfaced in rampant form during the 1982 Falklands War, Emma Wood started to dream of moving from her home in East Anglia to the Highlands of Scotland. She felt increasingly frustrated and marginalised as Thatcherism got a grip on the southern English psyche. The Scots she met on frequent holidays in the Highlands had no truck with Thatcherism, and she felt at home with grass-roots Scottish anti-authoritarianism. The decision was made. She uprooted and headed for a new life in the north of Scotland.

She was to discover that she had crossed a border in more than the geographical sense.

Loving her new life and friends in first Sutherland and then Ross-shire, she nevertheless had to come to terms with the realisation that in the eyes of some Scots she was an unwelcome 'white settler' who would never belong. She became aware of the perception that some English incomers were insensitive to the needs and aspirations of Highland communities.

Her own approach has been thoughtful and creative. In Notes from the North she sets a study of Scots-English conflicts alongside relevant personal experiences of contemporary incomers' lives in the Highlands. She gently and perceptively confronts the issue of racial intolerance, and sets out conflicting perceptions of 'Englishness' and 'Scottishness'; she argues that racial stereotyping is a stultifying cul-de-sac, and that distinctive ethnic and cultural strands within Scottish society are potentially enriching and strengthening forces. This book is a pragmatic, positive and forward-looking contribution to cultural and politicial debate within Scotland.

Notes from the North is essential reading for anyone who is thinking of moving to Scotland and for Scots who want to move into the 21st century free

An Inhabited Solitude: Scotland – Land and People
James McCarthy
ISBN 0 946487 30 8 PBK £6.99

'Scotland is the country above all others that I have seen, in which a man of imagination may carve out his own pleasures; there are so many inhabited solitudes.'

DOROTHY WORDSWORTH, in her journal of August 1803

An informed and thought-provoking profile of Scotland's unique landscapes and the impact of humans on what we see now and in the future. James McCarthy leads us through the many aspects of the land and the people who inhabit it: natural Scotland; the rocks beneath; land ownership; the use of resources; people and place; conserving Scotland's heritage and much more.

Written in a highly readable style, this concise volume offers an understanding of the land as a whole. Emphasising the uniqueness of the Scottish environment, the author explores the links between this and other aspects of our culture as a key element in rediscovering a modern sense of the Scottish identity and perception of nationhood.

'This book provides an engaging introduction to

he mysteries of Scotland's people and landscapes. Difficult concepts are described in simple terms, providing the interested Scot or tourist with an nvaluable overview of the country... It fills an mportant niche which, to my knowledge, is filled by no other publications.'

BETSY KING, Chief Executive, Scottish Environmental Education Council.

Wild Scotland: The essential guide to finding the best of natural Scotland

James McCarthy

Photography by Laurie Campbell

SBN 0 946487 37 5 PBK £7.50

Wild Scotland

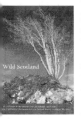

With a foreword by Magnus Magnusson and striking colour photographs by Laurie Campbell, this is the essential up-to-date guide to viewing wild-life in Scotland for the visitor and resident alike. It provides a fascinating overview of the country's plants, animals, bird and marine life against the background of their typical natural settings, as an introduction to the vivid descriptions of the most accessible localities, linked to clear regional maps. A unique feature is the focus on 'green tourism' and sustainable visitor use of the countryside, contributed by Duncan Bryden, manager of the Scottish Tourist Board's Tourism and the Environment Task Force. Important practical information on access and the best times of year for viewing sites makes this an indispensable and user-friendly travelling companion to anyone interested in exploring Scotland's remarkable natural heritage.

James McCarthy is former Deputy Director for Scotland of the Nature Conservancy Council, and now a Board Member of Scottish Natural Heritage and Chairman of the Environmental Youth Work National Development Project Scotland.

Blind Harry's Wallace

William Hamilton of Gilbertfield

ISBN 0 946487 43 X HBK £15.00
ISBN 0 946487 33 2 PBK £7.50

BLIND HARRY'S
Wallace
William Hamilton of Gilbertfield

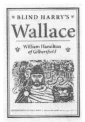

The original story of the real braveheart, Sir William Wallace. Racy, blood on every page, violently anglophobic, grossly embellished, vulgar and disgusting, clumsy and stilted, a literary failure, a great epic.

Whatever the verdict on BLIND HARRY, this is the book which has done more than any other to frame the notion of Scotland's national identity. Despite its numerous'historical inaccuracies', it remains the principal source for what we now know about the life of Wallace.

The novel and film *Braveheart* were based on the 1722 Hamilton edition of this epic poem. Burns, Wordsworth, Byron and others were greatly influenced by this version 'wherein the old obsolete words are rendered more intelligible', which is said to be the book, next to the Bible, most commonly found in Scottish households in the eighteenth century. Burns even admits to having 'borrowed... a couplet worthy of Homer' directly from Hamilton's version of BLIND HARRY to include in '*Scots wha hae*'.

Elspeth King, in her introduction to this, the first accessible edition of BLIND HARRY in verse form since 1859, draws parallels between the situation in Scotland at the time of Wallace and that in Bosnia and Chechnya in the 1990s. Seven hundred years to the day after the Battle of Stirling Bridge, the 'Settled Will of the Scottish People' was expressed in the devolution referendum of 11 September 1997. She describes this as a landmark opportunity for mature reflection on how the nation has been shaped, and sees BLIND HARRY'S WALLACE as an essential and compelling text for this purpose.

'Builder of the literary foundations of a national hero-cult in a free and powerful country'.

ALEXANDER STODDART, sculptor

'A true bard of the people'

TOM SCOTT, THE PENGUIN BOOK OF SCOTTISH VERSE, on Blind Harry.

'A more inventive writer than Shakespeare'
RANDALL WALLACE

'The story of Wallace poured a Scottish prejudice in my veins which will boil along until the floodgates of life shut in eternal rest' ROBERT BURNS

'Hamilton's couplets are not the best poetry you will ever read, but they rattle along at a fair pace. In re-issuing this work, the publishers have re-opened the spring from which most of our conceptions of the Wallace legend come'.
SCOTLAND ON SUNDAY

'The return of Blind Harry's Wallace, a man who makes Mel look like a wimp'. THE SCOTSMAN

The Bannockburn Years

William Scott

ISBN 0 946487 34 0 PBK £7.95

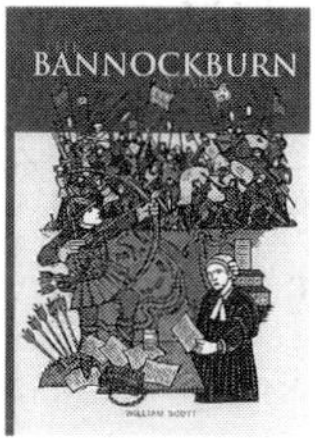
BANNOCKBURN

A present day Edin-burgh solicitor stumbles across reference to a document of value to the Nation State of Scotland. He tracks down the document on the Isle of Bute, a document which probes the real 'quaestiones' about nationhood and national identity. The document ends up being published, but is it authentic and does it matter? Almost 700 years on, these 'quaestiones' are still worth asking.

Written with pace and passion, William Scott has devised an intriguing vehicle to open up new ways of looking at the future of Scotland and its people. He presents an alternative interpretation of how the Battle of Bannockburn was fought, and through the Bannatyne manuscript he draws the reader into the minds of those involved.

Winner of the 1997 Constable Trophy, the premier award in Scotland for an unpublished novel, this book offers new insights to both the academic and the general reader which are sure to provoke further discussion and debate.

'A brilliant storyteller. I shall expect to see your name writ large hereafter.'
NIGEL TRANTER, October 1997.

'... a compulsive read.' PH Scott, THE SCOTSMASN

Over the Top with the Tartan Army (Active Service 1992-97)

Andrew McArthur

ISBN 0 946487 45 6 PBK £7.99

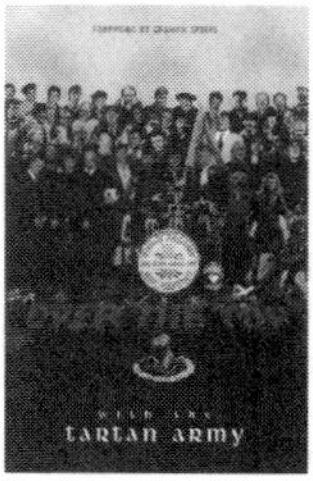
tartan army

Scotland has witnessed the growth of a new and curious military phenomenon – grown men bedecked in tartan yomping across the globe, hell-bent on benevolence and ritualistic bevvying. What noble cause does this famous army serve? Why, football of course!

Taking us on an erratic world tour, McArthur gives a frighteningly funny insider's eye view of active service with the Tartan Army - the madcap antics of Scotland's travelling support in the '90s, written from the inside, covering campaigns and skirmishes from Euro '92 up to the qualifying drama for France '98 in places as diverse as Russia, the Faroes, Belarus, Sweden, Monte Carlo, Estonia, Latvia, USA and Finland.

This book is a must for any football fan who likes a good laugh.

'I commend this book to all football supporters'.
Graham Spiers, SCOTLAND ON SUNDAY

'In wishing Andy McArthur all the best with this publication, I do hope he will be in a position to produce a sequel after our participation in the World Cup in France.
CRAIG BROWN, Scotland Team Coach

All royalties on sales of the book are going to Scottish charities, principally Children's Hospice Association Scotland, the only Scotland-wide charity of its kind, providing special love and care to children with terminal illnesses at its hospice, Rachel House, in Kinross.

LUATH GUIDES TO SCOTLAND

South West Scotland
Tom Atkinson
ISBN 0 946487 04 9 PBK £4.95

The Lonely Lands
Tom Atkinson
ISBN 0 946487 10 3 PBK £4.95

The Empty Lands
Tom Atkinson
ISBN 0 946487 13 8 PBK £4.95

Roads to the Isles
Tom Atkinson
ISBN 0 946487 01 4 PBK £4.95

Highways and Byways in Mull and Iona
Peter Macnab
ISBN 0 946487 16 2 PBK £4.25

NATURAL SCOTLAND

Rum: Nature's Island
Magnus Magnusson
ISBN 0 946487 32 4 PBK £7.95

The Highland Geology Trail
John L Roberts
ISBN 0 946487 36 7 PBK £4.99

WALK WITH LUATH

Mountain Days & Bothy Nights
Dave Brown and Ian Mitchell
ISBN 0 946487 15 4 PBK £7.50

The Joy of Hillwalking
Ralph Storer
ISBN 0 946487 28 6 PBK £7.50

Scotland's Mountains before the Mountaineers
Ian Mitchell
ISBN 0 946487 39 1 PBK £9.99

Walks in the Cairngorms
Ernest Cross
ISBN 0 946487 09 X PBK £3.95

Short Walks in the Cairngorms
Ernest Cross
ISBN 0 946487 23 5 PBK £3.95

SPORT

Ski & Snowboard Scotland
Hilary Parke
ISBN 0 946487 35 9 PBK £6.99

SOCIAL HISTORY

The Crofting Years
Francis Thompson
ISBN 0 946487 06 5 PBK £6.95

MUSIC AND DANCE

Highland Balls and Village Halls
GW Lockhart
ISBN 0 946487 12 X PBK £6.95

Fiddles & Folk: a celebration of the re-emergence of Scotland's musical heritage
GW Lockhart
ISBN 0 946487 38 3 PBK £7.95

FOLKLORE

The Supernatural Highlands
Francis Thompson
ISBN 0 946487 31 6 PBK £8.99

Tall Tales from an Island
Peter Macnab
ISBN 0 946487 07 3 PBK £8.99

BIOGRAPHY

Tobermory Teuchter
Peter Macnab
ISBN 0 946487 41 3 PBK £7.99

Bare Feet and Tackety Boots
Archie Cameron
ISBN 0 946487 17 0 PBK £7.95

On the Trail of Robert Service
GW Lockhart
ISBN 0 946487 24 3 PBK £7.99

Come Dungeons Dark
John Taylor Caldwell
ISBN 0 946487 19 7 PBK £6.95

FICTION

The Great Melnikov
Hugh MacLachlan
ISBN 0 946487 42 1 PBK £7.95

POETRY

Poems to be Read Aloud
Collected and with an introduction by Tom Atkinson
ISBN 0 946487 00 6 PBK £5.00

Luath Press Limited
committed to publishing well written books worth reading

LUATH PRESS takes its name from Robert Burns, whose little collie Luath (*Gael.*, swift or nimble) tripped up Jean Armour at a wedding and gave him the chance to speak to the woman who was to be his wife and the abiding love of his life. Burns called one of *The Twa Dogs* Luath after Cuchullin's hunting dog in *Ossian's Fingal*. Luath Press grew up in the heart of Burns country, and now resides a few steps up the road from Burns' first lodgings in Edinburgh's Royal Mile.

Luath offers you distinctive writing with a hint of unexpected pleasures.

Most UK bookshops either carry our books in stock or can order them for you. To order direct from us, please send a £sterling cheque, postal order, international money order or your credit card details (number, address of cardholder and expiry date) to us at the address below. Please add post and packing as follows: UK – £1.00 per delivery address; overseas surface mail – £2.50 per delivery address; overseas airmail – £3.50 for the first book to each delivery address, plus £1.00 for each additional book by airmail to the same address. If your order is a gift, we will happily enclose your card or message at no extra charge.

Luath Press Limited
543/2 Castlehill
The Royal Mile
Edinburgh EH1 2ND
Telephone: 0131 225 4326 (24 hours)
Fax: 0131 225 4324
email: gavin.macdougall@luath.co.uk
Website: www.luath.co.uk